Palgrave Macmillan Studies in Banking and Financial Institutions
Series Editor: **Professor Philip Molyneux**

The Palgrave Macmillan Studies in Banking and Financial Institutions are international in orientation and include studies of banking within particular countries or regions, and studies of particular themes such as Corporate Banking, Risk Management, Mergers and Acquisitions, etc. The books' focus is on research and practice, and they include up-to-date and innovative studies on contemporary topics in banking that will have global impact and influence.

Titles include:

Steffen E. Andersen
THE EVOLUTION OF NORDIC FINANCE

Seth Apati
THE NIGERIAN BANKING SECTOR REFORMS
Power and Politics

Vittorio Boscia, Alessandro Carretta and Paola Schwizer
COOPERATIVE BANKING IN EUROPE: CASE STUDIES

Roberto Bottiglia, Elisabetta Gualandri and Gian Nereo Mazzocco (*editors*)
CONSOLIDATION IN THE EUROPEAN FINANCIAL INDUSTRY

Dimitris N. Chorafas
BASEL III, THE DEVIL AND GLOBAL BANKING

Dimitris N. Chorafas
CAPITALISM WITHOUT CAPITAL

Dimitris N. Chorafas
FINANCIAL BOOM AND GLOOM
The Credit and Banking Crisis of 2007–2009 and Beyond

Dimitris N. Chorafas
SOVEREIGN DEBT CRISIS
The New Normal and the Newly Poor

Violaine Cousin
BANKING IN CHINA

Vincenzo D'Apice and Giovanni Ferri
FINANCIAL INSTABILITY
Toolkit for Interpreting Boom and Bust Cycles

Peter Falush and Robert L. Carter OBE
THE BRITISH INSURANCE INDUSTRY SINCE 1900
The Era of Transformation

Franco Fiordelisi
MERGERS AND ACQUISITIONS IN EUROPEAN BANKING

Franco Fiordelisi and Ornella Ricci (*editors*)
BANCASSURANCE IN EUROPE
Past, Present and Future

Franco Fiordelisi, Philip Molyneux and Daniele Previati (*editors*)
NEW ISSUES IN FINANCIAL AND CREDIT MARKETS

Franco Fiordelisi, Philip Molyneux and Daniele Previati (*editors*)
NEW ISSUES IN FINANCIAL INSTITUTIONS MANAGEMENT

Kim Hawtrey
AFFORDABLE HOUSING FINANCE

Jill M. Hendrickson
REGULATION AND INSTABILITY IN US COMMERCIAL BANKING
A History of Crises

Otto Hieronymi (*editor*)
GLOBALIZATION AND THE REFORM OF THE INTERNATIONAL BANKING AND MONETARY SYSTEM

Sven Janssen
BRITISH AND GERMAN BANKING STRATEGIES

Alexandros-Andreas Kyrtsis (*editor*)
FINANCIAL MARKETS AND ORGANIZATIONAL TECHNOLOGIES
System Architectures, Practices and Risks in the Era of Deregulation

Caterina Lucarelli and Gianni Brighetti (*editors*)
RISK TOLERANCE IN FINANCIAL DECISION MAKING

Roman Matousek (*editor*)
MONEY, BANKING AND FINANCIAL MARKETS IN CENTRAL AND EASTERN EUROPE
20 Years of Transition

Philip Molyneux (*editor*)
BANK PERFORMANCE, RISK AND FIRM FINANCING

Philip Molyneux (*editor*)
BANK STRATEGY, GOVERNANCE AND RATINGS

Imad A. Moosa
THE MYTH OF TOO BIG TO FAIL

Simon Mouatt and Carl Adams (*editors*)
CORPORATE AND SOCIAL TRANSFORMATION OF MONEY AND BANKING
Breaking the Serfdom

Victor Murinde (*editor*)
BANK REGULATORY REFORMS IN AFRICA
Enhancing Bank Competition and Intermediation Efficiency

Anders Ögren (*editor*)
THE SWEDISH FINANCIAL REVOLUTION

Özlem Olgu
EUROPEAN BANKING
Enlargement, Structural Changes and Recent Developments

Ramkishen S. Rajan
EMERGING ASIA
Essays on Crises, Capital Flows, FDI and Exchange Rate

Allesandro Roselli
FINANCIAL STRUCTURES AND REGULATION
A Comparison of Crises in the UK, USA and Italy

Yasushi Suzuki
JAPAN'S FINANCIAL SLUMP
Collapse of the Monitoring System under Institutional and Transition Failures

Ruth Wandhöfer
EU PAYMENTS INTEGRATION
The Tale of SEPA, PSD and Other Milestones Along the Road

The full list of titles available is on the website:
www.palgrave.com/finance/sbfi.asp

Palgrave Macmillan Studies in Banking and Financial Institutions
Series Standing Order ISBN 978–1–4039–4872–4

You can receive future titles in this series as they are published by placing a standing order. Please contact your bookseller or, in case of difficulty, write to us at the address below with your name and address, the title of the series and the ISBN quoted above.

Customer Services Department, Macmillan Distribution Ltd, Houndmills, Basingstoke, Hampshire RG21 6XS, England, UK

Basel III, the Devil and Global Banking

Dimitris N. Chorafas

palgrave
macmillan

Softcover reprint of the hardcover 1st edition 2012 978-0-230-35377-0

First published 2012 by
PALGRAVE MACMILLAN

Palgrave Macmillan in the UK is an imprint of Macmillan Publishers Limited, registered in England, company number 785998, of Houndmills, Basingstoke, Hampshire RG21 6XS.

Palgrave Macmillan in the US is a division of St Martin's Press LLC, 175 Fifth Avenue, New York, NY 10010.

Palgrave Macmillan is the global academic imprint of the above companies and has companies and representatives throughout the world.

Palgrave® and Macmillan® are registered trademarks in the United States, the United Kingdom, Europe and other countries.

ISBN 978-1-349-34610-3 ISBN 978-0-230-35842-3 (eBook)
DOI 10.1057/9780230358423

A catalogue record for this book is available from the British Library.

A catalog record for this book is available from the Library of Congress.

10 9 8 7 6 5 4 3 2 1
21 20 19 18 17 16 15 14 13 12

Transferred to Digital Printing in 2013

Contents

List of Tables and Figures

Tables

Figures

Introduction

Whether we are talking about the economy, about finance, about social issues or about political themes, the challenge is to leapfrog ahead of a looming crisis that no person is big enough to start single-handed or powerful enough to stop. Acting ahead of the next bubble, and its consequences, is the task the Basel Committee on Banking Supervision took upon itself in December 2010. Regulating global banking is a demanding task, because:

- there is nobody who really knows how to carry out this near-miracle, and
- there is an abundance of adverse reactions from embedded interests which had profited handsomely from previous bubbles and wish to retain the status quo.

Regulatory reform cannot happen in an economic vacuum. Many market players are affected by it in different ways, and some will suffer adverse consequences. Biology provides a paradigm. Whenever the habitat of a species changes, there are both winners and losers.

Economic systems behave in a similar way. Therefore the obstacles to regulatory reform are political rather than technical. While, under the aegis of the Basel Committee, agreements on stronger capital requirements and new liquidity standards for banks have been reached quite quickly but, as the 81st Annual Report by the Bank for International Settlements (BIS) points out, there are still a number of critical steps to be addressed. According to BIS, these include:

- the full and timely implementation of Basel III,
- the elaboration of measures associated with systemic risk by big banks (and their adoption), and
- the design of regimes able to ensure the orderly resolution of big banks in cases where they fail.[1]

The greatest of all challenges is quite likely to be an updated holistic view of global finance, its opportunities, its risks and the role played by increasing sovereign indebtedness. In no way should Basel III be considered a closed system of the banking industry, immune to the sea of red ink that surrounds it at sovereign, corporate and household levels. There is plenty of evidence of a closer than ever interconnection between:

- the global economy,
- the financing of government deficits,

- the financing of debts accumulated by private citizen, and
- the way the banking industry works.

An integral part of what still needs to be done in terms of taming the forces of globalized banking is the study and analysis of numerous lessons and legacies from the economic and financial hecatomb global economies have been going through since 2007. Central banks' monetary policies in the USA and Europe have come under close scrutiny as they have, inter alia, become a real and present danger to price stability. Overindebtedness and destabilization of the currency might superficially appear to be issues having little to do with Basel III, but in reality – for better or worse – monetary policy, fiscal policy and bank regulation and supervision correlate with one another.

The ultralight bank regulation and supervision that followed the repeal of the Glass–Steagall Act was flawed policy on the part of the US government, and it was also adopted by the UK and other member states of the European Union. The damage has been multiplied many times over by the acquired habit of citizens living beyond their means. The excuse that not thinking that something is wrong gives it the superficial appearance of being right is simply not acceptable.

Let's be clear on this. Time is running out for corrective action, far beyond what Basel III says. The market turbulence that followed the global big banks' descent into the abyss in 2008 would seem as nothing beside the devastation that would follow a major sovereign bankruptcy – and as far as this bubble is concerned, there are several candidates lining up to provide the trigger. If this bubble bursts, Basel III will be swept away in a moment and we shall be back again at point zero.

This sword of Damocles hanging over the global economy in no way diminishes the importance of knowing what the Basel III rules and modifications bring to the banking industry's economic habitat. The scope of the new regulatory regime is nicely described by a July 19, 2011 Basel Committee announcement. There are 28 systemic banks in the global market which must be watched with great care. The failure of any of them will trigger massive changes, not just in banking but also in the global economy.

* * *

I am indebted to many knowledgeable people for their contribution to the research which made this book possible, including their constructive criticism during the preparation of the manuscript; most particularly to Dr Heinrich Steinmann and Dr Nelson Mohler.

Let me take this opportunity to thank Lisa von Fircks, for suggesting this project, Gemma d'Arcy Hughes for seeing it all the way to publication, Elaine Towns for editing the manuscript and Keith Povey and his team for the book's production. To Eva-Maria Binder goes the credit for compiling the research results and making valuable suggestions.

DIMITRIS N. CHORAFAS

Valmer and Entlebuch
September 2011

Part I

The Financial Crisis Is Shaping Regulatory Reform

1
Basel III: An Overview and a Warning

A bird's eye view of Basel III capital rules

With the December 16, 2010 release of the Basel III rules, the Basel Committee (Basel) aimed to strengthen preventive measures that are at the heart of bank regulation and effective supervision. Examined strictly on its own merits, each of the revamped Basel II rules, as well as the new ones, is sound. There are, however, two major challenges which regretfully have been, and continue to be, outside the Basel Committee's remit:

- today's globalized financial markets are a far cry from the much simpler banking environment that Basel I, and by extension Basel II and Basel III, aimed to regulate, and
- no matter what the Basel Committee say, the different governments, particularly those in the West, continue to shield their badly wounded big global banks which they saved from bankruptcy through the use of lavish amounts of taxpayers' money.

If the latter continues, it will distort the regulatory system and will eventually make Basel III nearly irrelevant. The rules released so far by the Basel Committee say nothing about such an *event risk*, which will not disappear just by sweeping it under the carpet.

From an organization point of view, the Basel III rules divide into two classes: those representing an overhaul of existing prudential standards, such as capital requirements; and those introducing rules where hardly any previously existed. The emphasis placed on bank liquidity is an example. Taken together, these two classes aim to shield the banking industry from the next crisis as well as to reduce spillover risk.

The problem is that nobody today really knows precisely from where the 'next crisis' will come. In addition, if the past is any guide, the appearance of early signals of a crisis will be downplayed, and those responsible for watching over it will be inclined to turn a blind eye to the growing risk. Both Alan Greenspan, then chairman of the Federal Reserve, and Ben Bernanke, who succeeded him, said that they did not see the 2007 crisis coming. But plenty of bankers and hedge fund managers saw it coming and joined it.

Neither Greenspan nor Bernanke allegedly knew that many banks, and in particular the big global institutions, had too little capital before the crisis. Looking the other way has also been the erroneous policy in the UK and in continental European countries. For example, the Royal Bank of Scotland needed a huge bail-out because it went into the crisis with a dangerously thin capital cushion of only about 3.5 percent, rather than because its losses were too large.[1]

To better appreciate how big banks became undercapitalized without even breaking the letter of the law, one should recall that, in 1988, Basel I required that international banks hold capital worth 8 percent of their assets. Subsequently, Basel II allowed them to calculate how much capital they actually needed by estimating the probability of their own loans defaulting.[2] Here is precisely where the wave of abuses started.

One of the ways banks found to arbitrace Basel II and run on thin capital was to shield themselves behind their own unsound models.[3] In the years leading up to the 2007 crisis, an army of bankers, mathematicians and lawyers put together new kinds of instruments that were made specifically to provide an array of opportunities to arbitrage the Basel II capital requirements, using 'rocket science'.[4]

No wonder, therefore, that the central bankers who worked on Basel III have been faced with a challenge to thoroughly restructure the banks' capital requirements, not only by increasing them but also by providing more clear-cut definitions of *does* and *don'ts*. This has been the right policy, but it fell victim to its own success because it led many governments to soft-pedal on Basel III.

Gradually, sovereign policy-makers began to understand that applying the new rules requires huge sums of money to recapitalize the banks. According to McKinsey, European banks will need to raise €1.1 trillion in equity by 2019, while American banks will have to raise US$870 billion.[5] Here are, in a nutshell, the Basel III definitions of regulatory capital. (For a discussion on their strengths and weaknesses as well as for quantitative information, see Chapter 5.)

- *Tier 1 equity* is the bank's common stock and retained earnings, minus regulatory adjustments such as reduction for goodwill. Equity is the classical definition of a company's capital.

The fine print of Tier 1 equity is still evolving. The most recent agreement on Basel III came on June 25, 2011, obliging the systemically important global banks to hold an extra 1 percent to 2.5 percent of equity (see section below entitled 'The devil is in the detail…'). This has been the right step, though details have still to be thrashed out, including which banks will be named as being systemically important in a global sense. The surcharge comes on top of already agreed Basel III rules requiring all banks to raise their core capital buffers to at least 7 percent of their risk-weighted assets.

- *Tier 1 additional capital.* This includes preferred shares and other financial instruments complying with regulatory criteria. The latter aim to ensure that such capital can absorb losses while the bank is a going concern.
- *Tier 2 capital.* This consists of debt instruments answering regulatory criteria aimed at ensuring they can absorb losses when a bank fails. For example, that these instruments are subordinated and have a minimum original maturity of at least 5 years.

A common feature of Tier 1 additional capital and Tier 2 is that they can be written off or converted to common stock when the issuing bank is unable to support itself in the capital market. Other instruments being considered in the realm of Basel III are *contingent capital* (see Chapter 5 on CoCos) and *bail-in debt.* The latter is converted to Tier 1 equity when the bank reaches the point of non-viability.

Quite correctly, Basel III has eliminated *hybrid capital* instruments, which provided a stream of tools and incentive to make small game of the capital rules. It has also done away with *Tier 3 capital,* which consisted of short-term subordinated debt intended to cover market risk.

In contrast to Basel I and Basel II, which preceded it, Basel III also pays attention to *liquidity* requirements in the banking industry. Prior to the July/August 2007 implosion, many banks operated with narrow liquidity margins, using the sham excuse that they were relying on easy access to market liquidity. This excuse suddenly disappeared the day the gates of hell were opened.

To better appreciate the urgent need for strong rules for bank supervision, the reader should know that substandard capital, make-believe assets, poor liquidity, excessive leverage and very weak risk management have not been the misbegotten policies of only a few fat cats. Big global banks which became train wrecks through their imprudence, had friends in high places whose palms they were allegedly greasing via unprecedented political contributions.

This sort of occult investment, if it really existed, as it is rumored, paid dividends. Not only did these high-ranking friends see to it that none of the many wrongdoers was brought to justice, but they also acted while Basel III was being designed to put pressure on regulators to water down the Basel III clauses, and delay it by spreading its implementation up to 2019.

This is precisely where Basel III's downside lies: the lack of a rapid implementation timetable and of a system-wide view with close monitoring of potentially weak points. Such weaknesses reduce its impact. History at large, and most particularly financial history, suggests that it is not the apparently riskiest parts of the universe – and of financial markets – that legislators and regulators should keep an eye on, but the ones believed to be the least risky.

In addition, now and in the future, more and more attention must be paid to the deadly embrace of sovereigns and big banks. Not to do so will be a dangerous mistake. In the early years of the twenty-first century, for example, closer scrutiny of the housing bubble and its 'triple A' mortgage-backed securities would have revealed that they were far from being *risk free*. A similar statement is valid today about the complexity and opaqueness of the balance sheets of big global banks and of the governments that rush to support them while leaving in place the same inept management.

The concept underlying modern regulation

As noted in the previous section, the new capital adequacy rules by the Basel Committee on Banking Supervision is a set of regulatory standards targeting not only a sound capital ratio commensurate with the risks a credit institution takes but, in addition, the liquidity requirements and other issues relating to good governance. At least in theory, the rules and directives that succeeded and amended those of Basel II combine a more holistic view of what is needed to control exposure in the banking industry, and a pragmatic approach to the correction of Basel II's weaknesses exploited by individual banks, such as the fuzzy notion of hybrid capital.

To promote a comprehensive discussion around these two points, and of other critical issues of bank supervision, it has been a deliberate choice to present Basel III as a *discipline* rather than as a set of individual rules independent from one another. As the next section will explain, the devil is in the discipline's detail. Moreover, because not everything is as yet set in stone, the text uses case studies to expand a point – or to provide a warning that unless the current overall risk culture changes, the Western economy will be in great trouble.

It is no exaggeration to say that, some years from now, what we shall think of the regulatory activities of the Basel Committee as being divided into two major epochs: *before* and *after* the deep economic and banking crisis of 2007–12. This crisis has already fundamentally changed the sense of prudential regulation, but it has also brought into perspective many issues that have been downplayed but should now attract legislators' and regulators' attention.

The best examples can be found thorough analysis of the regulatory discipline that governs the mighty engine of the global financial market and its dynamics. Its moving gear is no longer loans but *derivatives*. Under the old rules, risks associated with steady financial innovation through derivative financial instruments did not quite fall into the Basel Committee's realm.

Yet, continuing to accept the current opacity and leaving them out of the legislative and regulatory equation, will ensure that, sooner rather than later, Basel III will be half-baked. Indeed, in accounting for the rapidly mounting risks from derivatives, thanks to the 2010 Wall Street Reform and Consumer Protection Act (WSRCP, FINREG, Dodd–Frank Act) the USA is, at the time of writing, ahead of all other nations in banking supervision. American regulators are putting the finishing touches to rules based on this legislation that will force many derivative instruments on to exchanges and into central clearing houses.

One of the great merits of the Dodd–Frank Act has been the recognition that the financial system had discovered ways to make risks, including lending risks, appear to go away. It therefore forces banks to take responsibility and make their risks transparent. This discourages inappropriate exposures and requires the private sector, not taxpayers, to provide funds to cover its assumed liabilities.

Another sound rule promoted by the Dodd–Frank Act in the USA is that failed firms will absorb their own losses, and their management will be removed. It would have been even better if the law had stipulated clearly that those in charge of failed banks must be brought to justice for gambling with shareholders' money, and for their mismanagement.

Indeed, it can arguably be said that it was a mistake not to include in the Dodd–Frank Act an explicit threat of sanctions, because without them there will be no improvement in either culture or ethics. Instead, any legislation will eventually be turned into a target-rich environment for banking industry lobbyists.

This is regrettable, because plenty of bad experiences revealed and documented by the economic and financial crisis of 2007–12, whose after-effects are still present, confirm the need for draconian (not just tougher) measures. To make it move, the human donkey needs a carrot and a stick, to quote an old proverb.

To its credit, the Act includes a critical innovation that should be implemented worldwide. It explicitly recognizes the shadow banking system as a source of systemic risk. Having done so, it then provides regulatory tools to mitigate the exposure by means of closer oversight and wider margins of safety.

It is by no means far-fetched to view the new American legislation as the alter ego of Basel III. In part, Dodd–Frank and Basel III overlap; for example, in requiring banks to hold more capital against retained risk. Most important, however, they complement one another by addressing issues that are an integral part of the sound governance of the banking industry. The union of Basel III and Dodd–Frank should be the enlarged domain of responsibility of the Basel Committee on Banking Supervision.

A similar statement is also valid regarding the integration of the 2002 Sarbanes–Oxley Act (SOX), which has squarely placed personal responsibility for accuracy of financial accounts on the shoulders of the chief executive officer (CEO) and chief financial officer (CFO) of a company.[6] It is very regrettable that, in 2007–8 the Bush Administration failed to apply SOX, which was at that time the law of the land.

As for the often heard critique from the bankers side that the Dodd–Frank Act is too long and complex, the critics are really missing the point. If they were not so near-sighted, they would have appreciated that problems in the modern economy caused by an interconnected system which can be severely damaged by:

- improvidently made loans,
- inappropriately packaged securitization,
- imprudently developed derivatives, and
- inadequately controlled risks.

As Barney Frank wrote in an article in the *Financial Times*:

> many business people complained about the adoption of antitrust laws ... [and] many predicted a serious blow to American capitalism with the adoption of the Securities and Exchange Act. Ten years from now, current objections to regulating derivatives and restricting imprudent residential mortgages will ... [be seen as] sensible reforms.'[7]

There have been good reasons for the Wall Street Reform and Consumer Protection Act. Over-the-counter (OTC) deals, which make both fat profits and huge losses for banks, have so far been opaque to regulators – and in many cases to the CEOs of the banks themselves. The way a recent article in *The Economist* put it, derivatives account for a third of J.P. Morgan Chase (JPM) investment banking revenues.[8]

Not only the new American legislation but also Basel's rules will force banks to hold more equity than they used to in connection with derivatives, but whether this will be commensurate with risks being assumed is as yet unknown. Still, the reason I never tire of repeating that global legislation similar to that of the Dodd–Frank Act is urgently needed, is that European, Asian and Latin-American regulators are moving slowly in the direction of targeting risks which create king-sized loopholes in global financial industry regulations, and encouraging bankers to stop migrating risks to darker corners of the global financial system.

Another example of Basel III weaknesses is the lack of universal standards for rating creditworthiness, following the independent rating agencies' great failure with the subprimes. This is a complex issue. In 2010, the Dodd–Frank Act made it illegal for American regulators to use ratings by independent agencies for regulatory purposes. Instead, its Section 939A stipulated that bank regulators must modify their rules to remove any reference to, or requirements of, reliance on credit ratings, using instead other standards of creditworthiness.

The question is: 'Which alternatives?' Any valid candidate must be comprehensive, simple to understand and easy to implement, as well as being generally accepted not only by the different jurisdictions but also by the globalized financial market. By allowing all sorts of financial institutions to use their own internal models and relying on diverse risk formulas, regulators are shooting themselves in the foot – particularly so as they have neither the funds nor the 'rocket scientists' (physicists, engineers or mathematicians who previously worked in aerospace or other high-powered projects and are now employed by big global banks for modeling, research and analysis) to control hundreds and thousands of models. In all likelihood, this will lead to chaos, and provide plenty of opportunities for regulatory arbitrage.

What happened with Basel II's internal-ratings-based (IRB) method documents was that internal models needed to be policed constantly to avoid their being used to understate risks, or even outright hide them. A case may as well be made that models will not be able to capture shifts in credit risk over time. And last but not least, parochial models raise the problem of heterogeneity in the control of credit and market risk by supervisors.

To be in control, the regulators of the banking industry will have to develop methods and tools commensurate with the complexity of modern finance, always keeping ahead of steady innovation in the banking industry. This cannot be achieved by continuing to rely on the simplistic and obsolete value-at-risk (VAR) model. Using VAR is like a policeman trying to catch a speeding Ferrari by using a horse and cart.

In my book *Risk Pricing*[9] I introduced the use of quantum electrodynamics (QED) to track higher-order risks. Every industry experiences strategic inflection points which offer promises as well as threats. When the threats increase by order of magnitude, the methods and tools used should be thoroughly revamped. It is a failure of Basel III that it has not paid attention to the power of methods and tools necessary for effective risk control.

The devil is in the detail of all decisions

For sovereigns[10] and leaders of industry, attention to detail is *a must*, not an option. 'Gains in quality come from meticulous attention to detail and every step in the manufacturing process must be done as *carefully* as possible, not as *quickly* as possible,' wrote David Packard in his seminal book *The HP Way*. Packard adds: 'This sounds simple, but it is achieved only if everyone in the organization is dedicated to quality'[11] – and, I would add, to detail.

I am raising this issue because a good many failures are nothing but the mistakes of individuals', made sometimes as a result of political pressures and bandwagon climbing, but more often than not because of scant attention being paid to ethics and no attention at all to detail. Charles V of the Holy

Roman Empire was passionate about detail. He believed that the order of this world is revealed by the little things, not the big ones.[12]

Take, for example, the way that regulators score the systemic risk of individual big banks. As stated, they apply an extra 1 percent to 2.5 percent of additional capital to the systemic risk factor; a good example of an important Basel III detail. But the way an article in the *Financial Times* put it, several Japanese and French banks appear to have benefited 'from the way global supervisors have decided to calculate extra capital requirements'.[13]

In terms of aftermath, what this means is that some banks face smaller than expected surcharges, while others are confronted by larger ones. At the time of writing, the Basel Committee had announced that it had scored 73 of the largest global banks. The criteria have been their size, complexity, cross-border presence, and extent to which they are difficult to replace in the financial landscape.

More than a third of these 73 would, in all likelihood, face additional capital requirements if and when the new rules were applied. There was no official announcement about the names of these banks when such news became public, let alone how much the capital surcharge will be for each of them.[14] For obvious reasons, however, analysts got busy guestimating how the dice would fall – and, by extension, what kind of detail has been considered when deciding on a classification.

According to some guestimates, America's BNY Mellon, Wells Fargo and State Street Banks will have only a 1 percent surcharge. The same is true of Spain's BBVA, Germany's Commerzbank, Holland's Rabobank, and Japan's Mizuho Financial. France's Crédit Agricole and Société Générale, the Franco-Belgian Dexia, Italy's UniCredit, Spain's Santander, Holland's ING and Japan's MUFG are reportedly in the 1.5 percent class of capital surcharge, while the 2 percent class includes Goldman Sachs and Morgan Stanley; BNP Paribas; and the Swiss UBS and Crédit Suisse.

A 2.5 percent capital surcharge will allegedly be applied to the Bank of America, J.P. Morgan Chase and Citigroup; BNP Paribas; and Deutsche Bank. The committee which reportedly made these choices was composed of regulators from 25 jurisdictions with a large financial industry. So far, the big banks in this tentative list originate from only 9 countries:

- 8 in the USA,
- 3 in the UK,
- 3 in France,
- 2 in Germany,
- 2 in Switzerland,
- 2 in the Netherlands,
- 2 in Spain,
- 2 in Japan, and
- 1 of French/Belgian capital.

Some analysts commented that the lack of detail regarding the criteria on which these decisions were based make them questionable. For example, curiously enough, Japan's Sumitomo Mitsui Financial and Nomura seem to escape surcharges entirely. In a consultation document, the Basel Committee promised that it will update the list of banks it is tracking every three to five years. Many experts questioned that detail because it seems to them that, in a fast-evolving market three to five years may be equal to half a century in the old, quiet financial times.[15]

In addition, the Basel Committee stated, in the same consultative document, that it will consider expanding the surcharge system to include other global financial companies. This preliminary decision is welcomed, but the reader should notice that, here too, the detail is missing.

- Will the amount of financial or commodity risk assumed by a company be the crucial factor? If not, what else will be?
- How will this risk be measured? And who will be *the supervisors' supervisor* to challenge the metrics[16] and the decisions?

Properly sized, the examination of future risks includes the analysis of the consequences of current decisions and of problems left unattended. The only way to properly confront ongoing challenges, and project on to those that may be coming, is by studying critically the most basic elements and, from that position, examining what the new rules should be – and how their correct implementation will be assured.

While guidelines and quantitative targets are helpful, the key principle is to formulate and express one's critical thoughts freely. 'A slave is he who cannot speak his thoughts,' said Euripides, the ancient Greek dramatic author. This was true in antiquity and it is just as true today.

Euripides welcomed critical analysis, and this is the way in which this book looks at Basel III: what are its strengths and weaknesses? Among its strengths is its attention to the banks liquidity and capital reserves commensurate with the risks each institution is taking. An example of weaknesses in the regulatory armory are compromises that make no sense but create huge loopholes. For example, the cynicism of deferred tax assets (DTAs) being accepted as core capital, as a result of sovereign pressure (see Chapter 4).

A compromise such as the DTAs is more curious (and amusing) as it is common knowledge that make-believe capital through deferred taxes was one of the failings of Basel II. Short-termism took precedence over sound management. In an article in the *Financial Times*, Bruce Anderson asked the question: 'If anyone understands the UK government's policy on Libya, would they please explain it?'[17] Precisely the same query can be made about the Japanese government's insistence on considering Mickey Mouse money as bank capital.

Even more serious is Basel III's failure to redefine in modern terms the meaning and membership of the *financial sector* in the economy. Speaking of banks in the way they were known in the past: retail, commercial and investment institutions, is like to trying to do away with the redefinition challenge:

- What about hedge funds and non-bank banks, which escape regulation and supervision?
- What's Basel III's hold on dark pools, special purpose vehicles, flash crash (see Chapter 2) and other biases of the economy, invented and operated by big banks under the regulators' noses?

No doubt, *moral risk* should also have been a focal point of Basel III, but it is not. In terms of what defines politics, a famous saying by former British prime minister, Harold Macmillan was 'Events, dear boy, events.' The same is true with what defines moral risk. Events bring it strongly into the picture and, foreseeing this, laws and regulations should include a strong message against its appearance and its contagion.

Moral risk is exactly the kind of thing the banking sector does not need, because it can be a fatal vulnerability. Yet it has been widely present in the dysfunction of the financial industry that led to the 2007–12 deep economic crisis. The system allowed greedy people to rise, take command, ruin the bank for which they were responsible – and do all this without being brought to justice, and with no questions asked.

The destructive power of moral risk has not held Basel III's attention, either in the headlines or in the detail. As we have seen, because of the 2007 hecatomb there are persistent doubts bout how credit risk should be rated, Basel III does not even include a reference as to how a bank's quality of management and its ethics should be appraised. This happens despite the fact that the foremost asset of a bank is not the money in its vaults, it is people: its clients, its employees and its executives.

As these references document, the more one looks into the Basel III details, the more one feels the need for reframing the bigger picture within which such details must fit. Such a restructuring has been the objective of the UK's Vickers Commission. In mid-June 2011, George Osborne, the British chancellor, threw his weight behind the proposals of the Independent Commission on Banking (ICB),[18] which has opened new perspectives in risk control. In an interim report, in April 2010, the ICB had recommended that banks:

- ring-fenced their retail operations, and
- set aside 10 percent of capital as a buffer against hard times.

Not only did what the Vickers Committee suggest make a lot of sense, but a similar directive should have been embedded in the rules of Basel III at least at an equal level with – if not a higher standing than – the capital surcharge above minimum requirements. Michel Barnier, the EU's internal market commissioner, plans to integrate this ring-fencing and capital provisioning concept into the framework of the EU's Capital Requirements Directive 4 (CRD4), on which he is currently working.[19]

The reader should notice that, while the 10 percent capital buffer mentioned above is a higher ratio than that put forward by Basel III, it is also more realistic. In addition, a crucial contribution of the Vickers Commission is the grand solution of ring-fencing retail banking arms into separately capitalized subsidiaries which can be salvaged if the rest of the bank becomes bankrupt.

Regulators should look at this as an important innovation, and I would expect that Basel III would lose no time in adopting it. Deposits, savings, loans, payments and settlements are basic banking functions that allow for no interruptions. In contrast, the banks' trading and investment divisions should be allowed to live or die without lavish handouts of taxpayers' money.

All told, it is pity that a third innovative measure studied by the ICB, that of breaking up banks 'too big to be saved', was in some way dropped from the radar judging from the way its report is shaping up. The break-up of misbehaving banks would have made a lot of sense – and the best headlines. The day may not be far off, however, when this concept comes back with a vengeance, the trigger for it being the next bubble. We shall see.

In conclusion, as this section has emphasized, both the detail and the bigger picture are very important elements in every piece of legislation and every regulation. What they have in common is that they go beyond guidelines and signposts. To help in this direction, a comprehensive discussion of Basel III should not be limited to explaining what the new rules are or what they mean to the banking industry and to the common citizen, but also to present them in a way that makes sense in terms of facts and aftermath. This is reflected in the book's organization and structure.

What the book offers the reader

Written for practitioners looking for guidance on the implementation of Basel III by the banking industry, and its after-effects, the book explains why a successful application of its directives must be organized in a way that leads to cultural change in the virtual economy. As such, the text is practical; it is not, however, a 'how-to' book, because, beyond the framework of a comprehensive approach, each bank has its own problems to confront and solve.

Banks take risks, but so does anyone engaged in any kind of entrepreneurial activity that commits present resources to future expectations. The essence of sound governance by no means eliminates risk-taking. Rather, it is to anticipate the adversity that probably lies ahead, and to question whether expected returns are commensurate with assumed exposure.

Considering future implications and challenges associated with current decisions and actions evidently involves uncertainty: while Basel III – like its predecessors, Basel II and Basel I – sets guidelines, standards and limits, uncertainty is certainly not taken out of the financial system; it is left to the managers of individual banks to confront it. That is all to the good, because people who absolutely need certainty in their life and work are unlikely to become captains of finance.

Part II looks at global finance as a perpetual motion machine. Chapter 2 starts with the central banks' *trilemma*, created by expanding financial markets, the impact of novel financial instruments and the search for financial stability. Chapter 3 makes the distinction between global banking and international trade which are often looked at (incorrectly) as being practically synonymous. Then it concentrates on the notion of systemic risk and its amplification by playing the system.

It has been a deliberate choice not to deal with Basel III specifics until Chapter 4, to enable its rules and regulations to be placed in the correct perspective. This allows us to bring to the reader's attention, in a more comprehensive way, what will most likely prove to be the new regulations' 'positives' and 'negatives'.

The four chapters in Part III examine Basel III's mechanics, as well as its unfinished business. Chapter 5 provides evidence that the need for a regulatory authority has been felt since antiquity, but then questions whether the global financial market is ready to accept it. Chapter 6 explains what a close watch over Basel III's implementation means in terms of adherence to capital adequacy and liquidity.

Chapter 7 concentrates on a theme which, to my mind, Basel III has underplayed. That is a pity, because if home and host supervisors don't work in unison this may well prove to be a death sentence for the new rules and regulations. The nature, deep roots and impact of home–host problems haunt both bankers and regulators, and will continue to do so.

The remit of Part IV is risk management. All practice rests on theory, even if its practitioners are unaware of it. The most important contribution of theory is the culture it brings with it. For Basel III to be successful, and perform better than its discredited predecessor, Basel II, it must not only instill a new risk management culture but also to introduce a theory that convinces people this is normal and, indeed, healthy (see also the second section above in this chapter).

Chapter 8 outlines a practical approach to the control of risk which has at its roots personal accountability. It then explains the notion of principal risks, gives plenty of examples on risk factors (which are specific), and concentrates on the outlier[20] events of risk distribution. The risk in the long tail of a trade, investment, loans pool or other position is technically defined as much higher than expected – challenging the now classical ways and means of its control, which assume normal conditions.

Chapter 9 examines the nature and impact of correlation risk, another group of exposures which have traditionally been downplayed and to which neither the global banking industry nor Basel III pay them the attention they deserve. Chapter 10 explains why the ability to say 'No!' is Step 1 in risk control. This is followed by an analysis of risk and return, organizational prerequisites for effective risk control action, and the reasons why risk should be treated as a business cost.

Part V looks at the duality characterizing banks and sovereigns at present, as the latter too have turned themselves into perpetual motion financial machines. Chapter 11 points out that that sovereign risk has become a real danger commensurate with that of banking risk. The European Union is taken as case study of how and why living beyond one's means is the way to oblivion. The problem is that this has become policy in the West.

Chapter 12 starts with a reference to Milton Friedman who questioned the central banks' independence. What happened with the 2007–12 deep economic and banking crisis proved Friedman right. The case studies included in the book explain why this is so. Central bankers would have been better off if they had followed Charles V's dictum: 'Never abandon even a small part of your rights; if you do, they will soon ask you for the balance.'

The reader may have a legitimate query as to how the last three chapters of the book connect to Basel III. The answer is that the state's intervention in trying to support financial institutions that are too big to be saved has altered the previously prevailing relationships between banks, their regulators and supervisors. Failure to take this into account will guarantee that Basel III fails in its mission.

Lacking a plan about what should be done if large and complex banking groups were to fail because of the huge risks they were assuming, sovereigns rushed to provide a torrent of liquidity and capital assets at taxpayers' expense. The presence of this *deus ex machina* enabled the banking industry to continue taking risks that it would have abstained from in the absence of the sovereigns' benevolent insurance. Governments and central banks thought they were in a strong position to bear those risks, but this was only an illusion. The broadening of the scope of economic activity by sovereigns:

- led to their unprecedented indebtedness in peacetime, and
- acted as a catalyst for the advent of a new economic and financial landscape that is still unfolding.

Whether one likes it or not, there is a long, pothole-strewn road from here to global financial stability, if this can ever be reached. Capital ratios and liquidity guidelines for banks are important, but now these are only a small part of the problem of protecting the world economy from a tsunami of systemic risk, and this is Basel III's goal. Giving *carte blanche* to the sovereigns will be like hanging the sword of Damocles over the global economy's head.

In conclusion, we don't yet know whether Basel III will be a success or a failure. What can be argued, though, is that there will be an important long-term impact on the banking industry, and in particular on big global banks – provided that governments don't alter the Basel III rules, delay their implementation or cancel them completely. Governments, however, are playing the devil with Basel's higher capital ratios and liquidity requirements, probably because they know the sorry state of the financial institutions under their watch.

Part II
The Perpetual Motion of Global Finance

2 Finance and Banking Are Time and Motion Machines

The central bankers' trilemma

Finance and banking are perpetual motion machines based on virtual rather than real assets and, more recently, on a rapidly growing mountain of debt. They sustain their perpetual motion by being inventive and marketing-oriented, creating business opportunities on a local, national and global scale, taking risks and facing headwinds that have the potential to destabilize the whole financial system.

While international trade and global banking correlate, the former having preceded the latter and depending on it for financial intermediation, payments and settlements, the two are by no means identical (see Chapter 3). The most vivid pattern of global finance resembles that of an individual in a play by Euripides, the ancient Greek dramatist. Euripides' heroes went toward their antithesis in their rise, then were caught in the net of their indecision, and while going forward in their course marched toward their fall.

The fall that follows the rise in business activities may create systemic risk. To avoid the after effects of crises that have the nasty habit of destabilizing the economy and the financial system, sovereigns try to regulate the banking industry. In a global setting, however, this is much more easily said than done – no matter how many 'summits' by heads of states and other tourist events are held in the hope of reaching a consensus on the right direction and amount of regulation.

The world of banking has been a mirror of history at large. An old proverb says: 'Money makes the world go round'. Banking activities resemble a wheel turning continually and, in its motion, first building then demolishing situations and conditions that (superficially) looked as if they were stable.

To put some order into the wheel's motion, since the late 1980s the Basel Committee on Banking Supervision (*Basel*) has created three successive versions of rules on capital adequacy and other issues affecting the management of banks. Released in 1987, the regulations that became known as

Basel I targeted a flat level of 8 percent capital adequacy for international banks and 4 percent for nationally operating banks. This was at no time gamed (arbitraged) through hybrid assets.

Basel II was partly aimed at correcting Basel I's flaws, and partly to make the regulatory system more sophisticated. It took a long time to come into existence.[1] Released in 1999, its draft paper went through a whirlwind of commentaries and tests, ending up with many compromises that made it ineffectual. Both Basel I and Basel II were characterized by the regulators' inability – because of political pressures – to exercise control over decisive issues which put the banking industry at risk.

Theoretically, but only theoretically, with Basel III (see Chapters 4 and 5) the Basel Committee on Banking Supervision is moving to correct the problems created by the cocktail of banking-and-politics that made the preceding two global regulatory versions ineffectual. Proposed reforms have centered on four areas:

- Weeding out hybrid instruments, which confuse debt and equity, thereby weakening the capital structure.
- Adding new capital buffers so that de-leveraging taking place in a crisis does not need to crush lending.
- Placing higher capital charges on riskier instruments, such as novel derivatives (section 5), and regulating over-the-counter trading.
- Providing for a liquidity framework, aimed at taking care of future liquidity crunches, so that the 2007–8 experience with liquidity's disappearance is not repeated.

Other reforms still being debated, but far from gaining unanimous acceptance in the global market, include an international leverage ratio which would (also theoretically) place a ceiling on overall gearing by credit institutions – in both good times and bad. The Swiss imposed a leverage ratio unilaterally on their big global banks, before Basel introduced the idea. By contrast, the French and German governments objected to this Basel III rule that banks have to declare their level of leveraging[2] – most likely because they know how highly geared their credit institutions are.

Revealing the leverage ratio of each bank is synonymous with promoting transparency. It also serves as a wake-up call, given the practice of too-thin capital cushions by reminding us that a bank management may underestimate the risks it is assuming. Political meddling by governments is most unwelcome, it is as well embarrassing to central bankers. As the Bank for International Settlements (BIS) put it in a commentary: 'Central banks face a credibility balancing act'.[3]

Capital requirements have classically represented the need for solvency posed by the most basic function of banking: that of being a financial intermediary between the private sector's excess of money and the public or private sectors' need for it. Reserve requirements are nothing new, but they vary widely from one jurisdiction to the next, often because of economic nationalism and protectionism – which is unacceptable in globalized finance.

Neither is it new that capital requirements tend always to be set in a way that leverages the economy. 'There is no limit to the amount of money that can be created by the banking system,' warned Marriner Eccles, a former chairman of the Federal Reserve, 'but there are limits to our productive facilities and our labor supply, which can only slowly be increased.'[4] Leveraging made through debt is behind the uncanny ability to have impact beyond one's reach, but the law of unintended consequences sees to it that when the economy takes a downturn, leveraging hits like a hammer.

Regulators have used their experience from current and past crises in setting the Basel III rules. On the other side of the fence, both the banking industry's lobbyists and governments themselves have been watering down the rules, or dropping them out of sight. Sovereigns and legislators do not really appreciate that they aren't protecting the banks by being paternalistic, giving them free reign or showering them with inordinate amounts of money, said Heinrich Steinmann, a former vice-chairman of the global Swiss bank, UBS (in a personal discussion). Because of the government's paternalism, the credibility of banks may increase temporarily, but the longer-term results are negative. Moreover, as the most recent massive salvage by using taxpayers' money has shown, the government becomes overwhelmed with debt it cannot repay.

As the 2007–12 deep economic and banking crisis showed, panicked governments have been foolishly throwing a lot of money at the problem, and central banks have been very eager to put their printing presses into overdrive. An unprecedented amount of debt does not jump-start the economy. What it does is to lower public confidence in those who govern – and in the bankers.

Essentially, both governments and central banks, and particularly the latter, are confronted by a *trilemma* – an impossible trinity – and find it difficult to make up their minds as to which way they should go. At risk is the central banks' credibility and their (hard won) independence. Solutions don't come easily, because of contradictions and conflicts of interest to be found in the triple goals of:

- Assuring financial stability, which provides the system with the ability to fulfill its key economic functions smoothly.
- Avoiding systemic risk on a control-as-you-go basis rather than flooding the market with capital and liquidity.
- Providing for full employment to placate governments, and therefore assure the central bank's continuing independence in a politico-economic sense.[5]

Without question, the central bank should be the guardian of monetary and price stability. Every economy has an inherent interest in a stable financial system, which is not only a precondition for the effective implementation of monetary policy measures but also the key to a prosperous economy.

Priorities, however, are not set in stone. The Bernanke Federal Reserve has put the third goal listed above in the No. 1 position – and judging by this perspective, its policies have been a failure, since US unemployment has stayed stubbornly above 9 percent. By contrast, with the trilemma being what it is, financial stability has been sacrificed, not only by the Fed but also by the Bank of England and (to a lesser extent) by the European Central Bank (ECB).

This is irrational, because all stakeholders: governments, business and the general public, benefit from monetary stability. When there is instability, sovereigns are obliged to apply restrictions on capital flows and controls, which bring distortions and corruption. Conflicts emerge because foreign and domestic players have different interests and agendas, which means that the three attributes of central banks' policies listed above are not working in synergy.

Effects of the 'New Economy' on the financial time machine

The reasons why financial markets resemble time machines do not need a great deal of explanation. Deposits, loans and securities are their raw material. Through equities and bonds the buyer of a financial instrument turns today's investment into a future stream of interest payments. A bond investor has a steady rate of interest income. An equity investor profits from the dividends stream s/he gets, and (if lucky) the equity gains in value.

On the other side of the equation, the seller of a financial instrument turns future income into cash at the time s/he makes the transaction. The raw material of this transaction is *perpetual*; the same instrument can be bought and sold many times over. A financial transaction may also be leveraged (again, many times over). Modern finance pools together different instruments, this pool is securitized and the new instrument is sold, bought, recombined and resecuritized.

Such a feature of perpetual financial motion needs players with a mathematical background to calculate the probability of risk(s) and projected profits and losses (P&L); as well as players who specialize in trading. Risk is mispriced for many reasons: greed, ignorance of a policy. or forgetting to analyze longer-term effects in terms of risks and return. If the players think only in the short term, then risks can run wild.

Among the players contributing to the perpetual motion of modern finance are the market makers. Without them, the markets would move slowly and might even not function. Still another population is that of risk controllers, who should scrutinize risk factors by 'rocket scientists' (see Chapter 8) – and estimates by traders; watch over the observance of limits; and take action to close down positions with unwanted risk and return.

This is a task requiring both skill and imagination. As every banker or financial expert should know, the gates of risk and return are adjacent and identical. Therefore, what an institution obtains from lending and trading is not necessarily what it thinks it is getting when it enters into a financial transaction. There is an asymmetric distribution of opportunities and exposures, which may work at the expense of the bank, the bank's stakeholders, the economy and society at large.

A sign that a financial institution is well governed, is that its management watches carefully over these asymmetries and takes timely corrective action. Post-mortem interventions are ineffectual, and government interference creates moral hazard, which is widespread nowadays and in all likelihood tops all other reasons that deeply affect banking, the economy and society in general.[6]

Part and parcel of moral hazard is rescuing big banks that are at edge of the abyss. Such cases have multiplied because of the increased correlation among financial assets and liabilities, including corrosive 'assets' of highly volatile or nearly zero value. Crises derail the perpetual motion financial machine, and compromise the banks' independence.

Even worse is the fact such intervention is largely made necessary by greatly increasing the sovereign debt. 'The *perpetuum mobile* will come to a standstill when the state creates money in excess,' says Heinrich Steinmann, pointing to the cash generated by the sovereigns via their central bank. 'In addition, 'The state in general works at low efficiency, and it is consuming more value than what is contributing positively to economic well-being.'

'Scaling up risks may cause them to cascade rather than cancel out. The bigger and more complex the structure, the greater this risk ... Because size and complexity increase the chances of cross-contamination,' wrote Andrew Haldane and Robert May in an article in the *Financial Times*. 'Errors do not cancel; they cascade. There is a flaw of large numbers.'[7]

These are large *red* numbers. In the past, 'red' meant communism. Now it stands for *debt and deficits* (DAD) which is worse than communism as far as the economy and the common citizen are concerned. It is the color of the State Supermarket, which wants to be everybody's *'daddy'*.[8]

'The present situation in banking is in many respects perverse,' say Haldane and May. They are right. Big salvage operations have an often overlooked any downside. The essence of it is that, by creating an excessive amount of money the state loses its credit standing, while the printing presses accelerate, resulting in a breakdown in business confidence and the value of money shrinks sharply.

Typically, this takes place within a pattern of misguided incentives, further encouraged by lack of transparency and inadequate risk controls. Since the 1980s, misguided incentives have accelerated the drift toward an economic precipice, leading to the question of whether Alan Greenspan's 'New Economy' was only smoke and mirrors after all.

If there was ever a 'New Economy', then its constituent parts were mismanaged.[9] The blend of technology, deregulation, globalization, innovation and high leverage proved to be toxic. Supergearing carried enormous risk. It is indeed ironic that instead of strengthening the financial system by increasing the robustness of the individual institutions, some of the 'New Economy's' basic elements did quite the reverse, inciting managers and traders to take inordinate risks and, comparatively speaking, reducing the banks' capability to absorb loss.

Technology was supposed to be been an enabling factor, and up to a point this was true. During the 1980s and 1990s it contributed significantly in enlarging the financial industry's business perspective. Theoretically it also assisted in the control of risk through real-time networks, mathematical models and processing power. In practice, however, computers, models and networks made possible more risk-taking and greater leverage. Bankers and other market players failed to account for the fact that a comparatively small change in the value of an underlying security can lead to a large change in exposure and, while gearing can increase profits in good times, it works against the leveraged entity in bad times, creating havoc in its finances.

It therefore comes as no surprise that in 2007 the financial machine sprang out of gear. As the number of leveraged parties – from investors to banks and sovereigns – multiplied, the financial game ran wild, with scant attention being paid to necessary controls. Age-old pillars of sound banking, such as liquidity, were put on the back burner.

There has also been a generally recognized capital inadequacy in vital financial industry sectors, most particularly in banking. No wonder, therefore, that some three decades since globalization began, there is a need for re-regulation; this time on a global scale. The unexpected consequences of globalization, rapid innovation in financial instruments and unbounded leverage have become key reasons behind the drive to re-regulate banking and other financial industry sectors.

The fact that there should be new norms became evident a few years after deregulation and globalization had worked their way through the system, but no one paid attention to this until the time and motion machine of finance caught fire. While globalization was hailed as something of a holy grail, since the late 1980s a much higher frequency of financial crises meant that investors' faith in the global economy began to get shaky. They are plenty to reasons to doubt what is written in the books of credit institutions, the accuracy of their earnings estimates, and the foundations of their creditworthiness, even if they carry an AA rating.

The lack of dependable figures on assets, liabilities, profits and losses affects the psychology of people dealing with the perpetual motion machine of global finance, and adds to the rough ride for the world's markets. The credit crisis that hit in the first years of the 2007–12 economic earthquake had a direct impact on the value of important real assets (such as real estate),[10] as well as on stock markets (particularly on bank stocks).

The problems that engulfed inventoried derivatives and structured financial products (see section below entitled 'Novel financial instruments...') has led to a prolonged malfunctioning of Western economies. Sovereigns and central bankers now appreciate that where the economic and financial system suffered most was in generating future growth, but there is no clear plan on how to repair the damage to ensure a longer-term efficient and resilient financial environment.

Expanding financial markets and their scams

After the end of the Second World War, and most particularly since the 1980s, financial markets have been expanding over three dimensions: geography, types of products, and the nature of the market participants, all of which require regulation and supervision. The 'shock and awe' necessary to convince investors and other market players that the train is back on its tracks, is not, however, necessarily provided by Basel III.

The financial markets' geographical expansion into uncharted territory, and the systemic risk this poses, is the theme of Chapter 3. This chapter is concerned with products and participants – two subjects that correlate between themselves and with geographical expansion.

Financial markets were originally established, and are still widely regarded, as *asset markets*. At present, this term is misleading but continues to be used because of lack of a term that includes the notion of *both* assets and liabilities. While, classically, trading in assets was the main focus, if the characteristics of the 1980s, 1990s and the first decade of the twenty-first century were to be condensed into just one sentence, that would be that these days financial markets deal much more in *liabilities* – hence in *debt* – than in assets. The difference is significant: investing and trading in physical goods and in some services has a longer time horizon, but for other services and practically all virtual goods (securitized debt being an example), to leverage their value, the time horizon is short.

Gearing up invites speculators and creates a vicious cycle, which has been joined by the banks. Investors use their own money, but speculators gamble with borrowed money: the assets of others. Since the 1980s, these 'others' were pension funds, endowments and high net worth individuals. More recently they are taxpayers, as sovereigns rush to salvage large financial institutions by using lavish amounts of public money.

Globalization permitted market participants to increase their reach significantly, and not always for the better. The story of the Bernard Madoff US$65 billion scam,[11] the largest to date in financial history, is well known and does not need to be retold here. What is new, interesting and unsettling, however, is that Madoff's catchment area, as defined by Irving Picard, the court-appointed trustee overseeing the Madoff estate's bankruptcy, was universal and included a wide range of people and companies who had been defrauded.

Picard has received more than 16,000 claims from people who believe they were Madoff's victims, and has filed nearly 80 lawsuits seeking more than US$55 billion from dozens of banks, hedge funds and individuals.[12] This flood of litigation has taken on international dimensions, and came as the trustee charged with recovering Madoff money reached the deadline for seeking compensation.[13]

The global nature of these lawsuits represents more than 1,100 subpoenas and two years of investigation. They allege that some of the biggest American and European financial institutions, including J.P. Morgan, Citigroup, Merrill Lynch (now Bank of America), HSBC, UniCredit and UBS either failed to spot Madoff's decades-long Ponzi scheme, or were allegedly so close to it that they might have enabled it.

One of the lawsuits takes aim at an Austrian bank, Medici, run by Sonja Kohn, whom Picard describes as Madoff's 'criminal soul mate'. Another, an awesome suit for US$9 billion, asserts that HSBC hired KPMG twice, in 2005 and 2007, to probe Madoff, but that the bank failed to act when concerns were raised by the certified public accountants (CPAs).[14] The credibility of some 'investment' schemes was already threadbare. Picard's revelations explain the reasons.

The banks and individuals sued by Picard strenuously deny the allegations and say they will defend themselves vigorously in court. This promises to be globalized banking's (see Chapter 3) battle royal, and the Basel Committee could learn a great deal from it to institute worldwide 'catch a thief' clauses in Basel III – assigning direct personal responsibility for their execution to each bank's top management. In HSBC's case, the CPA spent more than six months on each review, and each time came back with a laundry list of potential problems.

The findings by KPMG included a warning that by allowing Madoff to act as subcustodian for his own funds created the potential that the trades were 'a sham in order to divert client cash'.[15] But nothing reportedly caused HSBC's management to change its relationship with Madoff, whom it continued to serve as custodian for multiple feeder firms until his arrest in 2008. The lesson for the Basel Committee is that, if Basel III does not include rules for disciplinary action in such cases of oversight and business as usual, it will be no more than a paper tiger, and its wider adoption will change nothing about the way that banks are run.

Nor has this been an isolated case. The trustee charged UBS with a similar inactivity connected to feeder funds (which must also come under Basel III regulations). The bank replied that it was trying to accommodate clients seeking access to the Madoff business – a very poor excuse indeed.

Access International Advisors, a French firm that served as the investment manager for one of the UBS-affiliated feeder funds, hired a diligence specialist, who came back with a stark warning: 'If this were a new investment product, not only would it simply fail to meet due diligence standards: you would likely shove it out the door.'[16] But again, for unknown reasons, business continued as usual as though CEOs, chief operating officers (COOs) and risk managers did not understand that a myriad opportunities present themselves with:

- a market-wide geographical explosion;
- novel financial instruments popping up like mushrooms; and
- the changing nature of financial markets' participants – with bifurcation between large and complex institutions and single individuals.

This has become a very complex system, made even more so because a great many of the bets being made were on future values while leverage saw to it that, when the market turned against the bets, losses cascaded across a series of geared-up positions. Add to that the ignorance characterizing many of the players regarding financial market fundamentals and one can see the hurdles facing the regulators.

It is no surprise that, in return for shouldering greater risk, partly resulting from opacity, the clearer-eyed investors require a much better income – from transborder deals rather than from those in their own country. This is one of the reasons why transborder arrangements are never that straightforward. Investors take unwarranted risks in the hope of making a fortune, and banks do the same.

The opportunity presents itself because financial technology has developed a bewildering array of complex instruments (mainly derivatives – see the next section) which have made it possible to create more leverage than ever before. This has become a regulator's nightmare, as investments across the global financial landscape take place in a variety of jurisdictions. Transborder capital flows themselves are a broad, and sometimes, ambiguous term. They include different kinds of financial transactions:

- Bank lending, both short- and long-term.
- Foreign direct investment (FDI) in all kinds of projects.
- Investment in public and private equities.
- Ephemeral positions taken for a rapid gain.

Each of these examples has its own characteristics, and whether or not a given trade is within the margins of legality varies between one jurisdiction and another. It also has different implications for political leverage, moral hazard, profit and exposure to risk. Often, gains depend on a fast reaction, which is one of the characteristics of speculation, as well as on how successfully or how poorly the investment is managed – including scant attention being paid to creditworthiness, lobbying and other political factors (see the next section).

Novel financial instruments and their challenges

Basel III, or whichever other set of rules and regulations for the banking industry might arise, can only be effective if it also addresses banking activities, financial instruments and human behavior. Of these, human behavior is the most elusive. However, this does not mean that any attempt to reign in greed by bringing wrongdoers to justice would be a failure, or that lobbyists should be encouraged in their activities (see the section below – The activities of lobbyists).

The challenges posed by *financial instruments* start with the fact that they are telling examples of human inventiveness. As tradable contracts, they give rise to a financial asset of one entity and a financial liability (or equity) of another. Examples of *financial assets* are: cash, demand deposits, time deposits, commercial paper, shares, and a long list of contractual rights. Debt and equity securities are assets from the holder's viewpoint and liabilities when seen from the perspective of the issuer.

Financial liabilities are principally debt obligations, money contractually due to another party, as well as employees' rights, obligations under insurance contracts, and pension liabilities. These are the simpler examples, and while they still are valid that list is incomplete because it is being enriched by novel derivatives almost on a daily basis (see section below – 'Regulations do not match...').

There are many issuers of financial liabilities, including sovereigns who have joined the bandwagon amid torrents of red ink. This has happened throughout history. Britain's Henry III was deeply in debt, and his contemporary, Charles V of the Holy Roman Empire, was also swimming in red ink. His credit was so low that he was often paying for borrowed money with an interest rate of 43 percent per year. The emperor was still able to obtain funds, however, because his creditors were afraid that if they refused him new loans they could lose the whole amount they had already advanced to the imperial treasury.[17] Sounds familiar?

Even if extreme cases are ignored, though, sovereigns deal more in financial liabilities than financial assets. Paper currency is a debt security. A country's consumer-led economic model, like the one prevailing in the USA, the UK, France, and other Western countries, is fuelled by deficit-financed transfers. Hence the risk that too much debt may spiral upwards and get out of control – as has happened so often in the past.

Novel instruments are to a very substantial extent debt-based. Asset-backed securities such as collateralized mortgage obligations (CMOs), repurchase agreements and securitized packages of receivables are generally considered to be assets, but in reality they are liabilities to the issuer and assets to the holder. In fact, they are 'assets' only when the parties to which they pertain honor their financial responsibilities. The situation is similar regarding options, warrants, futures contracts, forward contracts and swaps. These are assets only when they have a positive value for their holder, but if they have a negative value they are either useless (as in the case of options) or they are liabilities (as with futures and forwards).

Whether a financial instrument is old or new, each of the two counterparties in a transaction seeks to expand its contractual rights and limit its contractual obligations. A *contractual right* is the legally supported right to receive cash or another financial asset from the other party; or to exchange financial assets or financial liabilities with another entity under conditions that are potentially favorable to the holder.

Contractual obligations are, to a large part, debtor liabilities that come due. This is not appreciated sufficiently by theorists, who look at debt as a better option than equity because, among other reasons, it exploits an anomaly in the tax code of most countries. Equity is taxed, debt is not. Taxation and 'easy money' reasons have seen to it that the debt culture works like an epidemic, at all levels of society and in all quarters. At the consumer level, 'Borrowers were urged to gorge on cheap credit like geese being stuffed to create foie gras,' says John Lanchester.[18]

At corporate and sovereign levels, debt has increasingly become a recycling business. Credit markets have the power of limiting debt-fueled expansion by increasing the costs of debt when the risks of added debt outweigh the rewards. However, this power is not always exercised, particularly in years of plenty. Therefore, it does not discourage the theorists from looking at the borrowing of funds (from the perspective of the debt issuer) as a purchase option in an enterprise with the capital as the premium, and the value of the business as the strike price.

In this approach, the level of debt and the volatility of the corporate value are the crucial variables for determining the *risk premium*, but there is no assurance that its estimation is even remotely realistic (which is true in a growing number of cases). If it were, we would not have been hit by a five-year-long economic and banking crisis that destabilized the Western financial system.

With debt having taken such a commanding position, it comes as no surprise that the lion's share of innovation in financial instruments revolves around buying, combining and selling of contractual obligations. Where regulatory initiatives such as Basel III should pay a great deal of attention is that there is much less interest (as well as skill) in looking at the downside of the synergy between: debt, leverage and the long tail of risk distribution.

There is a symmetry in financial analysis. Forecasts and projections largely focus on the positive side of the most likely events or developments.

Downside scenarios, which spotlight negative after-effects and their implications that might cause major harm to the investor, the bank or even the whole economy, are downplayed. Yet, though the probability of their occurrence might appear to be slight, tail events (see Chapter 8) bring with them risks with a major impact, and particularly so among large and complex financial institutions.

Basel III will be on the wrong track if it attempts to equalize the risk assumed by institutions of different sizes and complexity. Another challenge confronting Basel III is associated with the credit standing of issuers of instruments and of counterparties. How to evaluate creditworthiness in a dependable manner has been one of the weakest links in the chain of novelty in debt-based financial instruments.

Creditworthiness is a concept as old as banking. As far as loans are concerned, banks have classically used a basic credit rating system that is no longer satisfactory. One of the results of the financial market's globalization has been that there is now a plurality of incompatible and (often) contradictory credit ratings. To remedy this shortcoming, Basel II promoted the employment of credit ratings by independent agencies. This proved to be short-lived, because the alchemy of turning B-rated commercial paper into AAA securitized bonds destroyed its credibility. The 2004–7 rally in the market for toxic securities has led to unprecedented billions of dollars in losses for all the big banks (and many of the smaller ones).

Write-downs proliferated to such an extent that even the US government's supposedly deep pockets could not provide enough to fill the gap, and politicians twisted the arm of the Financial Accounting Standards Board (FASB) to abandon marking-to-market.

At the time of writing, nobody really has a clear idea on how to create a dependable approach to credit rating, let alone a global system able to judge credit risk. Regulators tend to encourage banks to use their own internal risk models alongside the independent agencies' ratings, but these may be the problem rather than the solution, as few of these models are truly reliable.

In addition, the globally stretched banks, as well as individual investors, do not have the resources to conduct extensive independent credit analyses or to develop and test fail-safe credit evaluation models. One of the reasons why ratings by independent agencies proliferated in the pre-2007–12 years is that they offered a relatively cheap and easy shortcut to the process of evaluating the creditworthiness of counterparties and financial instruments.

The problems regulators are confronting with Basel III in connection with new financial instruments and market players' creditworthiness at large, are complex enough in themselves, but they are made even more intractable by human inventiveness, which is great in itself but has cost the world dear.

Regulations do not match the complexity of derivatives markets

Books and articles on financial history suggest that the existence of derivatives markets dates back to as early as the seventeenth century, when shares were sold and bought at a forward date and share options were traded. (The father of options was Thales (640?–546 BC), in ancient Greece.) Trading of forward contracts on rice in Japan in the seventeenth and eighteenth centuries has also been recorded.

Originally made as bilateral agreements, a form of today's over-the-counter (OTC) deals, derivatives trades also benefited from exchanges. What could be regarded as modern derivatives exchanges emerged in Chicago during the second half of the nineteenth century. Traders dealt in commodities, a practice that gained importance as, for the first time, quantities and prices were standardized, margin calls were regulated, and the possibility was introduced of fulfilling contracts by means of offsetting trades rather than delivering the underlying.[19]

Commodities trading characterized the great majority of early derivatives. The first currency swaps (a more sophisticated commodity) appeared in the 1960s, but they were mainly used to circumvent British capital controls rather than for wider trading. Currency derivatives, as we know them today, really started in the 1970s, after the Bretton Woods Agreement of stable exchange rates and dollar convertibility to gold by sovereigns was relegated to history.

This wider derivatives market took some time to gain momentum and, because of its relatively small size when in the early to mid-1980s banks asked the regulators where to write such deals, the answer was 'off-balance sheet' (OBS). This decision introduced a great amount of opacity into deals involving novel financial instruments, and the regulators came to regret it.

Regulation had taken the back seat because for a dozen years, from 1973 to 1985 the derivatives market barely rose, keeping below a level of about US$3 trillion per year. But it doubled during the latter years of the 1980s, and by 1997, the year of the East Asian financial crisis, it had exceeded US$35 trillion. At that level, over US$25 trillion, or 72 percent, was in OTC bank-to-bank derivatives deals rather than trades executed through stock exchanges.

In terms of notional principal amounts (a term borrowed from swaps, representing an amount of money that is typically not exchanged but serves as frame of reference), today the derivatives market stands at around US$1.2 quadrillion. In a way not unlike that of the late 1990s, the lion's share is dealt over the counter, with:

- interest rate contracts representing about 77.5 percent of the total;
- foreign exchange contracts at a little over 9 percent;

- credit default swaps (CDSs) more than 5 percent[20]; and
- the balance of 8 percent or so being commodity contracts, equity-linked contracts and others.

Regulators are concerned about the risks associated with derivative financial instruments because the majority of them benefit from opacity, novelty and high leveraging. Even without such reasons, however, any massive amount evidently harbors major risks.

The first major derivatives crisis to hit a financial institution and reach global dimensions came in September 1998, when Long-Term Capital Management (LTCM), of Greenwich, Connecticut failed. Its meltdown nearly blew out the world's financial system in what became the earliest 'New Economy' earthquake. Others followed, such as:

- the stock market crash of 2000;
- Enron's and WorldCom's scandals of 2002–3;
- the Lehman Brothers' bankruptcy in 2008; and
- the wider descent into the abyss of 2007–12 – which began with securitized subprimes, and other derivatives instruments.[21]

A post-mortem reference to LTCM and its derivatives bubble can be an eye-opener on needed regulation, inasmuch as this hedge fund was an agglomeration of high-flying bond traders and big-name academics who were recipients of the Nobel Prize in Economics. Myron Scholes and Robert Merton, who acted as LTCM's consultants and top salesman, were joined by David Mullins, a former Federal Reserve vice-chairman and heir apparent to Alan Greenspan, the chairman.

Contrary to what the words 'long term' might suggest, LTCM was a day-to-day money machine engaging in the riskiest bets made possible by the deregulation of financial markets. Its management left much to be desired, and among other deficiencies featured a totally inadequate approach to the control of exposure – being a sort of predecessor to Lehman Brothers.

LTCM investors, including pension funds and several banks, rushed to put their money with the company, because from its launch in 1994 the hedge fund reported handsome profits: a 27 percent rate of return in 1994, 59 percent in 1995, 57 percent in 1996, and so on until it crashed. There was no regulation in place to deal with LTCM risk, and still there is none – not even in the trimmed-down Basel III. Yet, it was no secret that the hedge fund subscribed to the Arthur Andersen and Baring schools of creative accounting, and, allegedly, regularly failed to subtract from its income statement the losses suffered from the high leverage of its balance sheets.[22]

Many individuals and institutional investors got their fingers burned from the high-flying hedge fund's downfall. Money was poured in it without due diligence. LTCM had entered into business with what was at the time the largest ever equity pool: US$1.25 billion, gathered from around the world. At the outset, major firms, including Paine-Webber, Sumitomo Bank, Dresdner Bank, Bank Julius Baer, Liechtenstein Global Trust and many others acted as if blind faith had replaced sound governance. In theory, LTCM's trades were a financial innovation, but in practice they were black magic which eluded US regulation – a privilege held by all hedge funds until very recently.[23]

In a letter to *The Economist*, James Schofield put this black magic in perspective by stating that much of what passed as financial innovation in recent years, and helped to trigger the near-collapse of the finance industry, was little more than an ingenious sleight of hand.[24] (He also pointed out that, in his opinion, the term 'innovation' is improperly used in finance, because bankers are not on a par with those who invented the transistor, decoded the human genome, found cures for diseases or created other technological breakthroughs benefiting the real economy and society at large.)

All this is highly relevant to Basel III and the work being done by the Basel Committee. The many themes revolving around the financial time and motion machine, central bankers' trilemma, ever-expanding markets and their fast-evolving instruments have deliberately been included in this introductory chapter to remind the reader of the complexity of a holistic global regulation of banking and of the finance industry at large.

Basel III will be an irrelevant blip in the history of finance if it fails to compel banks to assume and uphold a *fiduciary duty of care* when dealing with other people's money, whether this comes from pension funds, state and municipal governments or common citizens. Or if it condones the behavior of bankers who try to prevent legislators and regulators from performing their duty.

For example, on September 29, 2010, Lloyd Blankfein, chief executive of Goldman Sachs, issued a thinly veiled warning that the bank could take its operations out of Europe if the regulatory crackdown on the industry became tougher.[25] These comments came only weeks after the Basel Committee on Banking Supervision released the new set of rules to increase banks' capital and liquidity requirements.

Unwarranted pressure from those who should be regulated weakens the politicians' will to enact new regulatory rules and laws. As an example, the most important provision of Basel III, aimed at allowing insolvent banks to exit the market without putting the functioning of the financial system at risk, did not gain the required consensus. Instead the door has been left open to give big global banks special treatment using taxpayers' money and sovereign over-indebtedness, the way it has happened during the recent major financial crisis.

Zero results have also been obtained (so far) in terms of regulatory requirements aimed at a tougher cross-border supervision. With the exception of vague concepts such as 'improving transparency for business partners and for the market', nothing has been achieved that is enforceable on a global scale and is worth mentioning. Yet, if all banks and other financial institutions of systemic importance are not explicitly forbidden from gambling anywhere in the world, then new regulations are hardly worth the paper on which they are written.

Dark pools, special purpose vehicles and flash crash

Precisely because they are so inventive, banks should be subject to a regulation characterized by insight and foresight. An example of recent developments crying out for regulation are the fast-growing *dark pools* (also known as *dark liquidity pools*). These consist of off-exchange trading platforms whose prices are not made public, and are run by big global institutions as interbank platforms. They are designed for buying and selling shares without tipping off other traders, and are doing so in competition with stock exchanges, but in a non-transparent way.

Because they work outside traditional markets, these dark pools are believed to be a potential threat both to the established exchanges and to principles of transparency. At present, however, there are no regulations obliging them to be transparent, hence equity trading may become a con game without the majority of market participants even noticing.

Of particular concern are dark liquidity transactions, becoming quite prominent in the USA, where they make up an ever-growing proportion of equity market trading. According to some opinions, they already account for more than 10 percent of all trades. Analysts suggest it is likely that various dark pool providers could eventually join forces, combining up to a point their individual dark pools, and applying for equity exchange status, but under conditions that will largely be under their own control – not of the regulatory authorities.

So far this has been uncharted territory for Basel III. The way an official statement put it, Basel's regulators gave themselves up to mid-2011 to find a solution to regulating *shadow banking*, an umbrella name which tends to include the dark business mentioned above. Since this is a mare's nest, a '2011' target is far too optimistic. The banks' reaction is sure to involve swarms of lobbyists (see also the next section).

One of the reasons why dark liquidity pools are popular for moving large blocks of shares is that they operate anonymously, and according to several opinions that's a privilege big banks would fight to preserve. Bonds may also become subject to dark liquidity trading. Some of the world's largest investment banks have already thrown their weight behind electronic trading between institutions and their customers, particularly for government bonds.

Critics say that unregulated dark pools promises to be the next big financial scam, emphasizing that one of the financial scams of the first years of the twenty-first century, securitized subprimes among others, have been promoted by the (also unregulated) *variable interest entities* (VIEs). This term is used by the Financial Accounting Standards Board to refer to a legal party (the investee) in which the investor holds a controlling interest not based on the majority of voting rights.

Nearly synonymous with the VIEs are the *special purpose vehicles* (SPVs). Most SPVs have been designed primarily to provide off-balance-sheet finance to the bank's clients and to the institution itself. Basel III is not taking a position in respect of the control of SPVs. Perhaps because they are difficult to value, they have been permitted to continue their 'good work' unsupervised.

This is regrettable because, typically, SVPs are thinly capitalized; therefore they are a danger to the financial system. Other entities, particularly their parent, must provide them with financial back-up. One of these other entities should be the primary beneficiary, which means that at least one of the entities that have variable interests in an SVP or VIE must assume more than half of the expected, or unexpected, losses.

As should never be forgotten, SVPs were designed to overcome regulatory constraints. Their business strategy gained significant momentum in the years preceding the 2007–12 deep economic crisis. They became popular because of the banking industry's desire to hide failed transactions, free up capital, carry out asymmetric maturity transformations, and proceed with regulatory arbitrage. The three main classes of SPVs are:

- structured investment vehicles (SIVs);
- asset-backed commercial paper (ABCP) conduits; and
- SIV-lites, mainly fed with mortgage backed securities (MBSs) based on subprimes and other dubious instruments.

The three are related. SIVs and SIV-lites refinance themselves in the money market through asset-backed commercial paper. However, if credit risk rises or there is market panic, then SIVs face liquidity problems and eventually a torrent of red ink. Up to a point, huge losses are hidden from the public eye because of *conduits,* which are carried off balance sheet by the bank that creates them, and the alchemy of presenting the SIVs themselves as being independent of the parent company (a false premise).

Conduits are *high risk* instruments employed to make a fast buck, since the underlying instruments are usually cheap, often rolled-over every few months. Since regulatory constraints are practically non-existent in this regard, conduits and SIVs are set up freely by a credit institution for its own use and that of its clients. The fact that there is no regulation makes possible high leverage, satisfies risk appetites and allows investment in equity and debt with greater than statutory exposure.

Recent experience with doubtful financial approaches has shown that SPVs-related junk can find a market as long as the good times last. Banks portray mortgage-backed securities (especially those using pools of subprimes incorrectly rated as AAA, instead of CCC) and other doubtful products as extremely advanced instruments appealing to the 'sophisticated investor'. In reality, however, these have proved to be rather primitive instruments, used for gambling on the economy without any supervision. To make them even less transparent, the large majority of the different SPVs are based offshore and theoretically constitute an 'arm's-length vehicle'. That is a false statement. What they do is:

- to buy the most highly speculative assets as long as these allow the declaration of fake profits,
- to build themselves up with immense leverage ratios, and
- to borrow money short-term, but invest it over the longer term – thereby violating one of the cardinal rules of banking.

Any regulation which forgets the lessons of the past is destined to fail. Investors, banks and other companies as well as state and local governments that have been 'SIV-positive' – that is, they have used their investment fund to buy toxic waste in the form of SIV financial papers – had plenty of wounds to lick after 2007, when the bubble burst. This is true of all industries, though, not just of finance.

Another novel financial process crying out for prudential regulation but untouched by Basel III is *high frequency trading* (HFT). This is an altogether different ballgame than the SPVs, capitalizing on high technology. Its risk comes from the fact that some technological advances in the financial markets can have unwanted consequences. What HFT offers is a number of conceivable advantages for the markets' efficiency, including greater liquidity and narrower bid-offer spreads.

There is also a downside, where such things as data input errors, technical glitches and malfunctions are found. Because of the large volume of order entries affected, these lead to a massive price volatility, which generates uncertainty among traders, impeding the smooth functioning of financial markets and creating hazards that can lead to systemic risk.

Unexpected consequences might also arise from inadequate control of operational risks by market participants, particularly in the case of manual or technical errors – triggering an extremely fast transaction in the wake of a large volume of order entries. The consequences can be worse when market players abuse or manipulate the system, thus posing a threat to market integrity.

For example, on May 6, 2010, it took less than 30 minutes for the Dow Jones Industrial Average (DJIA) to fall by nearly 1,000 points, before rebounding. In a sequel to this *flash crash*, a liquidity crunch then spread to the equity market, as the automated trading systems paused in response to the dramatic price movements. Many traders withdrew from the market, and others reverted to manual systems but could not keep up with a spike in volume.

'Stub quotes', placeholder prices provided by market-makers, caused some shares in household names to be sold as penny stocks.[26] The damage was, however, contained because, within a short time investors had a chance to analyze trading data and returned to the market, though still shaken by the rapid swing in equity prices.

Basel III does not deal with flash crash, nor do its regulatory activities address technological issues. This is a severe mistake. Today, because banking and technology have merged into a single financial process with unprecedented loss-absorbing capabilities, capital rules that do not account for technological after-effects and failures are very misleading, and may prove to be worse than nothing.

Nor are the authorities so quick to solve issues that involved technological challenges. It took five months for regulators to explain what happened with flash crash. On October 1, 2010, two regulators: the Securities and Exchange Commission (SEC) and the Commodities Futures Trading Commission (CFTC) said that on May 6 a convergence of events led to the event – but it was primarily brought about by mathematical trading models executed very fast in a skittish market.[27]

Opinion polls following this long-awaited regulatory explanation have shown that investors responded with loss of faith to the way interconnected markets work today, and some extended their criticism to the way markets are regulated. The flash crash has shown how interdependent financial markets have become and, through them, also the global economy. It is only reasonable to expect that Basel III should not only reflect this market interdependency but also to regulate it.

The activities of lobbyists

Back in the Roosevelt years, the legislation that aroused the greatest negative reaction by embedded interests was the Public Utility Holding Company Act. 'Swarms of lobbyists descended on Capital Hill, and one newsman calculated they outnumbered the members of Congress,' says Nathan Miller '... [moreover] a significant portion of the flood of telegrams and letters that poured in upon Washington were fraudulent.'[28]

Subsequently, it was revealed that the utilities behind this tempest had spent well over a million dollars in their fight against the bill. Even revalued for inflation, that would be a drop in the ocean today, because in the decades since the 1930s, lobbying has become a very expensive business practice, and the government now bends over to provide lobbyists with funds, as documented by the Clinton Administration's prosecution of Bill Gates and Microsoft.[29]

Lobbying has a long history. In the early years of the nineteenth century, Matthew Bolton, the British industrialist, said that intensive political lobbying permits laws to be turned to one's favor. This is essentially what people and companies paying the lobbyists ask them to do. Indeed, one of the prime targets of lobbying is influence on regulation – in a wide range of industries from pharmaceuticals to banking.

Lobbyists exist practically wherever there are markets, and they constitute the most unregulated, occult business in finance and politics. Their job is to act as advocates of special interests, exercising pressure and buying consciences through what they euphemistically characterize as expressing their 'points of view.'

One of the typical lobbying practices in a democracy is meeting with lawmakers and government officials to influence their minds and/or alter their decisions. The game is asymmetric because the government officials, on whose opinions and decisions the lobbyists leave an impact, are people whom they know already quite well, since previously in their careers they had been bureaucrats or members of parliament.

This occult business has gone so far that the last couple of decades saw the birth of the government-lobbying alliance in the USA, a metamorphosis of the *industrial–military* complex of which President Dwight Eisenhower spoke in the 1950s. The fear that new legislation or regulations will deprive the beneficiaries of the possibilities of extraordinary earnings, translates into the political will to step backwards – through lobbying. In its short life Basel III had had plenty of that.

A similar case can be made for FINREG.[30] During the 2010 Congress sessions aimed at restructuring the American financial industry's regulations 'K Street', Washington's fabled home of lobbyists, were ultra busy. Prominent lobbying groups successfully watered down regulatory clauses during months of congressional horse-trading over the nature and extent of the new rules.

In the minds of many people, neither the Senate nor the House version of the bill, which was given the names of its sponsors, Senator Dodd and Representative Frank[31], had gone far enough. Yet the banks still resisted it fiercely. To neutralize some of the lobbyists' actions, in mid-May 2010 over 2,000 demonstrators from 20 states descended on the nation's capital to 'lobby the lobbyists' and express their anger over their work for Wall Street.[32]

Simon Johnson, a professor at the Massachusetts Institute of Technology, said that, with FINREG, the critical question of being 'too big to fail', which provided the excuse for the massive salvage of big banks, was ducked because there was no broad bank break-up plan on the table. Other critics said that even if there had been a plan nothing would have been decided because of the impact of the lobbyists. In the aftermath, the attempt to force banks out of riskier activities and ban them from taking a different position in the market than that of their customers, fell off the radar screen.

In quite a similar way, in their opposition to Basel III, K Street lobbyists, and the financial institutions behind them, argued that, rather than preventing banks from using their insured deposits to gamble on risky instruments, the new rules would make legitimate hedging prohibitively expensive. That is nonsense. What has curiously been called 'legitimate hedging' is a misnomer chosen to hide gambling.

Nor are lobbyists operating only in Washington, DC. Brussels, where the European Union (EU) Executive is located, has a swarm of them – some 17,000 – just waiting for a budget and a signal to get on the move. (A week prior to Lloyd Blankfein's statement regarding Goldman Sachs, quoted earlier in the chapter, EU officials had approved a new system of pan-European regulatory bodies with additional powers – for example, to ban certain financial products or activities in times of market stress.

Consumer protection has been another victim of lobbying. In early March 2011, Mervyn King, the governor of the Bank of England, criticized banks that make profits from 'unsuspecting customers, particularly institutional customers'.[33] He also said that banks that are 'too important to fail' are tempted by excessive risk and bonuses.[34]

King is right. In the USA, in France and in the UK there have been grumbles about bankers' pay and outsize bonuses. Barclays, for example, revealed that salaries and bonuses of Bob Diamond, its CEO, and two top executives of Barclays Capital totaled £30 million (US$48 million).[35] The almost bankrupt Royal Bank of Scotland, saved at the eleventh hour through taxpayers' money, also paid millions of pounds sterling in bonuses.

Meanwhile, there is another political fuss brewing over the tax policies of big banks. In the UK, Barclays was forced to reveal that it had paid just £113 million (US$171 million) in British corporation tax in 2009, equivalent to 2.5 percent of its global pre-tax profit that year[36] – or less than four times what it paid its three top executives as bonuses for 2010.

As these and similar cases of poor judgment demonstrate, there are very good reasons why regulators want to see changes to the way bankers are rewarded. One of the better approaches is that larger banks should legally be required to defer 50 percent of executive bonuses for three years or more, and link the payments to performance. They would also have to:

- determine which of their employees trade in areas that could inflict substantial damage to the bank, and
- ensure that bonuses and other oversized compensation schemes do not encourage excessive risk-taking or contribute to systemic risk.

But while some banks have already introduced similar changes or are planning to do so, the majority of big global banks are opposed to such changes. The army of lobbyists is always ready to descend on legislators, regulators, central bankers and other government officials who even dare to suggest a change in the status quo.

3
Global Banking and Systemic Risk

Globalized finance is not a branch of international trade

The aim of this section is not to 'structure reality' but to *restructure around reality* the business of global finance as distinct from, but related to, international trade. The distinction that keeps these two notions apart is important precisely because it permits us to look at Basel III with the proper perspective. Quite often, there is confusion between global banking and international trade, even though each has its own set of risks and therefore requirements for regulation, and any successful regulation of global banking has to take note of the specific characteristics of financial markets and their instruments (Chapter 1).

It is a mistake to confuse global banking with international trade, and vice versa, if for no other reason than an interruption in international trade is bad enough, but its after-effects are as nothing compared to a breakdown in global banking. With the former event, the economies of many countries will suffer, but with the latter the whole global economy will freeze.

A snapshot of past events helps to better understand what we are talking about. By all evidence, the history of international trade started as the fourth millennium BC was coming to a close.[1] Trade with other than nearby cities and nations was promoted by maritime activities. Its evolution provides more evidence (if more is needed) that there is no order, no matter how old or important, which in its beginning was not novel, poorly understood and (for a variety of reasons) contested.

The word *trade* implies an exchange which may involve raw materials, other commodities, manufactured goods or services. Though trade contracts may span several years, each transaction is typically short-term, characterized by specifics that are not necessarily contractual. Travel agencies, for example, distinguish between 'imported tourism' when they deal with foreigners visiting the country in which they are based; and 'exported tourism', when they deal with their home country's citizens traveling abroad.

While in the 5,000 years of its existence international trade had its ups and downs, it has never really ceased to exist. One of its most recent significant 'downs' came with the start of the First World War, in 1914. Another 'down' has been the consequences of the 2007–12 major economic crisis and the ensuring recession, which hit trade hard. Global GDP fell by only 0.6 percent in 2009, the year following Lehman's demise, but the volume of world exports dropped by 12.2 percent, and the recovery of global trade has been uneven. Emerging economies of the G20: restarted their trading rather rapidly, and by 2010 were importing and exporting around 10 percent more than in their best pre-crisis years.[2]

This, however, does not mean that the globalization of banking – the way it sprang up towards the end of the twentieth century, is back on track.[3] The concepts underpinning international trade and financial globalization are by no means interchangeable; they differ because they are based on different criteria and business factors.

One of financial globalization's major differences from international trade is its longer-term perspective. With the exception of 'hot money', which is seeking quick gains or temporary diversification, foreign direct investments (FDIs) are not a short-term proposition. Usually, though not always, an *investment* is not a trade in the more classical sense of the term. To be profitable, an investment:

- must be properly researched;
- takes time to mature; and
- has to be managed in an able manner over a period of time.

In other activities, too, from loans to mergers and acquisitions, global banking requires continuity, which can easily be disrupted by event risk (see Chapter 8): counterparty failure to live up to its commitments, protectionism, civil strife, wars and other upheavals – for example, a significant drop in counterparty creditworthiness.

Because of the ravages created by the First World War, in the early twentieth century, the international credit system was ruined. The antagonists: Germany, the UK and France, who were also major exporting countries found themselves weighed down by mountains of debt; their currencies collapsed, and for the impoverished treasuries global credit (as compared to trade) became a scarce commodity.

This contrasted sharply with conditions in the second half of the nineteenth century, when a sophisticated system of *international credit* was developed in London, and this became the kernel of cross-border commercial exchanges. The First World War destroyed its infrastructure; and banks and sovereigns found that stresses affecting global credit had major effects on their business. This was less the case in trade, however, even though banking (in the way it is established today) has been a promoter of trade since ancient times.[4]

The classical concept of international trade involves activities taking place between two willing parties in an exchange of money and commodities, but global banking goes beyond money exchange, with its aims ranging from discovering profitable financial deals to providing credit, overcoming legal differences between jurisdictions and other challenges.

It is precisely because of this range of activities that Western banks have turned globalization into gold, not just in one but in four different ways. First, by following Western multinationals abroad, commercial and investment banks established bridgeheads in developing countries at practically no cost. By contrast, entering distant markets on their own would have required significant expense.

Second, they improved their position in the global financial market by providing the bigger companies in emerging economies with worldwide financial expertise, which local banks could not offer. As a result, they creamed off the wealth produced by industrial activities in developing markets in terms of investment banking, loans and other services.

Third, some credit institutions, for example, Citigroup, had the foresight to acquire or establish retail banking subsidiaries in the new markets they entered. This strategy provided them with low-cost deposits, since emerging markets feature many savers. (In the late 1980s, Walter Wriston, the then CEO of Citibank said that the US$3 trillion deposits by Japanese savers in Japan's postal banks kept him awake at night.)

Fourth, western banks brought and aggressively marketed abroad their novel financial instruments, finding or creating important outlets for them eventually to the dismay of local banks and other investors. Only late in the day was it discovered that the AAA rating awarded by rating agencies to derivative instruments in their portfolios, such as securitized subprimes, was a fake.

All this did not happen overnight. Many events underpinning the forces behind global banking discussed above started with the Smithsonian Agreement of the early 1970s, which unleashed a torrent of new forms of risk. In parallel with that came the ability to price new financial instruments in a way that found acceptance by the market.[5] Favorable winds connected to political aspects of financial globalization also helped. Working in unison for a couple of decades, these business factors created a totally new global financial landscape, which the 2007–12 economic and banking crisis shook to its foundations.

Global banking's challenges and the Financial Stability Board

The rapid growth of global banking, which contributed to the increasing importance of financial markets, and its synergy with international trade, have altered the dynamics of monetary transmission processes. This has had an evident impact on monetary policies, as globalization raised the degree of uncertainty with which monetary and fiscal decisions are taken. From a monetary policy viewpoint, two important questions have been:

- how, and by how much, globalization has affected price developments; and
- whether greater worldwide economic integration dampens inflation rates in the Western world.

Closely connected to the first query is if, and to what extent, globalization – and most particularly global banking – has altered the channels of influence of monetary policy measures through greater integration of economic activities and increasing interdependency of different economies. If it has, then greater coordination among monetary policy poles is needed, but so far The Group of Twenty (G20) has provided a weak leadership.

While both the G20 and the Group of Seven (G7), which preceded it, tried to address some of the problems confronting local monetary authorities, in dealing with global financial issues most countries continue to use national-centered policies. They approach bigger-picture reforms from a narrow perspective, applying measures which (apart from their heterogeneity) are not particularly effective.

By taking a narrow view of problems that have outgrown the straitjacket of local and national conditions, sovereigns show both nearsightedness and indiscretion – to their own detriment. There was a precedence for this at the time of the French resistance against German occupation. History books say that 95 percent of the *résistants* and agents who were caught owed their arrests to their own indiscretion.[6] The twenty-first-century's *résistants*:

- make decisions without due consideration of systemic risk (see next section), whose presence is talked about but is not handled in a rigorous way; and
- oppose the existence of a central authority, choosing to remain as a loose group of heads of state – which ensures that lessons from successive crises are forgotten and therefore the same mistakes are being repeated.

The Bank for International Settlements (BIS) has instituted the Financial Stability Board (FSB), a global club of regulators, to oversee systemic risk. This is commendable, but like the Basel Committee it works through inverse delegation. Moreover, the lack of vital information among regulators about deficiencies in banks' capital reserves, funding practices and other issues such as problems connected to asset management, handicaps its work.

As its name implies, the goal of the FSB is to promote financial stability. The term stands for a condition in which the financial system – including its intermediaries, markets and market infrastructures – is capable of withstanding shocks and the unraveling of financial imbalances.[7]

Financial stability helps to mitigate the likelihood of disruptions in the functioning of markets and in financial intermediation. Proactive approaches require the proper identification of the main sources of risk and vulnerability. These may be, for example, inordinate risk taking, unreliable risk metrics, inefficiencies in the allocation of capital (from savers to investors) and the mispricing of risk and return. To be effective, the monitoring of financial stability must be forward-looking, anticipating events rather than chasing them like a fire brigade.

At the top of the list of FSB's priorities is data on the links among big global banks as well as between them and other sectors of the financial system. Many European institutions, for example, were loaded with securities linked to the American housing market, and they lost heavily when securitized subprimes turned to dust.

Similarly, for the control of systemic risk, much more information than is at present available is needed about the banks' transborder exposure, as well as the nature of the asset classes underlying derivative instruments and specific concentrations. A couple of mammoth institutions capsizing can carry down with them the whole global financial system – and these institutions continue to grow in size. Between 2003 and 2007 the world's ten biggest banks more than doubled their balance sheets,[8] and since 2007 this concentration has increased as healthier big banks absorbed those on the brink of bankruptcy, while new threats have shown up outside regulated banking.[9]

The FSB's initiative is most welcome, because keeping vital financial control information close to one's chest has also contributed to the internationalization of a number of malfunctions, fed by sloppy errors and serious omissions. There is no better example than the US$65 billion Madoff bankruptcy (see Chapter 2), displaying supervisors' inactivity despite information they received from whistleblowers.

The principle is: what the Financial Stability Board, and the regulators at large, do not know will hurt – because the lack of vital information can greatly increase systemic risk. But really valuable information is scarce. Only after financial losses begin to mount is the absence badly felt, and by then it is too late, as news about insolvency and illiquidity heighten market uncertainty (see also Chapter 8 on home–host challenges). The 80th Annual Report by BIS aptly notes: 'Banks' liquidity and funding problems are greatest ... In addition, host countries suffered disruptions in intermediation as foreign banks experienced strains in their home market or in third countries.'

If economic and financial globalization has created such headaches, it would be normal to expect that it has also provided benefits. An often mentioned example of the pros is lower rates of inflation in Western economies. By early 2011, however, this example no longer applies, as inflation either has taken off, or is generally expected to do so. At the time of writing it is already over 4 percent in Britain (and 5.5 percent in China), while in December 2010 Germany, too, confronted an unexpected rise in inflation.

Bernanke says that he does not worry about inflation (even if in the US core inflation is picking up) because, according to prevailing economic theories, the influence of external price movements on the rate of change in domestic prices is often merely temporary. But what if this is not the case? With flexible exchange rates, inflationary trends ultimately hinge on the increase in the general price level supported by the central bank. If, and only if, the central bank is pursuing a clearly defined goal of price stability will it counteract pressures on the overall inflation rate resulting from changes in relative prices.

This is not, however, what Western central banks are doing nowadays. Leaving the globalized financial markets to do the central bank's job is tantamount to avoiding tough decisions by doing nothing. Global banking cannot pursue an expansionary or restrictive monetary policy 'on behalf of' central banks. Economists and central bankers who think that such miracles do happen have lost touch with reality. Critics say that, rather than targeting price stability: Western central banks have done their best to raise the heads of the inflation hydra, and global banking has also contributed to it through superleveraging, while regulatory scrutiny has been diminished as supervisors averted their gaze.

Under these conditions, it cannot be taken for granted that globalization has strengthened the monetary authorities' orientation toward price stability. Quite the contrary, in fact – the longer-term policy of nearly zero interest rates and quantitative easing (as practiced by Western central banks) will in all likelihood bring serious problems of its own. Neither is it an undisputed truth that much greater capital mobility engineered by global banking enhances the incentive for market discipline.

Another argument for the pros, whose proof has been anything than conclusive, is that advances in information and communications technology, as well as the deregulation of the banking industry, have been drivers of increased economic well-being. While these developments did affect up to a point the conditions under which monetary policy operates, they were related more to greater international competition than to financial stability.

The impact of the globalization of banking (see above) was double-edged: the rapid industrialization of relatively inefficient emerging markets meant that the cost of commodities (particularly oil and copper) rose rapidly, while the growing consumption of others, such as coal, had negative environmental effects.[10] This is not a theme of this book, but should be kept in mind as an example of collateral damage beyond the issue of price stability.

In mid-2007, just prior to the start of the major economic crisis, a study by the Organisation for Economic Co-operation and Development (OECD) attempted to quantify globalization's contribution to commodity price trends. It found that the fast growth of the non-OECD countries could have increased real oil prices by between 20 percent and 40 percent in the 2000–5 timeframe. An IMF study reached similar conclusions.[11]

Empirical evidence is also suggesting that important competitive pressure resulting from low-cost labor in developing countries has weakened the link between prices and production costs. The link between production needs and capacity build-ups has also been broken. In some industries, capacity utilization has fallen significantly, with car manufacturing providing an example of this. Sergio Marcchione, Fiat's and Chrysler's CEO, has been saying that, for a world consumption of about 50 million cars per year there is an installed production capacity of between 90 and 95 million cars.

Capacity under-utilization should be seen as one of global banking's major negatives, since new factories are financed through loans which cannot be served (let alone repaid) as there is no income. Housing also is confronting over-capacity problems. The glut of unsold houses in the USA, Spain and (more recently) China has severe financial and social consequences.

In conclusion, regulatory authorities do appreciate that global banking needs solutions which ensure that the institutions are not overleveraged, their assets are sound, gambling has no place in their business, and their lending is properly funded. However, economic and financial nationalism as well as other factors do not permit a devolution of authority able to make the supervision of global banking more factual and efficient. The result is that global bank regulation has one eye open and the other shut.

Contagion from global crises and systemic risk

On June 28, 1994, *Folha de Sao Paulo*, a leading business daily in Brazil, printed an article: 'Next Crisis Is in the Banks'. It was written by Clovis Rossi, who at the time was covering the G7 summit in Lyon, France, and probably got a closer look at the pains global banking was going through as well as the risks of contagion.

The central theme of Rossi's article was based on the pre-summit remarks by Michel Camdessus, at that time the managing director of the International Monetary Fund (IMF), who had reportedly said that the financial system was in pieces. The message from the IMF seminar preceding the G7 meeting was that the 'next earthquake' in the globalized world will be in the banking industry. Therefore, as Camdessus had said, according to Rossi, it was 'extremely urgent to tighten the screws'.[12]

This statement proved to be prophetic, and the fact that the global financial and banking cataclysm came a dozen years after the warning is proof that nothing was done in the intervening period to avert it. Nor was Michel Camdessus the only person ringing the alarm bell. Several warnings were given by other experts regarding forthcoming banking crises and the incompetence of the authorities to deal with them. Examples of subsequent crises include:

The 1997 severe banking crisis in Thailand, Indonesia and South Korea; and

The 1998 bankruptcy of Russian banks and the eleventh-hour salvage of LTCM.

No surprise, therefore, that financial imbalances such as credit and market bubbles built up over time and then suddenly unraveled, with detrimental effects on intermediaries and markets more or less simultaneously. In addition, the shared exposure to financial shocks had a negative effect on a range of financial players and led to contagion.[13]

Much of what happened in global banking in those go-go years of the end of the twentieth century was a result of the wild speculation fed by softening regulatory and supervisory standards. There were many warnings about the likelihood of systemic risk if proper controls were not established, but governments chose to ignore them because government control over banking and financial activities had lost its influence, and the pendulum had swung in the direction of writing blank checks and encouraging financial speculation.

As the twentieth century came to a close, politicians were more interested in spending money on unaffordable and unsustainable endowments, rather than focusing on good governance. The fundamental philosophy that underpins the ever-growing 'state supermarket' has become a case of robbing the thrifty to pay for the improvident – while, at the same time, bankers and traders who make a killing through all sorts of highly risky instruments have been admired as superstars.

Combined with the trend toward unlimited globalization,[14] the momentum of which continued to increase through the 1990s and early 2000s, the 'casino society' presented policy-makers with a series of challenges. One of them was the likely effect of growing interlinkages between national economies and large global banks.[15] Another revolved around early signs that the banks' balance sheets were increasingly falling outside the reach of national regulators.

Farsighted central bankers and regulators spoke about the increased danger of contagion, which was difficult to deny because the financial market's globalization changed the extent and manner in which monetary policy and regulatory measures can effectively apply. As was noted in the preceding section, a key question has been whether the growing integration of financial markets impaired, or even completely undermined, the influence of monetary policy and the reach and impact of the supervisory authorities.

Both of these points have contributed to the increase in global systemic risk. Bending the curve requires that heads of state, lawmakers and regulators understand clearly the global system's background risks and drivers; appreciate the power of plays and the players creating them; and are able to use Talleyrand's strategy of unstoppable negotiations with clear objectives in their minds. The essential part of such objectives is the need to:

- measure not only the level of intensity but also the effects of exposures accumulating at inflection points; and
- understand that the real source of the global systemic risk, and of its control, is found more in politics than in economics.

The major adverse event that will trigger a loss of confidence in the financial system, as well as a loss of economic value that has significant adverse effects on the economy, does not necessarily need to be financial. A major physical or economic event can have a severe aftermath. It is not something that comes out of a cloud and then simply disappears. The tsunami that hit Japan in mid-March 2011 was caused by a classical earthquake high on the Richter scale. The 10-meter-high tsunami was followed by the damage to four nuclear reactors at the Fukushima nuclear plant: each event was greater in intensity than its predecessor.

A classical example of systemic risk in the financial industry is the bank run, like the one that appeared in Britain in 2007 with Northern Rock. News or rumors about a bank's imminent inability to pay causes account holders to withdraw their money.[16] As market psychology turns negative and the rumors spread, the interbank lending market freezes, as happened during the first two years of the 2007–12 deep economic and banking crisis.

Bank runs, for example, can be contagious if depositors are imperfectly informed about the financial health of the credit institution they trusted with their money. They may also panic on the basis of runs they observe on other banks, which themselves might have been created by facts or by rumors.

Even if illiquidity rather than insolvency was the reason for the rumors, under certain conditions it is not easy to distinguish one from the other, particularly in a globalized financial environment. A consequence of bringing interbank lending to a halt is that other banks too become illiquid, or are seen as such. The worst case is that this leads to bank panic; however, a more common scenario is that, to improve their liquidity, banks issue no new loans and terminate existing loan agreements. This deprives companies of operating capital, forces them to postpone new projects, or to abandon existing ones, and obliges them to sell assets at fire sale prices in order to repay their loans.

Systemic risk can be exported. In the major bank run of the first Great Depression starting in 1929, about a third of all the banks in the USA became bankrupt. After this bank crisis, a system of deposit insurance was introduced, and capital requirements that banks had to meet were tightened. Economists believe that the reduction in the amount of credit available was a major contributory factor to the contagion.

The properties of the resulting measures of systemic risk closely parallel those of risk measures for portfolios of securities, according to the Bank for International Settlements (BIS).[17] The extra factor in the 2007–12 crisis is the failure of one or more large financial institution(s) that put the entire system at risk. Because economies and institutions are interlinked through globalization, none is immune from contagion.

Interbank markets panic in times of instability. If market players experience liquidity shocks through depositor withdrawals or changes in asset valuations, they react strongly and the overall amount of liquidity in the system may not be sufficient to honor all interbank market contracts.

An increasingly dangerous contagion in the global marketplace develops through asymmetric information leading to the inability of financially healthy banks to distinguish between good and bad counterparties, or to value their assets. This leads them to stop lending. To protect themselves, they hoard liquidity, and this renders the money market at best dysfunctional.

Eventually, poor functionality also becomes a channel of transmission of financial crises. In conclusion, in a globalized economic and financial environment banks are not only vulnerable to an economic downturn in their country of origin, and/or in one of the major markets where they operate, but also to a number of other factors, many of which have been magnified by transborder operations and asymmetries in worldwide financial information. Widespread imbalances in financial systems, lower creditworthiness accompanying lending booms, and other events affecting many intermediaries adversely have a negative impact on markets.

Regulatory arbitrage[18]

The severe economic and financial crisis of 2007–12 was strictly a creation of the banking industry. Unlike previous crises, this one was not caused by an external event such as a stock market crash or an emerging country's meltdown. The banking industry itself created it as an after-effect of lust and greed, but also because of generalized bad management and massive *regulatory arbitrage*, which itself is evidence of poor governance. Typically, the role of an *arbitrageur* is to make a quick profit via an investment. Arbitrageurs don't produce new financial instruments or own assets as patient investors. Their strategy is to come rapidly in and out of financial products already trading in the market – an activity which, to be successful, requires:

- first-class information;
- considerable financial acumen; and
- a fair amount of notoriety in the market where one operates.

Regulatory arbitrage is different in the sense that it is carried out over the medium to longer term and has as its aim the circumvention of laws and regulatory rules, particularly those connected to capital adequacy. An example is using hybrids instead of equity with Tier 1 capital (see the next section).

The real aim of this policy of gaming the financial system's regulations is to gain a quick profit from pure arbitrage to promote higher portfolio returns compared to ordinary market returns. Ethics aside, the downside is that, most often, the risks being taken are not covered by capital resources or available liquidity.

It is therefore no surprise that one of the reasons that contributed in a significant way to the 2007–12 crisis was the lack of global coordination to stop regulatory arbitrage before it became the supervisory authorities' nightmare. The Basel Committee is a place where central bankers meet to discuss their worries and wishes but, as has already been brought to the reader's attention,

- its authority rests on a process of inverse delegation,
- it does not have the power to take a bold initiative, and
- it cannot oblige national regulators to exercise timely control.

In addition, the need to strengthen financial supervision worldwide requires not only a deep understanding of systemic risk, which is the remit of Basel and of the Financial Stability Board (see the second section, above), but also earnest political decisions giving regulators the right to take bold action. Because of wide mobility and the growing dependence on debt of nearly all financial activities, there is a crying need for a supranational entity with the mission of watching over systemic risk. This entity should be given:

- a great deal of authority to act without consulting the different governments, and
- a charter that covers all components of the financial system and all sources of risk – including feedbacks, non-linearities, excessive greed and regulatory capital arbitrage.

It is no secret that regulatory capital standards set by the Basel Committee or any other supervisory authority are increasingly distorted by ongoing innovation in financial products. With Basel III, even before it is fully applied, banks have put into operation projects and models aimed at making small game of its higher capital ratios.

The big global banks perceive their technological leadership as their asset that is able to mitigate what may be the 'adverse effects' of higher capital requirements and other regulatory constraints on their profit-making. The supervisory authorities are well aware of these practices, but they don't have the budget to hire physicists, engineers and mathematicians who are able to counteract them.

It follows quite logically from this that the Basel Committee and Financial Stability Board should be endowed with a staff that includes 'rocket scientists',[19] clear-eyed bankers and traders willing and able to study and test the effects of financial innovation on the structure and risks of global banking as well as on capital standards. Experimentation and analysis should include the two-way relationship between financial systems and the economy, with an emphasis on:

- worst case scenarios,
- global interdependencies,

- conflicts of interest, and
- ways and means of weeding such conflicts out of the system.

Apart from such facilities and objectives, it is an illusion to talk about global banking supervision aiming at worldwide risk control in finance. As long as the mammoth money-center banks have their research laboratories well staffed with 'rocket scientists' – which the supervisory authorities are lacking – regulatory arbitrage will be the order of the day, not the exception.

Experimentation leads to invention, and to an understanding of the laws underpinning a given domain of activity. One of the issues that should attract the regulators' attention in terms of analysis and experimentation is the benefits, costs and risks of OTC versus exchange trading, not in the abstract but in direct connection to:

- types of instruments,
- market characteristics,
- creditworthiness of counterparties,
- amount of daily trading, and
- level of exposure assumed by each major counterparty both on- and off-balance sheet.

Closely connected to the themes associated with this research are the roles of OTC trading and central clearing, with a particular emphasis on derivatives. Other important research themes include *policy analysis* and its after-effects (all the way from monetary policy to fiscal policy); as well as regulatory policy and the way it is exercised in different jurisdictions, and cross-border with regard to money-center banks and other global financial entities.

Regulatory arbitrage will not suddenly stop because the supervisory authorities undertake such research and analysis projects, but experimentation can be instrumental in revealing the most and least negative aspects of current banking practices from the viewpoint of inefficiencies in the ultimate allocation of *credit risk*. Another theme to be brought under the magnifying glass of research are the asymmetries in *market risk*. In principle, risk allocation is inefficient if exposures end up systematically with parties that: have less than the necessary knowledge or experience in dealing with the distribution of risk, or they have only a marginal equity capital buffer to absorb losses because of unexpected tail events (see Chapter 8).

Several research papers, mainly from academia, have demonstrated that regulatory arbitrage tends to trigger asymmetric risk allocation, with credit exposures moving away from banks to less regulated financial entities. Since the start of the twenty-first century this has happened time and again with special purpose vehicles (SPVs). Indeed, as we saw in Chapter 1, SPVs were invented by banks to circumvent the capital requirement of covering risks with equity, as stipulated by supervisory rules and regulations.

Suggestions that the market can correct the emergence of unexpected exposures and inexperienced participants by penalizing poor risk control practices with losses, are pure theory. At worst, it is at the root of concerns by supervisors that capital arbitrage is a mechanism generating systemic risk, because market participants do not hold sufficient equity capital to guard against their assumed exposure.

At the beginning of the 2007–12 crisis, a case in point has been that of monoline insurers, who are comparatively less capitalized than is required by the trades they are doing and the guarantees that they give. A 2010 example is investment bankers who have begun to develop ways through which credit institutions might be able to circumvent the most punitive of the new capital rules drawn up in the context of Basel III. New financial products are being developed at present that would permit banks to circumvent the new capital rules by using novel, difficult to untangle, financing structures.

The way that anecdotal evidence has it, these novel regulatory arbitrage instruments, which will masquerade as 'assets', could be sold at a discount of 20 to 30 percent, either by means of actual sales or through other derivatives. In this way, they have–have found their way into Basel II capital, and they might also sneak into Basel III capital. One of the most interesting initiatives has focused on outlawing deferred tax assets (DTAs; more on them in Chapter 3)[20] from capital adequacy under Basel III, but this effort capsized under pressure from the Japanese government.

The Ponzi gamers support this sort of unethical finance as 'good creative thinking'. Critics look at it as the latest evidence that banks have learned nothing from the present crisis and will always invent ways and means of focusing on arbitraging the regulations. If, for example, pensions were manipulated in similar ways, one day pensioners would find out the hard way that the money they depended on was gone, and all that is left is useless paper.

There is a contagion effect associated with such scams. One bank does them because another has. But this cannot go on for ever. Disturbances in the underlying market can rapidly spill over to the widely used derivative instruments, in particular unsettling those entities that are the most leveraged. Experience has demonstrated that spot disturbances may pick up speed in the derivatives market and bounce back with a vengeance on the spot markets.

In studying the likelihood and impact of such events, experimentation can be of invaluable assistance. A good approach to simulating systemic risk is to employ interbank exposures and capital-to-assets contagion from this or that newly invented instrument which was. In a stress test, one or more large global banks can be assumed to fail, with the objective of emulating the number of other banks that would fail as a consequence.

An integral part of the aforementioned simulation should be mimicking each bank's 'hedging' and regulatory arbitrage. Sometimes, though by no means always, hedging is asymmetric and this can have disastrous consequences. If a number of market participants pursue similar strategies, particularly with leveraged derivative instruments, an unanticipated price movement in the spot market can have a devastating effect – and a shortage of capital because of regulatory arbitrage may lead to systemic risk.

Gaming Tier 1 capital should be a criminal offense under Basel III

Financial engineering was intended to be a creative process, but instead, it has allowed a small number of people and oversized banks to generate nothing but illusions, taking advantage of investors. While global banking could have benefited from the introduction of scientific methods and experimentation with largely subjective financial processes, scientific know-how has been used to create financial instability. The unwarranted changes can be expressed as manipulation of the 'facts' to become what some people want them to be, as opposed to what they really are does not happen only in banking. In the wake of the recent dramatic explosions among four nuclear reactors in the Fukushima power plant in Japan, it was revealed that, over several years, quality control reports had been faked.[21]

The creation of highly questionable 'assets' inflated the banks' balance sheets and 'justified' inordinately large salaries and bonuses. Through derivative instruments and other products, financial engineering has enabled unscrupulous individuals to hide losses and disclose only 'profits' as opposed to the true status of year-on-year financial results.

As noted in the previous section, many of the twists that have been brought to financial reporting and to the markets by way of 'rocket science' relate to regulatory capital arbitrage. In their way, such unwarranted practices contributed to the 2007–12 crisis. The good news is that evidence exists on how destructive these practices are; but the bad news is that, allegedly, they are still mainstream.

Novel instruments specifically designed for gaming Tier 1 (equity) capital are, among others, *perpetual deeply subordinated bonds*.[22] In the early 2000s, with the equity market in the doldrums following the bust of 2000, regulators permitted banks to add to their core capital (eligible Tier 1 regulatory capital) perpetual deeply subordinated notes that were callable 10 years down the line. These pay the investors a higher interest rate capped to a maximum coupon, but not every investor appreciated that.

Deeply subordinated bonds are at par with equity holdings in terms of capital at risk, but in contrast, they do not benefit from equity's upside. Therefore, they are not necessarily a good deal.

In spite of this, demand was strong and there was a rush of issues. For example, Compagnie Financière of Crédit Mutuel issued deeply subordinated bonds in June 2004 on a nominal amount of €100 million, subsequently increased because of market demand. The Anglo-Irish Bank followed in September 2004 with €200 million, increased to €600 million perpetual bonds that could be bought by the bank after 5½ years.[23]

Repurchase agreements announced in advance carry plenty of credit risk. The issuer may say s/he will buy the deeply subordinated bonds back, but may be unable or unwilling to do so. After all, they are perpetual. At the same time, however, their popularity among issuers and investors highlights the growing use of hybrid capital because of its misunderstood equity-like features.

Equally misunderstood has been the issuer's creditworthiness, as subsequent events have shown. The Anglo-Irish issue paid a coupon of 6 percent in the first year. That was the trap. Subsequently bondholders were to receive a coupon payment 25 basis points above the 10-year Euribor interest swap rate, that payment being capped at 9 percent.

The instrument's novelty capitalized on the fact that the issuance of hybrid capital had grown in popularity among banks, and not only among average investors. The perpetuals coupon acted as the hook, and Irish regulators presented no objection to this deal. For Anglo-Irish and other issuers it was a cheap way of acquiring funds, and (at least theoretically) it did not dilute shareholdings. The alternative would have been to issue equity.

What was publicly stated at time of issue is not what the Irish government and investors think today of the Anglo-Irish deeply subordinated bonds. With the benefit of hindsight it can be said: 'If I had known then what I know now', and the most up-to-date knowledge is that investors were very wrong when they allowed themselves to be attracted to these bonds, offering as they did higher yields than older notes. Claims from 'Tier 1' (a misnomer) bondholders rank at the bottom of the pecking order, just ahead of shareholders. This subordination was reflected in lower credit ratings for such deals.

There has also been plenty of credit rating hype, as with the subprimes of US fame.[24] The Anglo-Irish debt transaction was rated Baa1 by Moody's Investors Service, two notches below the bank's senior unsecured rating. Fitch Ratings assigned an A rating, one level below its senior rating.[25] By 2009–10 both credit ratings had turned to dust. Like the AAA ratings of subprime securitizations, they were a virtual reality that faded when confronted by the facts. The whole scheme amounted to unwarranted leverage that turned the Anglo-Irish into the 'Anglo-Toxic' Bank.[26]

This is precisely the theme of the present section. That investors are taken for a ride is their business, but when the government and regulators turn a blind eye is public business – and 'looking the other way' should never happen. When it does, it costs dozens of billions in currency, even in a relatively small country, as Irish citizen have found out the hard way.

When the crisis hit, the Irish government threw a great deal of taxpayers' money (as well as that of the IMF and the EU) at the problem. In fact, by the end of 2010, some of the 'novel instruments' of fake Tier 1 capital have been nothing else than straight taxpayers' money. (With hindsight we can say that how the perpetual deeply subordinated bonds fared depended on the issuer and on the market's appetite for risk.)

Banks are vulnerable to their own games because these are mainly asymmetric in terms of market risk and credit risk on the one side and of capital adequacy on the other. When credit risk rises, the hydra of leverage raises its heads and can eat up banks for breakfast. If risk management does the job it is supposed to do (see Chapter 8) then the vulnerability of banks to major shocks might be attenuated. Practical experience, however, teaches us that: banks are weakened because in good times risk control is less vigilant, and, moreover, they fake the data on their capital reserves, thereby depriving themselves of cash when they need it badly.

In an effort to create a level playing field, which would increase the banks' capital resources, on January 7, 2011, Basel issued the final elements of the reforms to raise the quality of regulatory capital. The terms and conditions of all future non-common Tier 1 (T1) and Tier 2 (T2) instruments of internationally active banks must have the option to be written off or to be converted into common equity. In this sense, T1 and T2 instruments going forward will look like contingent capital instruments.

The trigger would be at the point of non-viability, or when the bank would otherwise have collapsed without outside (mainly government) support. However, as was explained above, banks are actively searching for ways and means to jump the gun on new regulations before they are implemented – and regulator arbitrage is going unpunished.

It is difficult to conceive a worse policy. The message to commercial and investment bankers, as well as to governments, central bankers and regulators, is clear. Gaming Tier 1 capital can have catastrophic consequences not only for the institution doing it but also for the economy and financial system as a whole. Given the precarious state of the banking industry, and most particularly that of big global banks, the aftershocks can bring them down like a house of cards. Therefore, gaming Tier 1 capital should be a criminal offense under Basel III. But is anybody listening?

Banks too big to be saved should be allowed to fail

The way an article in *The Economist* put it: 'Rescuing banks can be like filling a bath with the plug out. It won't work if water flows out faster than it pours in.' The same article also provided an interesting statistic: 'deposits of non-residents in Irish banks were nearly €203 billion ... a figure larger than the €166 billion held by domestic residents and than Irish GDP.'[27] Because of gambling and of an unprecedented mismanagement of risk, Irish banks had lost large chunks of that money, and a careless snap decision by the Irish government guaranteed depositors all their assets, at the taxpayers' expense.

No questions were asked and no limits imposed, as a reasonable deposit insurance would do. The decision was dictatorial, because politicians assumed that Irish citizens had nothing to say about this unwarranted suffering. They had to endure the pain while the Irish economy looked like *The Economist's* bath with the plug out. This does not make sense.

Ireland has been a basket case in financial history, which suggests that systemic crises emerge through excesses, poor governance and the unraveling of widespread imbalances. Drift is the road to economic agony because nobody is really in charge; and when personal accountability is out of the picture the problems are intensified, particularly when times are bad.

In the absence of sound governance, even small events can lead to a repricing of risk. When this happens, not only does it adversely affect many financial institutions and markets, but it also generates its own momentum which, through feedback, sets in motion a self-reinforcing mechanism. This is how runaway risks in individual credit institutions spread throughout the financial system, with contagion channels acting directly by means of contractual relationships between market players, and indirectly, because of a general loss of confidence on the part of investors and of the market.

The significance of these negative effects for the banking system stems partly from the number of interbank linkages and partly from market psychology when bad news hits. This is particularly true when the authorities either try to suppress unfavorable information or it is revealed that they have been negligent in performing their duties.

In every financial institution, part of the failure in exposure control lies at the board and CEO level; while another part reflects the regulator's ability in applying the letter of the law (more on this later). A third part is because risk management models are primitive (for example, value at risk – VAR)[28] failing to incorporate effects of big market shocks.

In addition, banks dig, so to speak, their own grave by manipulating risk management models with the aim of reducing the amount of capital needed to enhance their financial staying power.[29] One way of doing so, and a frequently used one, is by underestimating correlation coefficients among instruments, counterparties, markets and other crucial variables (see Chapter 6).

This underplaying of exposure, and of capital adequacy, is most curious because even the banks themselves admit that they are taking big risks. Though they do not communicate the size of their positions or their concentration in markets, instruments and counterparties, by how much risky positions have increased can roughly be estimated from what banks report to regulators through value-at-risk.

Introduced with the Market Risk Amendment in 1996,[30] the VAR algorithm is an obsolete and tired model covering only certain principal risks and some risk factors. But even so it is an alarm bell, and the only one whose reporting is required by regulators in their efforts to determine the amount of capital banks should have against their trading positions. Put briefly, VAR is showing how much money a bank might lose should markets turn against it; if VAR is rising, this means the institution is taking a greater risk.

This happens all the time. The specific case this section brings to the reader's attention is VAR's rise in the early 2000s as rock-bottom interest rates set by Alan Greenspan (in the wake of the 2000 stock market crash), fed the fires of speculation by global banks. A weak risk management model and the low cost of money created the conditions for the 'perfect storm'. But even a weak risk management model may sometimes provide a useful signal. After 2001, VAR figures grew for nearly every global bank, to the point that some experts were saying that several banks could no longer be distinguished from hedge funds.

As reported in *The Economist*, in February 2004, UBS had stated that 'with markets and investor sentiment starting to improve' it would gradually increase credit and trading risks.[31] This was shown in its exposure: at the end of 2003 VAR exposure was US$260 billion compared to US$180 billion at the end of 2002 – a 50 percent increase. At J.P. Morgan Chase, VAR exposure was US$180 billion at the end of 2003 compared to US$120 at the end of 2002, also a 50 percent increase.

The value-at-risk exposure at the Morgan bank grew just as fast in 2003, but UBS held the lead with more than a quarter of a trillion dollars of value at risk. And behind the 'exposure giants' came other banks. Table 3.1 shows statistics worth keeping in mind in terms of exposure measured through value-at-risk. When these statistics became available, I asked a number of regulators what the reasons might be, and what they thought about them. To the first question, their answer was that there may be 'a number of reasons' (VAR cannot be more explicit, because it is a primitive model); and answers to the second question were not forthcoming, which I found to be quite curious.

Therefore, I pointed out in the course of these meetings that, in my opinion, two things were important with these VAR statistics: the *order of magnitude*, and the *annual increase* in exposure, which should be contrasted

Table 3.1 The zooming VAR that did not worry regulators

	2002 (US$ bn)	**2003 (US$ bn)**	**Increase in exposure (%)**
UBS	180	260	50
J.P. Morgan Chase	120	180	50
Citigroup	50	70	40
Morgan Stanley	50	60	20
Goldman Sachs	45	60	33
CSFB	40	50	25

with volatility. In 2003, with the exception of treasuries, markets became less volatile (for example, equity markets were less volatile than they had been for almost a decade).

In terms of background, *theoretically*, but only theoretically, if markets are half as volatile then the banks' positions could be twice as large for the same amount of capital reserve. In practice, this is the wrong hypothesis because volatility changes steadily, with unexpected spikes. Accounting for all that, the most important warning signal from the figures in Table 3.1 can be phrased neatly as: volatility was halved in 2003, but VARs rose by up to 50 percent.

This suggested that at some banks risk positions were reaching astronomic levels, compared with what they were at end of 2002. And the situation might even have been worse, because banks had increased their trading exposures in other ways too, such as by proprietary trading and direct investments in (and ownership of) hedge funds. In short, even an observer with dark glasses could see that a crisis was coming – which, of course, it did.

Nothing was done in time to deleverage the oversized global banking institutions. Instead, apart from throwing taxpayers' money to the four winds because, as a policy, the American, British and continental European governments decided to 'save' the global banks that were too big to be saved.

The Japanese government had invented that silly policy in the early 1990s and again 10 years later by lavishing public money on failed private banks, but was reluctant to bring wrongdoers to justice. This emboldened bankers into taking even greater but very poorly studied exposure on thin capital buffers, since they were faced with a win–win situation, and they had no worries about ethical fallout, penalties or prison terms.

What I call *Japanification*[32] – the easy but wrong and ineffective way out of a financial and banking crisis, has been followed on a large scale by Western governments unable to deal in a sensible manner with the 'too big to be saved' institutions. Their bail-outs have both created moral hazard and exacerbated the whole problem of bank supervision.

This did not escape the attention of some central bankers. On October 20, 2009, Mervyn King, governor of the Bank of England, told businessmen that regulation was not enough to keep banks from becoming 'too important to fail'. Instead, he said, banks should be split up[33] while:

- public money should underpin only those banks that operate as economically-necessary utilities, such as being responsible for payments systems and intermediation activities; and
- risky operations, such as proprietary trading and derivatives – in short, 'casino banking' – should be spun off to entities that do not benefit from sovereign guarantees.

Mervyn King did not say that bail-outs must be abolished, but he emphasized that regulators should be extra careful of individual and widespread imbalances that build up over time, making financial systems vulnerable. They should also sanction early herd behavior in financial markets (an example being the pattern identified in Table 3.1), which leads financial institutions to invest in similar risks.

For their part, governments must appreciate that throwing scarce and good money into a sea of bad debts not only creates a greater moral hazard but also consolidates leviathan banks into unmanageable entities whose sole salvation hinges on receiving a torrent of government support. To kick that habit, oversized institutions should have much higher capital requirements than other banks, and their activities should be regulated and supervised in the most rigorous manner on a global basis. Without that the recurrence of banking crises will never end.

4
Basel III Is a Grand Compromise, Not a Bold Initiative

Basel III should not repeat the errors of Basel II

Damaged by the Great Depression – though not by a self-inflicted injury, as happened in 2007 – banks used the capital they obtained from the Reconstruction Finance Corporation (RFC)[1] to redress their balance sheets rather than lending. Global banks in the USA, the UK, Germany, France, Belgium and the Netherlands repeated that practice with the lavish amount of money they received from governments during the recent economic crisis. And Japanese banks have done the same, on and off since the early 1990s.

Governments were forced to intervene in 2008–9 because the amount of risk that big global banks had assumed made small game of their capital ratios. This led the regulators to reevaluate capital requirements upward and to apply other rules, such as liquidity criteria. Some countries, such as Switzerland, also put a limit on the amount of leverage that banks could take on. In a nutshell, these were the principal means, up to the time of writing, that regulatory authorities put forward under the umbrella *Basel III*, whose aim is to:

- improve the quality and consistency of capital,
- avoid the excesses of leveraging on the balance sheet, and
- bend the banks' overreliance on short-term funding, which contributed greatly to the recent financial crisis.

The Basel Committee on Banking Supervision[2] presented its proposals for new capital and liquidity regulation on December 17, 2009. Initially Basel's documents were only proposals, but they still aroused a great deal of opposition and 'horse trading', as will be discussed briefly in this section. Basel III's consultation process has not been as lengthy as that of Basel II. The novelty was that governments became involved in changing several of the proposed new rules from capital adequacy to leverage ratio, treatment of financial stakes and minority interests.

While many jurisdictions tried to trim Basel III, some went well beyond its rules, directives and recommendations. In Switzerland, a commission of experts appointed by the Federal Council has proposed that, over and above a 10 percent Tier 1 capital, big Swiss banks should, in future, be obliged to set aside an additional capital buffer of 9 percent of their risk-weighted assets in the form of contingent convertibles (see the next section).

Critics of Basel III say that it follows too closely on the heels of Basel II,[3] which failed to do its intended job of keeping systemic risk at bay, and eventually became an embarrassment for regulators. According to experts, Basel II failed for four principal reasons:

- It took too long to implement.
- It gave commercial banks a free reign on amendments.
- It based itself too much on creditworthiness defined by independent rating agencies.
- Its rules did not benefit from rigorous supervisory control, with the result that laxity turned it into a 'free lunch' for the banking industry.

As governments and regulators turned a blind eye to the risks of hybrid capital, fake credit ratings and speculation with unsavory financial instruments (such as securitized subprimes), the perpetual money machine worked for itself rather than for the fulfillment of social and business aims. Commercial bankers, curiously, forgot that first and foremost their organizations had been depositary institutions. For their foray into uncharted territory they capitalized on:

(i) the repeal of the Glass–Steagall Act in the USA, which separated commercial banking from investment banking; and
(ii) deposit insurance, which turned the taxpayer into a guarantor of deposits wiped out through the folly of bank managers (see Chapter 12).

What Basel III should have done was to reintroduce the Glass–Steagall principle on a global scale, in appreciation of the fact that, without secure commercial banking, individuals, households and companies would not be confident about the safety of the money they deposit in a bank. Neither can they depend on payments, settlements, money transfers and clearing, nor on credits and loans.

Main Street and Wall Street came unstuck. In contrast to consumers, and small and medium-sized firms, big global manufacturing and merchandising companies don't really need the banks. They issue bonds on the capital market. But households and local firms don't have access to the capital market, so their best course is to borrow directly from the banking industry, which is why the credit institution's solvency and liquidity is so important.

It comes as no surprise therefore that the Basel Committee on Banking Supervision decided to act. Table 4.1 presents a quantitative comparison between the capital requirements of Basel III and those of Basel II. What exactly comes into core Tier 1, Additional Tier 1 and Tier 2 capital was presented briefly in Chapter 1 and is explained farther in Chapter 6, which focuses on the mechanics of Basel III. The purpose of Table 4.1 is to provide a bird-eye's view as well as a frame of reference for this chapter's themes.

Theoretically, total capital requirements remain at 8 percent but in practice, in the general case, Tier 1 capital has been strengthened because of the emphasis placed on *core capital* (equity capital), while several jurisdictions demand well above 8 percent from their banks. In addition, as we shall see in subsequent sections, there are liquidity requirements and other demands to be met – or at least this is the Basel Committee's intention. The irony with Basel III now is that regulators have decided to do something that promotes financial stability, but governments are asking them to do less because they know that financial institutions under their jurisdiction are in very bad shape.

In addition, banks will be obliged to hold an associated capital conversion buffer of 2.5 percent for losses in times of crisis. With this, as Table 4.2 shows, the core capital requirements increase to 7.0 percent (this 7.0 percent of *core* capital must not be confused with the 8.0 percent of *total* capital shown in Table 4.1). It does not take a genius to appreciate that, because of what was outlined above, capital conditions are going to be rather different with Basel III than they were with Basel II. In the wake of the financial crisis, the Basel Committee drafted tougher new rules, with the aim of ensuring that the shortage of liquid funds and the weak capital cushions that made

Table 4.1 A quantitative comparison of capital requirements: Basel III versus Basel II*

	Basel III	**Basel II**
Core Tier 1		
Common equity, retained earnings	4.5%	2.0%
Additional Tier 1		
Preferred shares, subordinated instruments**	1.5%	2.0%
Tier 2		
Subordinated debt***	2.0%	4.0%
Tier 3		
Reserve for market risk	Abolished	Fuzzy definition
Total	**8.0%**	**8.0%**

Notes: * Capital ID identification into a revamped Tier 1, Additional Tier 1 and Tier 2 have basically followed Basel III terminology, albeit with a tightening of definitions. See Chapter 6.
** Which can absorb losses while a bank is a going concern.
*** Which can absorb losses when a bank fails.

Table 4.2 The impact of buffers on capital requirements

	Common equity (after deduction)
Minimum Core Tier 1	4.5%
Capital Conservation Buffer	2.5%*
Minimum plus Conservation Buffer	7.0%
Countercyclical Buffer	0%–2.5%

Note: * Starting from 2016, the conservation buffer will be 0.625 percent, becoming 1.25 percent in 2017, 1.875 percent in 2018 and reaching 2.5 percent in 2019. Because of the conservation buffer, the minimum total capital will be 8.625 percent in 2016, increasing to 10.5 percent by 2019 – if the banking industry as we know it is still a going concern by that date.

the 2007–12 crisis spread so fast might not happen again. However, Basel's proposals attracted much more opposition than many expected, and resistance by big banks, as well as resistance by governments, exceeded the level that characterized previous regulatory efforts.

Delays in Basel III implementation have been one of its major handicaps. The value of Core Tier 1 at 4.5 percent will not be reached until January 1, 2015, which is too far in the future. Even worse, the security buffer at 2.5 percent has been postponed to January 1, 2019. Even the implementation of the new minimal requirements has been delayed because of a transition limit of two years; it is scheduled to start in 2013. Though the background reason is lack of money (among banks and sovereigns) financial crises do not wait until everybody is ready for them.

The Basel Committee works by inverse delegation, and its proposals must be adopted by national authorities to become binding – which is a long and painful process. Privately, few governments and credit institutions openly dispute the need for strengthened finances across the banking industry. Many are, however, concerned that Basel III asks for a recapitalization that is difficult to realize under current conditions, and one that would cut banks' profits if new capital standards were applied by 2012, as originally envisaged. On the other hand, if capital reserves are not increased significantly, the next banking crisis will be at the door.

Some of the arguments against Basel III rules are pure hypocrisy. In a bid to win political backing, big global banks have centered their opposition on the 'damage' that could be done to the global economy if they are 'so handicapped' by capital needs that they cannot lend effectively to businesses, as if lending was their primary preoccupation.

Another argument by the banks, that they will have to increase their fees for deposits, is plainly ridiculous. It does not need to be explained that, rather than gambling their depositors' money away through over-the-counter (OTC) bilateral derivatives trades, and paying exorbitant bonuses, banks should hold on to more of their earnings, and improve the quality of their assets to guard against producing extreme events and crises.

Nor did the Basel Committee on Banking Supervision act alone, as was the case with its previous rules. In September 2009, it was charged by the members of the Group of Twenty (G20; see Chapter 11) to come up with tighter rules to discourage excessive risk-taking by banks. Also to curb the use of off-balance-sheet accounting which essentially ends in keeping double books.

Behind Basel's decisions lies the goal to bring core capital and equity much closer together. Equity capital is the first to absorb losses in a crisis (see also in the next section, the new concept of CoCos). Because Tier 1 capital under Basel II was perverted, banks estimated that if core capital is equity capital, this would be equivalent to raising the minimum capital requirement to 10 percent. Those who pressed this argument (including some from the government side), conveniently forgot that under Basel II, core capital had become largely smoke and mirrors, with the result being a deep economic and banking crisis.

Contingent convertible instruments

One of the novelties introduced with Basel III is the adoption of *contingent convertible instruments* (CoCos) as supplementary capital. To a significant extent CoCos are a new species of the old *perpetuals* traded OTC, revamped and renamed. Other specialists, however, consider them to be new and more rigorously defined supplementary capital assets.

To better appreciate the difference between these two opinions, the reader should know that, up to now, the way to look at perpetuals has varied from one jurisdiction to another. By contrast, what they shared was a high price volatility which, when marked to market, altered their weight as bank capital.

Supposing other things to have been equal when valuing a perpetual bond, at the time of Lehman's crash it was sold at 75 percent to 80 percent of its nominal value. Later, this rose but then dipped again with the next financial crisis. For example, with the crises of Greece and of Ireland (always with other things being equal) a perpetual bond's price has sunk again from, say, 98 percent or par to about 90 percent.

The attraction of perpetuals to investors arises from the fact that, because they are a sort of capital in the frontline (like equity), they pay good interest. As with dividends, a bank's board can cancel payment of interest if there are no profits. In the UK, Lloyds and the Royal Bank of Scotland paid no interest on their perpetuals. In practice, in the more general case, this is easier said than done.

In some countries – for example, Italy – perpetuals are sold to the public as savings instruments. Therefore, the central bank and the government would not look kindly on a credit institution that deprives retail savers of their income, unless it becomes bankrupt.

Other reasons, too, ensure that today as far as their use as a proxy for equity capital is concerned, old-style perpetuals are in for a rough ride. They are hybrids, and in the original version of its proposal Basel III prescribed that the value of hybrids written in the books must be reduced by 10 percent in first year of implementation of the new rules – and more following that. It is generally believed that if this rule is applied it will incite banks to call in the perpetuals.

While subsequently that proposed Basel III rule has been called into question as opposition to it rose in the banking industry, at the time of writing nothing is clear in terms of how perpetuals will be treated. It is nevertheless likely that, precisely because of various ambiguities, beginning in early 2013 with Basel III's implementation, they will start to be called in. It seems likely that their place will be taken by contingent convertibles (for doubts concerning CoCos, see section entitled 'Gaming Basel III...' below).

Contingent convertible instruments may (but only may) well be the basic Tier 2 capital. The best way to look on them is as debt products with strong loss absorption features that are senior or subordinated. They convert automatically into equity if the issuer's core capital ratio falls below a predefined level.

The *contingency variable* is very important in this connection, because it is defining the capital ratio breach. In terms of pricing, as the probability of a breach rises, the instrument's value will decline. Avoiding a breach would enable these instruments to trade in line with broader market sentiments and/or company-specific credit developments.

According to Moody's, the independent credit rating agency, CoCos' ratings would be positioned no better than non-cumulative preferred securities. In the opinion of Standard & Poor's, the CoCos would be rated at least one notch below similar securities without a contingent trigger.

Since the trigger is be the capital ratio falling below a fixed minimum level, its definition may vary between jurisdictions. The so-called *bail-in* procedures are being discussed among supervisors as a way of dealing with systemically important banks; but they have yet to be tested. In this case, a conversion of debt capital into equity capital, or a percentage cut in the claims of senior creditors, would be either a *contractual* or *statutory* bail-in by regulatory directive.

What is not yet clearly defined is how bank deposits will be treated. This is important, because for any practical purpose deposits are also debt capital. They will probably have to be handled in a separate way in the case of a bail-in procedure, with exemption given to depositors from other creditors who carry a remote risk of extreme loss.

Several experts suggest that, under this perspective, CoCo bonds can be viewed as a kind of catastrophe insurance for which a premium is received in return for a small chance of a big loss. The market appears to be interested but not, or at least not yet, overwhelmingly so. British and Dutch institutions[4] have been the first to issue CoCos, while Swiss banks seem reasonably confident of handling them in a profitable way.

On December 12, 2010, Brady Dougan, chief executive of Crédit Suisse, said he hoped to begin issuing billions of dollars in contingent capital bonds in 2011, to help shore up the bank's financial strength well ahead of new Swiss regulations. While Crédit Suisse has until 2019 to meet the new contingent capital rules, the CEO told the *Financial Times* that 'he would aim to issue CoCo bonds soon to assure investors and regulators that there was adequate demand for the debt'.[5]

This has been one of the positive signals that the market has started to give its response to contingent capital. Indeed, investors' reactions to CoCos via Crédit Suisse provided a proof that there is demand for *loss-taking bonds*.[6] That is positive news for the banking industry, particularly for credit institutions of good standing.

Other things being equal, the better that regulatory authorities define the perpetuals' characteristics, the better it is for all players, because what distinguishes CoCos from the now classical perpetuals is that they have to comply with the required criteria for Tier 2 capital. Up to now, however, the definition has been more jurisdictional than global. For example, in Switzerland, two types of structures are envisaged a high-trigger paying 7 percent; and a low-trigger paying 5 percent.

Not everybody, however, is sure that CoCos are the answer to the additional capital sources urgently needed by banks. The big question is whether they will be available in a bank's treasury in large enough quantities to be able to ensure that the institution's capital reserves can absorb losses if it is unable to survive without an injection of taxpayers' money. This boils down to the query: can CoCos guarantee a bank's long-term resilience?

According to some experts, in times of crisis, investing in contingent capital carries the risk of unrecoverable write-downs on claims, or being obliged a priori to accept a conversion into shares. Moreover, hybrid instruments are not necessarily covered by investment mandates, and there is the issue of determining an appropriate price for convertible capital in the short, medium and longer term, as with perpetuals. If market liquidity is found to be wanting, then the price could be subject to major fluctuations, and market-based approaches for triggering conversion have an inherent potential for manipulation.[7]

Some financial analysts also think that, with CoCos, contingency planning does not go far enough. One big European bank is said to be pursuing a plan to put all investors on the line in the event of its failure. That would probably necessitate a rewriting of corporate law. Other queries regarding CoCos revolve around the banks' willingness and ability to abide by Basel III rather than attempting to get around it. Still others center on the proposed liquidity measures: *liquidity coverage ratio* and *net stable funding ratio*, both of which are discussed in Chapter 6.

A snapshot of new regulatory rules in the making

One of the problems encountered by bank regulators when they establish new rules is that these are designed to have general applicability. Large, medium-sized and small banks are essentially being confronted by similar rules, while it might have been more rational that highly upgraded capital and liquidity requirements are projected for specifically and apply to global banks as systemically important financial institutions.[8]

As we have seen, Swiss regulators follow that policy. Short of extra capital and liquidity buffers, when big global banks encounter severe problems or there is a transnational financial crisis, it will always be the taxpayer who has to bear the losses when the choice is between recapitalization and bankruptcy.

Aware of the need for rules and procedures that automatically raise an institution's capital ratio, hence its resilience to losses, the Basel Committee has various types of stabilization mechanisms under discussion. These differ in terms of their form, but more than any other difference is the one concerning the timing of Basel III's capital increase.

In terms of timing, the best answer evidently is 'the earlier the better'. But not every jurisdiction agrees with this principle. Those who do are saying that delaying the implementation of the new rules is a major negative, diminishing the rules' impact over the precise period that stronger capital adequacy and liquidity regulations are the most necessary.

Another subject on which regulators from different jurisdictions must agree are the exceptions. The best of all answers is 'no exceptions', and no way to dilute what should be a pristine Tier 1 capital. This is contrary to human nature, however, and as such it raises the issue of safeguards.

Because of what has happened with the dilution of Tier 1 capital under Basel II, the Basel Committee has narrowed the definition of what banks can count as the core Tier 1 capital ratio. Indeed, gaming T1 has proved to be one of Basel II's major weaknesses and therefore one should consider it a bad omen that, under pressure from the Japanese, Basel admitted DTAs as part of core capital (see the penultimate section of this chapter).

On the positive side, in mid-September 2010 Basel ordered banks to raise their minimum core Tier 1 capital from 2 percent to 7 percent of their risk weighted assets (see Chapter 8) by 2019 or face restrictions on pay and bonuses. That was too weak a penalty to have an effect, unfortunately, even though banks protested rigorously. Banks were also given the bonus of being able to add tax credits and some minority investments (see the last section of this chapter) to equity and retained earnings.

The opposition to the rules it introduces or promulgates is one of the best tests of a regulation's legacy. Another, and more important one, is the quality and endurance of the structures it leaves behind. Time and usage always put pressure on a system of rules, which it may or may not be able to bear.

One piece of evidence of opposition by stakeholders to Basel III's capital requirements is the 7 percent of risk weighted assets referred to in the preceding paragraph. This comprises a minimum common equity target of 4.5 percent of assets to be reached by 2015, and a conservation buffer of 2.5 percent of assets. The latter can be drawn upon with restrictions in times of stress and it should be in place by 2019, while certain exceptions will apply until the end of 2022.[9]

It goes without saying that such delays have been the result of opposition by stakeholders, and they are counterproductive. Extending the timetable of implementation might not have been a major problem if the big global banks had been truly solvent, but they are not. Their governments are therefore afraid that: they will have to pour into private bank coffers even more taxpayers' money than they did during the 2007–12 economic and financial crisis, and this will be political dynamite, over and above the fact that Western sovereigns are themselves bankrupt.[10]

Critics of implementation delays and of the watering down of capital measures are saying that an important issue which required, but did not get, special attention is the common frontier that exists between enhanced capital buffers and liquidity on the one hand, and financial reporting standards as well as new securities guidelines in the other. Unlike prior regulatory decisions, the evolution of the banking business recognizes that Basel III has common frontiers with both accounting standards (see Chapter 10) and securities regulation (more on this later).

In the early 1950s there was a professor at the University of California who told his students, 'if you give me the freedom to choose my accounting system I can prove anything to you'. A debt-ridden company can become one of the best capitalized around town, and a highly profitable one can document extraordinary losses. Universal accounting standards are very important, but while we talk of globalization today no homogeneous accounting system exists.[11]

Credit institutions that are self-respecting and have the assets to beef-up their balance sheets have no difficulty in building up the necessary capital buffers. But others that are at the edge of chaos will be tempted to use accounting differences to their advantage. After the irresponsible policies followed in the first years of the twenty-first century, can anyone be sure that banks will not do so?

One of the ironies with capital is that typically it is available in abundance to those who do not really need it. Banks that are well-governed and have plenty of earning power find no difficulty in raising their capital ratios, and can further add to them by showing restraint on dividends and bonuses. This is not true, however, of poorly managed banks.

Probably to deal with the worries of these not so well managed banks, and to ease the transition, the Basel Committee delayed the meeting of its most demanding targets to 2019, which is far too long a timetable. And it should not be forgotten, whether we have Basel III or not, the market needs higher capital ratios *now*, and sooner rather than later it can be expected to press this point home by applying an extra premium akin to the *Japan premium* of the 1990s. If the regulators don't accelerate the implementation timetable, or allow governments to water down Basel III's clauses, market pressure will push banks to meet higher capital ratios and liquidity standards without any major delays, and penalize them if they don't do so.

Indeed, the market is already uneasy that many of the details on Basel III still have to be resolved, and the devil is in the detail. This is not favoring the global banks themselves as they do not know if they have to raise equity to replace hybrids and other Mickey Mouse financial instruments (such as DTAs, discussed below) that might not qualify for long as Tier 1 capital under the new rules.

Stated in a different way, no wise institution should be tampering with capital standards. After the fundamental reasons for the descent to the abyss in 2007 and 2008 were decided, it became clear that *solvency* rather than *liquidity* was the No. 1 reason for the debacle. It is no accident that when in September 2010 an agreement on Basel III was reached, a core element of it has been the need to strengthen the banks' resilience. In future, credit institutions must hold not just 'more' but also better-quality capital.

Basel III also provided that, according to circumstances specific to a given jurisdiction, national supervisors may as well introduce a counter-cyclical capital buffer (particularly when they identify excessive credit growth; see Chapter 6). For many years, the Bank of Spain has required that banks under its authority hold counter-cyclical capital. This has proved to be a very good measure, though it has presented some accounting problems leading to the notion that banking rules and prevailing accounting standards are not adapted to work together synergistically.

The International Accounting Standards Board (IASB)[12] and Financial Accounting Standards Board (FASB) should work hand-in-hand with the Basel Committee to synchronize their actions. Other parties that should work hand-in-hand with Basel and the accounting standards bodies are the supervisory authorities of the securities industry. Both the Securities and Exchange Commission (SEC) in the USA and the European Commission (EC) have been advancing new regulations for derivatives trading. These aim to take most derivatives deals out of OTC and into clearing houses.

In addition, in conjunction to the new financial regulation (FINREG) of 2010, the Obama Administration wants to exact a levy of 0.15 percent on any bank balance sheet over US$50 billion to cover bank liabilities. Known as the *Obama levy*, this would feed into a fund earmarked to repay the cost of rescuing the financial system should problems arise in the future (emulating the deposit insurance tax perceived by the Federal Deposit Insurance Corporation: FDIC). The majority of banks have been deeply opposed to this new taxation,[13] but it seems to me that such a levy should become a global practice – and therefore an integral part of Basel III regulations.

Management's accountability with capital adequacy

Surprisingly, nobody has been talking about management's accountability with regard to capital adequacy and liquidity, and the urgent need to upgrade management skills and ethics. Not only in banking but in all sectors of the economy, poor management decisions have played a critical role in the decline of formerly prosperous enterprises and their decline into oblivion.

Here is an eye-opening example from the energy industry (see also, in Chapter 5, the discussion about management's responsibility for compliance). In January 2011, the US presidential commission investigating the causes of the 2010 oil spill in the Gulf of Mexico released a chapter containing the key findings of its final report. The chapter stated that 'Most of the mistakes and oversights (leading to the explosion [at BP's well]) can be traced back to a single overarching failure – a failure of management.'[14]

In an almost identical manner, poor management augmented by lust and greed brought down the banking industry. And when we know that this was and continues to be the case (nothing has really changed, apart from a few bosses losing their armchairs) regulators:

- should provide for higher capital requirements rather than those that please the politicians, by trimming them down; and
- should make the CEO, CFO and board members personally accountable if and when the bank's capital resources or liquidity dry up (see Chapter 8 on personal accountability in risk management).

Basel III does not link personal accountability to effective risk control, and this is a mistake. If such a link becomes law, then top management will have to run fast to ensure that both capital and liquidity are properly controlled and that steady evidence is provided on their sufficiency. Alternatively, that the bank immediately reduces its risks and assets.

Under these conditions, the CEO, CFO and board members will be personally motivated to ask for daily reporting on capital adequacy, supported by plan-versus-actual financial evidence. To better explain this argument, Figure 4.1 presents a snapshot of capital structure under Basel III, with levels ranging from CoCos to equity. This structure is composed of elements that enter into the capital definition of the new regulations. An effective daily reporting structure can be instrumental in improving capital governance, and it can contribute to financial stability because the sum of bank balance sheets is a pillar of the global banking system.

Nobody can argue seriously that the major crisis triggered in 2007 has not demonstrated clearly that both quality and amount of capital, as well as the

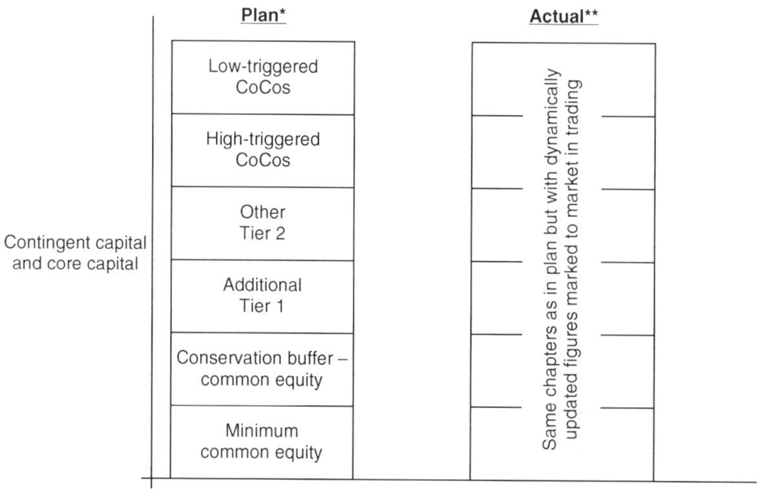

Figure 4.1 A financial reporting structure on capital adequacy, both on-balance sheet and off-balance sheet, using Basel III definitions

Notes: * Approved by the Board in compliance with Basel III rules.
** Daily marked-to-market fair value in conjunction with risk-weighted assets (RWA). It is better to have 2 *actual* columns: *n*th and *n*-1.

ability to convert all kinds of assets into liquid ones, are the base of an institution's financial staying power. At many global banks (as well as in smaller ones) their base was utterly insufficient to withstand severe economic shocks. It is understandable that, at their Pittsburgh summit in September 2009, the leaders of G20 agreed to strengthen the international financial framework and go ahead with new and tougher rules for prudential regulation.

Quite correctly, the job of producing these new rules was not given to theoreticians but to practical people with wide experience in central banking and financial regulation, who are members of the Basel Committee on Banking Supervision. The resulting consultation paper (see the first section above) was itself a compromise between what had to be done and what was possible given the prevailing conditions. The pity is that, subsequently, it has been watered down.

In its July and September 2010 meetings, the Group of Governors and Heads of Supervision (GHOS) – the oversight body of the Basel Committee – endorsed the proposed measures, which were then presented to the G20. But the politicians and their agents, as well as the bank's lobbyists (see Chapter 2), bend these rules and by doing this they did a great disservice to global financial stability as well as to their own banks.

Sunshine is the best disinfectant, Louis Brandeis of the US Supreme Court once said. However, instead of sunshine, the changes made to the original

Basel III rules (see the following sections) reduced its effectiveness, and this was bad management. Credit institutions and other financial entities, particularly global banks, would have been better off if they were made to face tough criteria obliging them to:

- change their culture,
- restructure themselves,
- rebuild their balance sheets, and
- come out from behind the skirts of patronizing governments.

Let's face it: because of its excesses the banking industry today needs an iron discipline. Trimming capital rules and other disciplinary measures worsens rather than improves its condition. While the price of restructuring is not just money (the whole culture of banking has to change), core capital and liquidity are crucial – and if high capital requirements reduce growth, as some people argue, so be it.

The argument that 'higher capital standards will result in less economic growth' is not acceptable. Nothing paralleled the growth of the British economy in the nineteenth century and the first years of the twentieth (prior to the First World War) when the capital adequacy of British banks was much higher than the Basel III rules. Beyond this, growth for growth's sake is the philosophy of the cancer cell.

Herman Daly, former chief economist of the World Bank, and several others have been challenging this 'faster growth' state of mind, pointing out that too much economic growth is *uneconomic* in a microeconomic sense. One of the reasons is that marginal costs eventually exceed marginal gains.[15]

As banks overleveraged themselves and the economy, these ever-growing large marginal costs – with risk being their underlying factor – have been kept off balance sheet, with the result that their visibility was low to nonexistent. In the aftermath, large banks and sovereigns continued to pursue the policy of outsized marginal costs regardless of the longer-term aftereffects. This has been another management failure.

Nothing can change the fact that global banking must reduce its leverage factor by a significant ratio. As long as it is overleveraged, it will remain badly undercapitalized. This is true not only in absolute terms but also in reference to the recent past. In a speech given in mid-December 2009 on the implications of changes in the financial industry, for both the economy and monetary policy, David Miles, of the Bank of England, estimated that, excluding global business, the British banks went into the 2007 economic crisis holding about half the capital relative to assets they held 50 years earlier, and only a third of the capital they controlled at the beginning of the twentieth century.[16]

Worse still, according to Miles, British banks held far less in truly liquid assets, which he put at about one third of the level of 1960. Yet, in the years following 1960, Britain was no longer the global economic and industrial power it used to be before the First World War, and therefore the excuse that the capital adequacy of British banks was reduced because they were financing the empire could not be sustained.

What really happened is that British banks, like the American, French, Dutch and German banks, overplayed their hand, gambling with new financial instruments such as derivatives; overspread themselves and their skills (this was particularly the case of the Royal Bank of Scotland); and made high use of leverage. In the so-called 'good times', when asset prices are high, leverage is a recipe for profits and growth. However, since Ancient Egypt there has existed the saying about seven fat cows followed by seven skinny ones, and when the time of skinny cows comes, high leverage becomes the best recipe for failure.

At the end of the day, this is a failure of management, BP style. The lack of steady attention to assets, liabilities and assumed risks (see Chapter 8) meant that nobody in the top echelons of large financial organizations noticed that the bank was running out of capital. Therefore no precautions were taken and reserves were not built in a way commensurate with the bad times. Perhaps the greatest risk Basel III is facing is that the bad practices acquired by gaming Basel II will persist.

Gaming Basel III through arbitrage and speculation

Basel III is still a long way from its completion day, which will come when it is voted on by the parliaments of its signatory jurisdictions. Some regulators are concerned about these ratifications. The trimming of its provisions will still go on, particularly regarding some of its key rules such as capital reserves and liquidity management, which have already either been diluted or their implementation period has been extended.

Populist politicians involved in clipping Basel III's wings say that this downsizing has allayed fears about funding, which is a problem for practically all European banks.[17] Analysts, too, point out that a puzzling question is how banks will manage to replace the estimated US$300 billion or more of subordinated capital they are currently using.

The careful reader will recall that the answer provided earlier in this chapter is by means of contingent convertible instruments (CoCos) which, as new hybrid forms of capital, differ from traditional convertible bonds in that the conversion is conditioned by the occurrence of predefined triggers, making it mandatory. However, the fact that it does not take place as a result of an option being exercised raises another query: will investors go for them for a very large amount like US$300 billion?

Critics say that, if this is the case, there is little doubt that banks and speculators will find ways and means of bypassing the Basel III rules. It is not unreasonable to expect a new game in town, which makes it an option that subordinated debt is either converted into equity or is written off at a certain percentage rate in capital restructuring – or by creating an artificial but contractual margin call.

Another derivative instrument might differentiate between institutions coming under stress but nevertheless have a 'realistic' chance of remaining going concerns, and those that are past the point of no return but are still salvaged by taxpayers' money. Notice that the word 'realistic' is qualitative and subject to a variety of interpretations.[18]

Still another Basel III domain where arbitrageurs and speculators might have a field day is the liquidity level. While some banks are already observing a short-term liquidity ratio, the net stable funding ratio (see Chapter 6) is a new concept. Several credit institutions are said to hate it – some for technical and others for financial reasons. For example, currently available data (for the banks' side) covers a limited amount of what is required to calculate that ratio. In addition, several local specificities would have to be considered to be able to compute it in a dependable manner.

A further major problem with Basel III is that the slow implementation period for its capital and liquidity regime, which will not be phased in fully until 2019, leave plenty of time to develop new derivative instruments that will game the new rules and their provisions before they are even applied. Not enough attention seems to have been paid to the fact that the world, and most particularly the West, cannot afford to have another large-scale banking crisis in the next eight years. That would mean the end of banking as private business, and capitalization as we understand it.

Critics add that, over and above all that, the modern Wall Street culture has become pervasive and has spread to Europe and Japan. This has created the most powerful and concentrated financial lobby in history, responsible for both the financial crisis of 2007–12 and for ensuring lavish bail-outs for its own benefit. Surprisingly, however, it has failed to understand that, with the new big economic crisis, it is digging its own grave – a likelihood that is increasing because the huge scale of the bail-outs bred extreme moral hazard, and it has opened up vast risk appetites with other people's money, which is a big warning signal for the future.

All this happens in an environment where playing the system is not only acceptable practice, but also seen as a sign of intelligence and sophistication. Even the talk that banks are busy rebuilding their balance sheets fast to foster their competitive advantages, is a half-truth, because such strengthening of capital is not uniformly positive from a systemic risk perspective.

One of the unexpected consequences of the 2007–12 crisis is that there is at present a more heavily concentrated risk in the vaults of banking leviathans that are 'too big to be saved'. The fact that over the past few years nobody apart from Madoff has been punished for malfeasance, in spite of there being plenty of it around, implies a win–win situation and bolsters the bankers' incentives to play the system.

Engaged in regulatory arbitrage and finding ways of taking increasing risks to generate paper profits and distribute fat bonuses has by now become a sport; and everyone wants to look sporty. The irony is that, by being busy working out how to break the rules, bankers have overlooked the three cardinal principles of speculation:

1. Knowing yourself.
2. Money management.
3. Appreciating the 60–40 end of a proposition.[19]

One could win by determining which contemplated investment has odds that are mispriced, choosing the odds on the 60 percent side. But with complex derivative instruments building layer upon layer of gearing and adding to each layer an inordinate amount of risk, pricing is an illusion and what is left is no more than throwing the dice.

Money management is toted by many banks as their forte. This is, however, far from the truth. If they were astute money managers CEOs, CFOs, investment experts and traders would not have led their institutions into bankruptcy or near bankruptcy in 2007–12. In fact, they would not have created this self-destructive economic and financial crisis in the first place. What they did was akin to a person cutting off the tree branch on which he is sitting – most definitely, this is not good money management.

As for 'knowing yourself' this has been the greatest of all illusions. The bankers who brought down on the West, and the world, the nearest thing to a second Great Depression knew neither themselves (and their capabilities) nor the market. Plenty of evidence provided by the 2007–12 deep economic and banking crisis points to the fact that the bankers and others, rather than 'markets', have failed in some very important ways. One of the reasons has been over-reliance on the 'efficient markets hypothesis' – a chimera, and another, just as critical, is that the financial system has both grown exponentially and become more complex, and hence unmanageable using current tools and by second-raters.

To be in charge, regulators and CEOs of commercial banks and other financial institutions must now pay much greater attention, both individually and in the systemic risk sense, not only to the exposure of each global bank but also to risk correlations (see Chapter 9), which can trigger a mega-failure with snowball effects.

At a risk of being repetitive, let me add that a good example in the direction needed in terms of banking industry regulations are the measures applied in Switzerland (see the first section of this chapter) which are much more severe than the new global standards prescribed under Basel III. Such measures are a reflection of the desire of the Swiss authorities to create a more robust environment, and to protect the country's position as a leading financial center.

In Britain, too, Lord Turner says that bankers should take fewer risks, and be made more responsible for better understanding and managing the exposures they are assuming. Details are crucial. In an article in the *Financial Times* on December 8, 2010, John Kay stressed the necessity for regulators to stop encouraging banks to outsource their credit analysis to rating agencies. Other voices point to the fact that bankers should be much more prudent in their dealings. But there also exist conflicts of interest concerning Basel III rules, particularly by governments.

DTAs: the Japanese spoke in the wheel of capital adequacy

From all evidence, there has emerged an axis against certain provisions of Basel III, formed by the Japanese and other banks who are supported by their respective governments. This alliance has multiple objectives, conceivably the worst of them being the legalization of *deferred tax assets* (DTAs), followed by manipulation of the clause on minority interests, dealing with pension liabilities, and turning intangible assets to the banks' advantage.

What deferred tax assets means is that taxpayers' money, representing past, present and future financial losses,[20] can be used as a tax deduction or credit in the tax return in present and future years. The DTAs' counterpart, known as *deferred tax liabilities* (DTLs), generally represents a tax expense recognized in the financial statements for which payment has been deferred, or expenses for which the company has already made a deduction on its tax return.

First, the bank's management must establish valuation allowances for deferred tax assets, when the amount of expected future taxable income is not likely to support the use of the deduction or credit. Novel derivative financial instruments help in fulfilling this requirement so that, for tax purposes, real (or invented) losses in one year can be offset against future profits.

Originally invented by the Japanese in the 1990s to beef up their big banks which were falling apart, the practice of DTAs became popular and today they are treated as capital in many jurisdictions. Under Basel III they were intended to be largely barred from capital calculations. But the Japanese government insisted that they should still be used for capital purposes, because the country's banks have traditionally used them to buttress their capital ratios.

Serious individuals and institutions do not agree with this thesis. The December 2003 monthly report by the Deutsche Bundesbank had this to say on the wide use of DTAs by Japanese banks:

> The tense situation at Japanese banks can also be seen from the unfavorable composition of their capital. For example, external auditors now have to assess whether the volume of deferred tax assets (DTA) in the

> balance sheet is appropriate. Given the difficult earnings situation of the banks, the fact that at the end of March 2003 DTAs accounted for half the core capital of the big Japanese banks also put pressure on the banks' creditworthiness.

This was true in 2003 and is still true today. DTAs are pure creative accounting, not serious business, and the fact that they are now widely used speaks volumes about the sick state of the banks employing them. One of the reasons why banks in particular have become addicted to DTAs is that profitability in their core businesses has not improved much over the years lending margins hardly grew, while the volume of lending has fallen.

Japan's financial industry was also hit by a wave of disintermediation, because banks remain reluctant to take on more risk by making fresh loans. As for borrowers, in particular small and medium-sized companies, because of the depressed state of the economy they have been wary of increasing their levels of debt.

Analysts who know what they are talking about did not fail to notice that falling numbers of bad-loan write-offs do not necessarily indicate that the worst of the banks' woes are over. Statistics indicating fewer bankruptcies do not always mean that the malaise has lifted; it may well be continuing to grow beneath the surface. Many small and medium-sized Japanese companies have been kept alive by government loan guarantees and other financial help. Banks were also bailing out their worst-hit borrowers by: forgiving debt, setting up fresh credit lines for them, and taking equity in lieu of repayment. It does not really pay to deceive yourself that a person, a company or an industry is healthy when it is sick, and the maintenance of DTAs under Basel III as pseudo-capital speaks volumes about a continuing sickness.

One of the best examples of lying with pseudo-capital comes from 2003, which was an important year in the history of creative accounting using DTAs. The financial figures of the end of June 2003, published after a delay on November 25 of that year, falsely indicated that Japan's big banks were on the road to recovery:

- the country's top four biggest banks reported a sharp rise in net profits, and
- the way to bet when massive amounts of red ink suddenly disappear is that an invisible hand is behind that miracle.

It has happened in Japan, and it will happen time and again all over Europe and America if Basel III retains the DTA. In 2003, Resona, the fifth-largest Japanese bank was the only exception from 'profits, profits, profits'. Resona managed to lose ¥1.8 trillion (equivalent to US$15.5 billion at the time) in the six months to September 30, 2003, despite being given two trillion yen of public money in May that year.

Resona's teetering on the edge of the abyss was particularly interesting because it had come to life in March 2003 through the merger of Asahi Bank and Daiwa Bank. Both of these credit institutions were troubled, and the recipients of a torrent of public money prior to their merger. After they combined their debts, their capital adequacy was theoretically 6 percent but it stood at only 2 percent if deferred tax assets to the amount of ¥700 billion yen were excluded.

Resona was a great deal sicker than the other Japanese megabanks, but this did not mean the top four were in good health. Much of their improvement in profits was not easy to sustain, even with DTAs. Rising markets helped them to record paper gains in equity portfolios and they made profits from bond trading in the spring of 2003. However, these were recognized, not realized, gains.

There was also an equally make-believe tax rebate that boosted profits. Still another popular practice was to cut general reserves against bad loans, on the assumption that the Japanese economy 'was getting stronger'. Having done that, the banks recorded the write-backs as profits. Yet the Japanese economy was flat at best, and over the decades did not come out of the coma into which it was put by its big global banks.

Nor are DTAs the magic products guaranteeing the banking industry's health. Following the 1990–1 debacle in the banking industry and the economy, the Japanese government has been permanently ready to inject public funds into its troubled banks. This fact alone should have been enough to persuade the Basel Committee to reject DTAs as capital under Basel III.

Indeed, the reason for this deliberate flashback to a decade or two ago is to bring to the reader's attention to the fact that creative accounting is an enemy of financial health and stability. DTAs are not only a bad practice but also a covert subsidy. They materialize only if an entity makes enough taxable profit within the following five years to recoup its losses. As long as the outlook for profits is weak, DTAs are worthless – unless the sovereign fills the private banks' coffers.

It is highly unwise that Basel III accepts a flat 15 percent share of DTAs into the redefined and restructured Tier 1 capital. This shakes the confidence that might be placed in the new regulations and will revive in broader global terms the infamous *Japan premium*.

As will be recalled, what became known as the Japan premium reached 40 basis points, because of growing doubts about the soundness of the country's financial system. Uncertainty about what was to follow forced even the biggest Japanese banks to pay high premiums to borrow money, and obliged several of them to retreat from some Asian bond markets, leaving Asian companies with fewer, and more expensive, sources of finance available (some years later this led to the Asian Tigers crisis).

'Confidence in Japanese banks is currently falling dramatically on the Euromoney markets, and many Japanese banks are unable to raise funds even if they pay a *Japan premium*,' said Richard Koo, an economist at the Nomura Research Institute in Tokyo, in a report in 1995 to the broker's clients.[21] Keep that in mind in 2011 and for the rest of the coming decade. Biasing the Basel III rules to make life easier for mismanaged banks and accommodate pressure by sovereigns is the worst possible policy. DTAs are a poke in the eye to Basel III.

Minority interests, mortgage serving, capital for contingencies, pension deficits, intangible assets and leverage ratios

In an article published in the *Financial Times*, Sheila Bair, former head of the Federal Deposits Insurance Corporation (FDIC) wrote that 'critics of higher capital requirements tend to understate the extent to which equity can be substituted for debt in financing new loans, and fail to account for the social costs created by insufficient capital cushions'. In conclusion, she added: 'What is really at play here is that some in the industry are arguing their own self-interest.'[22]

Bair took aim at a leading trade association that represents many of the largest global financial institutions and coordinates their lobbying. Banks uneasy with the new capital rules have 'predicted' that Basel III will raise the cost of bank loans in major industrialized countries by an average of 132 basis points. Part and parcel of this unsubstantiated, inflated and fictitious 'prediction' was that the result will be a loss of 3.1 percent in gross domestic product (GDP), and between 2011 and 2015 some 9.7 million jobs will disappear.

The boss of FDIC was right in her anger. Such cavalier statements based on the most frivolous kind of 'forecast' do not bring credit on those who make them. Quite the contrary, in fact – they document the low ethical standards of the organization(s) behind them. Nor can one be proud of governments that wish to bias the utterly necessary tougher rules of Basel III, and substitute a wide laxity as the way to cure the ills of credit institutions in their jurisdictions.

The previous section brought to the reader's attention the Japanese government's (unjustified) objection to the planned ban on DTAs. Another objection to the Basel III rules, this time by the French, concerns the capital treatment of subsidiaries held alongside minority investors. This is a big issue for some French banks.

For a number of reasons, Basel proposes to exclude the equity from a minority interest from a bank's Tier 1 capital, but include the entire venture when calculating the risk-weighted assets. Crédit Agricole is reckoned by analysts to be among the most at risk from this solution, which would oblige a bank to account for 100 percent of the capital requirements of a subsidiary, though another shareholder holds a rather substantial minority interest.

If this was the only compromise, namely that the Basel Committee softened its prohibition on counting the equity held by minority shareholders in overseas subsidiaries towards Tier 1 capital, one could only say let it be so. But this is not the case. Every country has tried to obtain special benefits for its banks, making small games of rules designed to protect financial stability, and be applied universally through the global banking industry.

With regard to intangible assets, the original Basel III thesis was that goodwill and other matters should be deducted from equity capital, because their value is sometimes questionable. American banks with a mortgage servicing license, and their regulators, objected to the rule. In contrast, European banks accepted it as they already have to deduct intangibles under their accounting regulations.

German supervisors, too, made a number of objections. They were concerned about the impact of the Basel standards on smaller savings banks that fund many small and medium-sized enterprises (SMEs). These banks do not raise equity capital; rather, they rely heavily on retained earnings, which may not be enough to cover the amount that must be held relative to a bank's risk-weighted assets.

A compromise reached in late July 2010 would have an asset tally being reduced in line with capital, which seems to have half-way satisfied the Germans. The French have been pressing that their versions of hybrid capital, such as French banks' loss-bearing preference share structures, will be exempt from any iron-out connected to the new rules.

Another Basel III original proposal which raised objections was that of additional capital for contingencies. The compromise decision is that of instituting debt-to-equity conversions. With regard to liquidity (see Chapter 6), the original proposal was the creation of a new net stable funding ratio to match assets and liabilities more closely. The compromise has been that the original ratio was changed and its implementation delayed until 2018.

Another unwarranted change concerned uniform handling of pension liabilities, which are at present treated differently in different jurisdictions. The Basel Committee proposed that the whole of a pension fund deficit is to be deducted from capital, rather than just the top-up liability for the following five years (as is now the case). This is a potentially big problem for some banks, particularly British ones, which have large defined benefit pension schemes. Here again, a compromise is being worked out but its details are still unclear.

Other unwarranted pressures for changes favorable to special interests concentrated on the net stable funding ratio (see Chapter 6). The Committee wanted, and still wants, to force banks to hold more long-term assets to match long-term liabilities. But the future of this is uncertain and in any case, whatever remains will be implemented toward the end of the coming decade.

Establishing a universal leverage ratio has been one of the topics that encountered the greatest resistance. There is a net and a gross leverage ratio. The estimated *net leverage ratio* takes into account the (guestimated) netting of financial derivatives and repos, elimination of insurance assets, elimination of minorities' related assets, elimination of cash at central banks, and elimination of intra-group transactions. By contrast, it includes undrawn credit commitments.[23]

The estimated *gross leverage ratio* asset base is equal to the net asset base before the netting of repos and financial derivatives. It also includes the notional value of *credit default swaps* (CDSs). The Basel Committee introduced a leverage ratio as a supplemental measure to reinforce the risk-based requirements with a simple, non-risk-based backstop reflecting gross exposure; and constrain the steady increase of leverage in the banking industry, thereby avoiding highly risky 30x, 40x, 50x or higher leverages, as well as establishing a potential de-leveraging procedure.

To account for risk associated with the leveraging of a credit institution, the Basel Committee had set a basic rule requiring banks to hold Tier 1 capital equivalent to 3 percent of all assets, including those held off-balance sheet, which are far from being transparent. A compromise saw to it that banks will not have to publish their ratios until 2015, and they will not have to comply with the 3 percent minimum until the end of 2017.

More than any single item in this long list of Basel III compromises, it is their overall pattern that is disturbing. This sort of steady pressure aimed trimming the rules for personal benefit is exactly what made Basel II so impotent. Let us never forget that the resulting laxity led to the deep economic and banking crisis of 2007–12, which at the time of writing continues to punish the Western economies.

Along with the pattern of bending the rules to please special interests comes the extended timetable adopted for implementing the new rules, whatever these may be. This, too, is a very bad policy, also followed with Basel II and the results of that are well known. The global banking industry is sick, and the regulatory medicine has to be administered *now*. The contemplated implementation in 2015, 2017 and 2019 leaves the door open for a new and much deeper crisis which may well sweep away Basel III with its different compromises, several of the 'too big to fail' banks and some sovereigns.

Part III

Basel III and the Notion of Global Risk

5
Is It Possible to Regulate a Global Financial Market in Perpetual Change?

The need for a supervisory authority has been present since antiquity

In the fifth century BC, Athens was the center of a prosperous empire characterized by a market economy spanning part of the then known world. Its citizens were known to be open-minded with a good deal of tolerance, but they also appreciated the role of regulation and the need for it.

The Athenians were not blind to the realities of a free market, as well as its risks and opportunities. The regulators closest in function to today's bank supervisors were the *sitophylakes*. They guarded wheat supplies by monitoring its traders, dealers and warehouse agents, to assure that there were no shortages, no scams and no price-fixing conspiracies. It was their business to guarantee that traders did not violate the city's laws protecting the provision, storage, distribution and price of grain.[1]

In a similar way, and for the same reason, nowadays banks and other financial intermediaries, as well as players in other industry sectors, must be supervised and with assurances provided that they keep within allowed margins of freedom of action. Nothing follows a straight line. Now, as ever, upper and lower control limits are indispensable, particularly when dealing with commodities and instruments that are inherently risky. A global watch over the banking industry is important, because exposures can build up rapidly as banking deals with maturity transformation by taking deposits, issuing medium- to longer-term credit, and executing trades, while often lacking capital buffers to absorb a spike in exposure or major write-downs and write-offs.

In regard to the first two listed, the mismatch between deposits and loans – the former being short-term while the latter extends over the longer term – ensures that risks often develop that are recognized too late or are being managed wrongly. For example, wrong-way hedging[2] may not only wipe out the contemplated protection but also add to the exposure because, quite often, the hedge's results are asymmetric.

Regarding the third item in the list, it is not the purpose of regulation to eliminate risk but to control it within limits acceptable to the economy and commensurate with the bank's capital.[3] This is very important because the functions of the banking industry, particularly those provided by deposit-taking institutions, have basic economic and social characteristics. A modern economy will not revert to barter agreements without a significant amount of stress and upheaval.

The reader should also appreciate that there practical and political reasons behind bank supervision. Whether in a single nation or in the global economy, the management of wealth must observe checks and balances established a priori. In a globalized economy these supervisory duties should take place across countries with different economic and financial structures, and address a whole range of heterogeneous financial instruments.

Like the *sitophylakes* of ancient Athens, the duty of bank regulators is to ensure that ingenious manipulators and speculators are kept in check. Regulatory laxity can make the devil of a mess, so the health of the banking industry should be restored through prompt action, no matter what kinds of conflicts of interest come into play, promoted by politicians and exploited by lobbyists.

Regulators need much more than authority, however, to make their job truly effective. To know precisely where, when and how to intervene, they must be involved in steady monitoring with an impressive amount of detail. They should also have rich databases of bank profiles – including not only accounting and financial but also managerial references. Monitoring alone is not enough. As experience of past crises suggests, weaknesses in credit institutions tend to be repetitive, persistent and builds up over time.

This dual action of close monitoring and database mining is torturing the banks' profiles to make them reveal their secrets. The need for it has increased significantly because of the rapid, global and transborder movements of financial assets and liabilities by banks, hedge funds, institutional investors and other entities. This amplification of financial services leads to significant structural problems as the amount of money in circulation in the global economy is too large for primitive or flimsy regulatory structures. Nor is a sophisticated regulatory task a matter of theoretical diatribes and idealized solutions gambling on the discipline and goodwill of all involved.

The difference between theoretical/idealistic and pragmatic premises has not yet been understood appropriately in terms of the global coordination of important home–host issues (see Chapter 7). The precedence that exists from the United Nations (UN) to the World Trade Organization (WTO) and to the G20 is not particularly convincing as it more-or-less follows the nineteenth-century communist principle of establishing a societal model, including its laws and regulations, on the premise of an ideal people living in an ideal social environment and working under ideal economic conditions.

Needless to say, this has nothing to do with reality. Not only is such an idealization of human nature and of socioeconomic structures pure utopia, but also, compared to the nineteenth century, many jobs have evolved in a way that needs sophisticated training, and their environment has become much harder to manage than in the past.

But, in contrast, as far as human nature and turning a blind eye are concerned, nothing has changed. Arthur Levitt and Harvey Pitt, two former chairmen of the Securities and Exchange Commission, said that the US government ignored tips regarding the manipulation of mortgage-backed securitized instruments.[4] And it was a similar scenario with the Madoff affair – and if such events can happen within the same jurisdiction, think of the opportunities for dishonesty in global regulatory activities.

Lax controls, unfulfilled promises, illusions and utopia aside, it is no less true that banking, trading, lending, investing and other financial services have, so to speak, outgrown the age of classical finance. As a result, the motives and decisions of its agents are no more constrained by old standards, such as the ethical rules of another age. On the moral side, many people think that they owe the public nothing, and they find nothing objectionable in bypassing the existing system of rules and regulations.

In conclusion, as with the wheat trades of ancient Athens, global financial checks and balances should not only be set but also enforced, even if it means that banks must operate with less sail exposed to the wind than they are in the habit of doing today. That constrains the range of activity, but the ships of the banking industry are not as reliable as they used to be with regard to their capital adequacy and liquidity to meet adversity at a moment's notice.

It would be a serious mistake to believe that everyone in both sides of the banking industry – its players and its high priests – always care where the limits lie (see also the final section of this chapter, on compliance). Ever-growing aspirations, and instruments such as derivatives, the implications of which are much harder to understand than the former straightforward instruments of banking, require a thoroughly studied and updated control structure. The global mission of bank supervision has to be clear to both the controlled and to the controllers.

The regulator's arsenal is never really complete

To be in control of the game of cat and mouse in the global financial industry, regulators have to be concerned about what happens to each entity and whether or not it has the ability to steer clear of systemic risk, confront unexpected events, and absorb shocks and adversities that hit simultaneously at the most inappropriate moment. To do so, they must pay attention to a complex range of instruments, markets and financial intermediaries.

Plays which, for whatever reason, escape the regulators' attention can have disastrous after-effects in both the present and in the future. Over a span of three years, the subprimes were looked on by bankers as the incarnation of the perpetual motion machine for business and bonuses, but by 2007 they were producing casualties on a scale that no one had even remotely envisaged. A few clear-eyed regulators and some bankers spoke of terrible '*ifs*' but US President George W. Bush fired the boss of the Securities and Exchange Commission (SEC), who wanted to act, and opened Pandora's box while the terrible *ifs* continued to accumulate.

The clear-eyed few were right, because one of the major regulatory preoccupations is the ability to anticipate financial imbalances that might lead to bubbles. Even if they don't, they might contribute to something suddenly unraveling with effects just as disastrous. There exist a myriad of forms of systemic risk, and proper oversight requires a modern, efficient infrastructure able to bring the regulators' attention to complementarities and contradictions in the existing financial system. For example:

- Fire sales and debt deflation can be as bad as excessive maturity mismatch.
- High leverage leads to instability, and it can be promoted through the amplification of speculatory bets.
- A misperceived asset–debt loop can be worsened by an unconventional monetary policy, such as zero interest rates or quantitative easing.[5]

Improperly appreciated financial events can be the source of future turbulence, such as the 1986 US tax law that made it possible to slice up and recombine mortgage-backed securities. Because many cause-and-effect relationships are nonlinear, to deal with sources of trouble and monitor exposures, regulators need clear concepts, methods and metrics. The measurements at their disposal have to be able to picture accurately[6] stresses, shocks and other externalities.

The information being obtained should be examined critically through experimentation, assessing likely individual failings as well as any developing distresses using instruments, the market and counterparties. Default probabilities must be computed using data sources relevant to the problem at hand. Risk should be priced at a level of sophistication commensurate with the instruments being used.[7]

Short of becoming a beggar for public money which, like all rents, is a detestable practice, banks must have the capital resources to face adversity when it comes. As far as reserves are concerned, the military has a similar principle. For almost every action there might be a reverse. In the Second World War, Winston Churchill looked at reverses as unfortunate but inevitable events, to be seen in the context of an overall strategy for final success.

Resources must be confronted as they develop, before they gain momentum. But in the period preceding the 2007–12 deep economic and banking crisis, politicians, regulators and bankers showed no urgency, no decisiveness and no sense of the shortage of time in establishing capital and liquidity countermeasures.

Precisely because of political indecisiveness and foot-dragging, political support, the most precious weapon in the regulators' arsenal, has been nowhere to be found. Another thing in short supply has been the will to act, along with the knowledge and ability to apply analytics. Analytical tools are necessary because regulators confront polyvalent requirements addressing a wide ranging issues – while the method to be used should be simple.

Four and a half centuries ago, Tommaso Campanella, an Italian author, wrote a seminal book, *Città Solaris*.[8] Campanella's thesis has been that laws should be few and very simply expressed. Precisely the opposite is happening today, with legislation and regulations being filed in unprecedented volumes, and we see the results.

What makes simplicity possible in an environment where everything seems to be so complex is the wisdom (and willingness) to *admit some ambiguity*. There can be a certain margin of error, but it will not be known in advance because a number of factors arise that make a priori clarity all but impossible. The speed on the highway may be set at 120 km/hr, but if it rains it will be lower and in dense traffic lower still.

Let the banks guess what might be the real limit of exposure, as market conditions change, instrument complexity and/or opacity increase, and the market starts to become volatile. But they should know in advance that if they go over that dynamically defined limit there will be penalties – sometimes heavy, commensurate with the bank's contribution to the likelihood of system risk.

This is quite different than the *pre-commitment* American banks wanted to apply in connection with Basel II. Ambiguity can be a most valuable addition to the regulators' arsenal, because it will make it difficult to game the system. If the exact parameters are not known in advance, the banks have to account for a margin of error. Such a policy will also ease the *agency cost*, or friction, between banks and regulators, because there are no clearly established positions to defend.

Another major advantage of introducing ambiguity into capital and regulatory standards is that it allows the people at the top level of the global regulatory structure, such as the members of the Basel Committee on Banking Supervision, to integrate into their decisions social issues – a task that is becoming increasingly necessary for well-rounded financial supervision (see the section below, 'Which organization and structure...?'). A certain degree of uncertainty about the limits will significantly improve the regulators' arsenal and help them to get ahead of the market.

Is the banking industry ahead of the regulator?

'The market is well ahead of the regulators,' admitted Richard C. Breeden in 1990, at that time chairman of the SEC. Perhaps not the whole market, but surely the big global banks and the regulators have no alternative but to catch up. This will not be easy, but it is do-able by thinking outside the box.

With trading splintering away from established exchanges (see Chapter 2), regulatory authorities are running hard to police complex transactions and control what is happening in a broad range of different jurisdictions, because of the dark pools and other gimmicks invented by banks to bypass the laws. The financial markets' globalization and dominance of institutional trading are forcing them to rethink some of the basic tenets underlying decades of securities law and other banking activities.

Dark pools were not a response to generic needs in banking from the viewpoint of using financial services. Rather, they were the result of hubris (as well as greed), and greed is usually accompanied by folly. In a nutshell, this is what propels the shadow banking system. To be ahead of the curve, the regulators' thinking must look for a new start that outfoxes shadow banking. The regulators must also have their own research laboratory well staffed with 'rocket scientists'.[9] Make no mistake, however, that while using technology is necessary, it is not sufficient, and neither are simple pronouncements about better-focused systems and procedures the solution. Theoretically, the shift from manual to automated trading creates better audit trails. However, in practice, this is not so. Developing surveillance systems to monitor trading on global scale requires:

- A great deal of system expertise that few regulatory bodies currently possess, and
- Instead of using high technology to be ahead of the masses, regulators have fallen in love with old technology. Target, the BIS payments system, was written a few years ago in COBOL – a 53-year-old inefficient programming language.[10]

In other words, not only is the regulatory arsenal incomplete, it is also using outdated technology. Radical change is always postponed because the men at the regulatory top are bankers and do not understand information technology (IT). Yet, if they are good managers they should appreciate that any organization that has to design and monitor the execution of regulatory laws, rules and directives must be ahead of those implementing them, or trying to cut corners.

As Campanella wrote four and a half centuries ago, a very few, simply expressed laws and rules are by far the best approach by governments and regulators, provided that they are properly applied by those for whom they are intended. Expert systems (not COBOL) should be the regulators' technology with transgressors being brought swiftly to justice, no matter whether they might say that they 'did not know' they had overstepped the mark.

Fines alone are not a suitable answer because they are typically paid by shareholders or an insurance company, leaving the wrongdoers to pursue their 'good job'. This is not only true of banking but of all industrial sectors. Here is an interesting example from the aerospace industry.

In a coordinated agreement with the US Department of Justice and Britain's Serious Fraud Office, BAE Systems settled charges involving its dealings in a number of countries. The defense contractor had to pay a US$400 million fine in the USA for making false statements to the government in regulatory filings (but nobody went to Court in spite of the Sarbanes–Oxley Act (SOX), and a £30 million (US$47 million) penalty in the UK for its accounting procedures in relation to its activities in Tanzania. Officially, these deals settled allegations of corporate bribery, but there was an outcry from critics, saying that former BAE executives should have been prosecuted.

Let's face it, the fear of the policeman is a concept unknown to the big global companies.[11] To perform their role in an able manner, regulators must ask aggressive questions in the course of their examinations of financial and industrial entities, their processes, products, instruments, transactions and – most particularly – their books.

There has recently been a long list of scandals and failures in supervisory duties, with the Madoff Ponzi game, Lehman Brothers, Bear Stearns and AIG, to mention just a few cases, which demonstrates that regulators have not been doing their jobs in a professional, consistent and focused way. That is a pity, and one of its unwanted consequences is that the market perceives the regulators as paper tigers.

It does not need to be explained that this state of affairs is counterproductive. It makes no sense to pass new legislation if, because of political pressures or for other reasons, regulators cannot (or do not) exercise their responsibility to maintain public confidence in the financial system – even if everyone knows that this is very important to avoid globalized banking business crashing disastrously.

Even if political pressure is behind the paper tigers' attitude, the result is unhealthy both for society and for the financial industry itself. Some people who do know the risks being taken say that, given the global economy's reliance on the financial sector, it is important to restore it to health while also building in appropriate safeguards. As the present crisis has so well demonstrated, financial staying power is *not* served by light regulatory involvement. The worst of all policies is to try to bluff the market into believing that there is a tough regulatory policy in place, when this is only half true. Yet, this is the policy that has been chosen, as politicians from a multitude of countries pull out those of Basel III's teeth that might bite their countries' banks.

At the risk of being repetitive, allow me to return to SOX. The basic concept underpinning the Sarbanes–Oxley Act of 2002 is that reliable financial reporting is a prerequisite to the assurance of sound governance of the economy and a reliable management of wealth. Fraudulent financial reporting and the risks it presents to the financial system, the business community and the general public have long been recognized as a problem by sharp-eyed people.

But as the law of the land has moved to reduce this risk by means of supervision, those engaged in fraudulent reporting have come up with new inventions. Therefore, it is necessary both to reinforce and modernize the weapons in the regulatory arsenal, as well as to raise the level of reference by increasing requirements and by exercising steady vigilance. This is what Basel III was projected to do prior to being watered down, as we saw in Chapter 4.

Which organization and structure for effective global regulation?

Financial services regulation has multiple roles: to ensure that systemic risk is under control; to promote the protection of investors, depositors and other counterparties; and to guarantee the integrity of financial markets in spite of political experience aiming to ease one rule or another. An integral part of this role is also to guarantee that business and the public have confidence in the ability of the financial industry to fulfill its duties to society and to ensure an adequate level of business continuity.

This requires leadership. Nelson Mandela said that to be a good leader one must act like a shepherd. A shepherd walks behind the sheep, but takes care to keep them safe. Regulators should work in the same way, without forgetting that to keep the flock safe in the valley the shepherd also depends on watchdogs. In finance, this is the role played by auditors, examiners and inspectors.

Performing duties well is complex enough at the national level; but it is much more so on a global scale. The execution of their duties by supervisory authorities, described briefly above, requires organization and structure, with the added difficulty that a sound solution should work cross-border but laws and rules vary widely from one jurisdiction to the next.

One way to respond to the dilemma outlined by the factors mentioned has been that chosen for the Basel Committee of Banking Supervision which, as already discussed, works by inverse delegation. The careful reader will recall the comment that inverse delegation is a weak liaison because any decisions by Basel have to be confirmed by each jurisdiction individually, which is a complex task, is open to pressures for changes, and deprives the Basel Committee of the authority it needs for decision-making.

Will the alternative structure of a centralized global authority, with full decision-making powers in its regulatory and supervisory duties, be a better solution? Before addressing that question, it is wise to ask another: is this a feasible project? Or is resistance to it is going to be so intense that it is better to forget about it altogether?

The answer to the feasibility query is negative. Jacques de la Rosière is a well-known and respected banker, a former governor of Banque de France and a former president of the IMF. Not long ago he was asked by the European Commission to examine whether a centralized regulatory authority for the banking industry would be agreeable to the European Union's (EU's) member states – a very good question, indeed.

After a diligent study, de la Rosière's answer was that this was not a solution acceptable to the EU's governments, and therefore suggested that the idea of centralized supervision should be dropped. Instead, in September 2010 the European Commission, European Parliament and the European Economic and Financial Affairs Council (Ecofin) agreed to establish *three* new European supervisory authorities (ESAs):[12]

- the European Banking Authority (EBA),
- the European Securities and Markets Authority (ESMA), and
- the European Insurance and Occupational Pensions Authority (EIOPA).

These find their precedence in the present financial supervisory committees, the Committee of European Banking Supervisors (CEBS), the Committee of European Insurance and Occupational Pensions Supervisors (CEIOPS), and the Committee of European Securities Regulators (CESR). The plan is that the new entities will be endowed with wider powers than are the present committees.

Only time will tell whether this wider distribution of supervisory duties is effective or just wishful thinking. Let us, however, consider the hypothesis that a centralized global supervisory and regulatory authority would be acceptable not just to the EU government but also to the G20 heads of state. Moreover, say that, under that hypothesis, plans are made to move ahead with global centralization. This would bring us back to the original query regarding how effectively such a centralized supervisory system of banking and finance might work.

To cover the financial industry worldwide in terms of regulatory responsibilities would require a mammoth organization with a great deal of bureaucracy, accompanied by a throng of lobbyists. Experience from the European Union Executive in Brussels would be enough to cool any enthusiasm for such a project. But there also exists a worse risk – that of reinventing the Communist Party and of repeating the experience of the failed Gosplan[13] in the former Soviet Union.

In his book *The Oligarchs*, David E. Hoffman gives a startling account of what the Gosplan bureaucracy amounted to:

> By the 1970s ... an elaborate blizzard of paper was nightmarishly complicated. Just the supply and distribution plans ... totaled seventy volumes of nearly twelve thousand pages and dealt with over thirty thousand commodities ... The wide bureaucratic planning system had become a strange, never ending undisciplined bazaar.[14]

Centralized control of the global financial industry versus Gosplan is not a far-fetched comparison. Today's failure in the management of the mammoth global banks has interesting Gosplan characteristics. Big global banks are run by a bureaucracies having quantitative targets measured in individual bonuses, and their whole structure features a striking resemblance to Soviet-era institutions. The risk that the structure of global supervision would fall into that trap is a real and present danger. As in the old Soviet model in the G20, and prior to it in the G8, there have been no simple master guiding directives. The overriding rule was and is bargaining. Practically everything pertaining to the direction of a global financial control system would be traded as in Soviet life: status, laws, regulations and power, as well as the right to violate established laws and regulations.

Moreover, to crown the reinvention of the Soviet state there would be a total lack of accountability. No head of state and no big bank boss is going to take the new super-authorities' pronouncements and directives seriously, because it is known in advance that nothing will happen to those who do not observe the rules.

Instead, creative accounting will have a field day, because even in countries where the law is supposed to punish wrongdoers, bank bosses directly involved in the demise of their enterprises (and of the economy) were allowed to go free. Nobody appears to really be bothered if false or inaccurate financial information is included in annual statements. For example, in the USA, the Sarbanes–Oxley Act has been in existence since 2002. As for the G20, to make the comparison with the Soviet era more meaningful, it has been unable to define a global code of ethics, or a system of sanctions that makes living outside the laws and rules for financial behavior too expensive to be affordable.

It needs no reminder that, over the years, the absence of carrot-and-stick control has created widespread disrespect for what is agreed – if and when an agreement is reached by global political leaders. In addition, even in the best cases, these decisions are nothing more than general lines; they pay no attention to implementation details and this makes it very easy to get around them.

A control system that is, or even tends to be, deeply and pervasively out of joint with real business life is worse than nothing at all. As in Soviet times, it will increase moral hazard rather than inducing people, banks and states to prize the common good, by getting their act together, and by doing so on a considerably higher footing than in the past.

An example provided by David Hoffman helps us to appreciate some of the similarities that will most probably develop between a supranational High Authority on Banking Supervision and the Soviet era. Hoffman quotes Yuri Luzhkov, the former mayor of Moscow who, when given the mission of managing the vegetable warehouses of the Russian metropolis asked his deputies for the spoilage rate.

The official answer was 1 percent, but the real answer was up to 30 percent.

As Lushkov put it, 'It was only then that I realized the pervasive cruelty of the system. With all the monstrous losses ... in the storage process ... [it] had the nerve to demand a loss of only 1 percent.'[15] It is interesting also to know that, in Hoffman's opinion, a deeper source of discontent was rotten leadership rather than rotten vegetables. The people running the Soviet apparatus continued to punish the economy with shortages, and never stopped producing low-quality goods, because they never faced any penalty for doing so.

Experience taught them they were above the law, as the more lobbying they did, the more they were let off the hook, and the more exceptions they asked for, the more irresponsible they became. This is precisely what happens when organizations become too big and so complex that they defy management principles. An almighty centralized High Authority for Bank Supervision is definitely not the solution to look for, but there is scope to redefine the supervisory duties that under Basel II were named Pillar 2.

Redefining important Pillar 2 risks

The financial industry's re-regulation, and most particularly that of global big banks and other mammoth financial institutions, is not only urgently needed but also has to be enacted in a way that is respected globally. However, as we shall see from Chapter 6, focusing *only* on solvency, and therefore on capital adequacy, would be a nearsighted solution. This has been evident since Basel II, which has included under Pillar 2 risks other than solvency, that coinvolved the banks' top management.

A basic principle of Pillar 2 has been the so-called *use test*. The concept underpinning it is that banks must have a capital adequacy assessment process (CAAP) as part of their compliance procedure (see the section below entitled, 'The Board's watch over compliance'). The use test specified that regulators should ensure that:

- the bank's board is aware of the capital adequacy assessment process,
- financial analysis and examination has incorporated all risks,

- capital adequacy assessments are used routinely in management decisions (which is the use test's core), and
- there is a process of review of internal control, compliance and quality of risk management.[16]

Under Basel II, however, capital adequacy assessment processes have never been among the priorities of boards and CEOs in the banking industry. Nor did supervisors intervene proactively to prevent capital from falling below a minimum commensurate with the bank's risk profile. In fact, the bank's risk profile was more hype than real life. Look at Lehman, AIG, RBS and the dozens other big financial conglomerates that hit the rocks.

Not everything about Pillar 2 was, however, negative. One of its little-appreciated contributions is that it brought into perspective risks related to factors other than capital adequacy. It is indeed a pity that these were not used intensively by regulators in their supervisory activities prior to the 2007–12 economic crisis. Examples are:

- concentration risk,
- reputation risk and
- legal risk[17]

Not only is, in general practice, *concentration risk* in the bank's portfolio poorly examined and updated, but also the big financial conglomerates themselves are contributing to concentration risk in a systemic sense. Based on data from the Bank of England, some analysts have calculated that, up to the mid-1990s, the share of the financial industry's total aggregate assets of the top three American banks was for six decades steady at the 10 percent to 12 percent level. A short time prior to the 2007–12 economic and banking crisis, however, this shot up to 40 percent.

The British picture has not been much different, and on both sides of the Atlantic there are practical reasons behind this unwarranted and risky concentration:

- the more financial business flows across a bank's trading desk, the more power it has over smaller rivals, and this leads to a self-feeding cycle, and
- such a win–win situation continues as long as the big bank can survive losses that wipe out its competitors, but it turns against the bank when it runs out of liquidity and/or faces solvency problems.

Had Basel II's capital adequacy assessment been put into action, and had bank supervision in Western countries been satisfied with use tests, some of the most spectacular failures that have been seen in recent years might have been avoided. But neither was the case. Bankers fought for their privilege to make highly leveraged decisions the way they wanted them to be. 'A people that values its privileges above its principles soon loses both,' former US President Dwight Eisenhower once said.[18]

Fraud aside, the biggest blow to the investment banks' reputation is the perception, often confirmed by surveys of its clients, that they put their own interests ahead of those of the customers they supposedly serve. Not long ago, one of the best-known Wall Street banks paid a hefty SEC penalty precisely for this reason – with its unwarranted policy being confirmed by more than 200 of its counterparties.

Which leads us to *reputational risk*. In the broader sense, reputation risk is what happens when the long-term business standing of an entity is traded for short-term ill-gotten profits. Designed in novel ways, complex securitized instruments made small game of the rules of credit rating and carried the indulgence of independent rating agencies along with them. Stamped 'AAA' by 'helpful' rating agencies, subprimes were sold freely to investors, and used as collateral by their buyers when raising new loans.

This sort of wild (and unethical) securitization divorced lenders from the risk of default and reduced their incentives to look carefully at the credit of their borrowers – which is one of the lender's basic duties. As the wheels of this novel perpetual motion financial machine turned faster and faster, the whole securitized subprimes business amounted to outright fraud.

Issuers have taken other bankers and lots of investors for a ride. Eventually, however, this light credit rating structure started to unravel. But mid-October 2007, three months into the crisis, Moody's cut the ratings of 131 securities backed by subprime mortgages, and said it was reviewing the grades of 136 others. Rating downgrades affected the collateral of many portfolios, and made these securities increasingly hard to value, to sell and to borrow against.

As in several markets, liquidity evaporated, the infection spread more widely into the banks' books, and their off-balance-sheet subsidiaries found they could not sell their 'asset-backed' commercial paper (ABCP). The banks deserted each other, and the interbank market froze. But, for the wrongdoers, *legal risk* has been swept under the carpet – because of political pressure, as supervisory authorities turned a blind eye to what was going on.

It might be different the next time around. A silver lining to the crisis is that regulators are now more likely to place rogue financial products under scrutiny. In the UK there is a growing likelihood that banks, insurers and investment firms will have their new products scrutinized as they are developed, under a regime being formulated by the Financial Services Authority (FSA).

In March 2010, in what the FSA said was its biggest investigation yet into insider trading, police and FSA officers raided 16 premises and arrested six people, among them employees of Deutsche Bank, BNP Paribas and Moore Capital, one of the world's biggest hedge funds.[19] That same month,

Lord Turner, the FSA's chairman, gave a hint of what might be coming as he lamented the failure of the regulator to anticipate and head off consumer scandals in the past. In the USA, consumer protection is an integral part of new financial regulations (FINREG; the Dodd–Frank Act).

Fraud is one of the domains where reputational risk and legal risk correlate. There is a widespread opinion that the regulatory system current at the time of writing (including Pillar 2) is not fit to uncover fraud, hence the need for an upgrade. As an article in the *Financial Times* had it, in America the Securities and Exchange Commission (SEC) displayed a remarkable tendency to bark up the wrong tree at almost every point.[20]

Critics say that, with regard to securities supervision in general, the SEC might have collected too many different factors under the same roof. Andrew Lo, who heads MIT's Laboratory for Financial Engineering, suggests separating regulations from forensics, in a way similar to what was done in the airline industry. The USA's National Transportation Safety Board is more independent in its investigations and resulting opinions because its mission is to investigate crashes, not to set rules after the event.

With Basel II, legal risk has been integral part of operational risk, which often finds its way into both credit risk and market risk. Globalization significantly increased the likelihood of legal risk, as different laws prevail in different jurisdictions, thus making compliance much more complex. Experts say that, if tested in court, many of the current transnational agreements would not stand up to scrutiny. This will have a very negative effect on business confidence. It will also have a negative effect on global banking and international trade, because confidence is at the heart of business.

The concept of market discipline and the CDSs' contribution

There are two types of *market discipline*: direct and indirect. '*Direct*' refers to the fact that anticipation of higher refinancing costs may constraint banks from excessive risk-taking, while '*indirect*' signals the market's response toward an institution, which can help superiors to detect weak credit and other ills afflicting financial institutions. Using the market as a criterion of good governance and creditworthiness is an interesting concept, but it is confronting two headwinds moral hazard and lack of transparency.

Time and again, a tsunami of moral hazard is created by the bail-out of lenders and other financial institutions at the eleventh hour, just before they become bankrupt. Because this has become common currency, saying that it is possible to apply a rigorous market discipline is at best a half-truth. The market can punish offenders only if and when it knows who they are – and this is applies equally to banks and sovereigns.

For example, many central bankers and financial analysts believe that easy money, such as soft loans from the IMF, have created a culture of government bail-outs. This, they think, has been behind several bubbles in the world's financial markets that burst after the end of the Second World War. The irony is that the sovereigns and central bankers themselves repeated the same mistakes, particularly in connection with the 2007–12 crisis, though they know very well that easy money is never part of a lasting solution, and a policy error will reveal itself sooner rather than later.

By contrast, if the big global banks and other financial institutions knew they would be allowed to fail, and their bosses might even face prosecution, then they would have an incentive to pay close attention to the quality and impact of their decisions, trade investments and speculation. This is also true of borrowers. If a borrower knows there is no salvage on the horizon s/he would be less likely to overborrow and overleverage him/herself.

In spite of the headwinds which can, in extremis, make market discipline meaningless, Basel II institutionalized it under the heading of *Pillar 3*. Basel III's position on this issue is still ambiguous, though the developing guidelines are that it will let it be known that it will require globally active banks to disclose a range of information about

- the risks they take,
- the way they assess risks,
- changes in their regulatory capital position, and
- behavioral issues that reinforce regulatory supervision by requiring transparency regarding an individual bank's exposure and the quality of its risk control.

Theoretically, several central bankers and supervisors have already espoused these concepts, though with a varying degrees of enthusiasm. One of the earlier comments at the time of Basel II had come from the Bank of England, emphasizing the expectation that Pillar 3 would lead to greater transparency in risk-taking and financial reporting. That commentary did, however, express the reservation that numbers that are published mainly reflect a financial institution's past risks and past performance.

In practice, the regulatory authorities have not been particularly enthusiastic about policing the transparency of banks under their watch. Nor did Pillar 3 go into sufficient detail, or define what sorts of fines would confront violators. Another failure has been the lack of a systematic approach. For a publicly listed financial institution, market discipline is a multiple feedback loop providing evidence about

- management's risk-taking practices and their results,
- market reaction to disclosed financial information,
- evaluation of the aftermath of risk and return on shareholder value, and
- information on changes in strategy by banks seeking to correct their mistakes and survive while there is still time to do so.

For these reasons it is absolutely inadequate just to state that 'for market discipline reasons information from banks must become more open and more generally publicly available'. This can range from slightly more detailed information posted in an institution's annual report, to a thoroughly honest evaluation of assumed exposure linking such figures to risk-weighted capital (see Chapter 6).

Attention should also be paid to the fact that banks do not all have the same interpretation of what *market discipline* means: 'We have concern about some disclosures required by CAD 3,'[21] said a senior executive of a leading commercial bank during our meeting, 'For instance by collateral type, industry exposure, and so on. But if we disclose by industry, then we give out competitive information. The same is true of credit provision in a certain segment like the retail portfolio.'

This executive also made reference to some of his colleagues in other credit institutions who are of the opinion that disclosures using a more detailed frame of reference is 'information out of proportion' regarding its release into the public domain – as opposed to confidential information provided to the supervisor. The counterargument is that information released into the public domain by banks and other financial institutions will only then serve the purposes of transparency if it stimulates an investigating mind to spot wrong results and outcomes outside the range of what is permitted.

Transparent information means a data stream that is uncompromisingly frank about each risk and/or faulty step. The message it provides should be strong enough to save its readers from self-deception. Another contribution of market transparency is to change the policy of

- overweighting favorable evidence,
- underweighting negative happenings and paying no real attention to the error ranges that inevitably accompany all financial reports.

In globalized banking, information that covers market discipline should be unambiguous to its users anywhere in the world. *Credit default swaps* (CDSs) come close to fulfilling this requirement. The power of CDSs is that they have a generalized system of metrics of financial health (specifically of creditworthiness), and because their market is so vast they cannot easily be manipulated.

CDSs play an important role beyond distributing credit risk. At the same time, however, there are risks inherent to the CDSs and their market, particularly with regard to event risk and insufficient transparency of over-the-counter (OTC) deals. In a nutshell, three metrics are important in estimating exposure:

- the *gross notional amount*; which is the outstanding volume of all concluded CDS contracts,

- the *net notional amount*, equal to the sum of netted risk positions, of individual institutions across all instruments, and
- the *market value* of a CDS contract, which reflects the replacement cost in case of counterparty default.

What interests us in this discussion is market value. When a CDS deal is concluded, this market value is close to zero, because the sum of premiums corresponds to the present value of expected loss. But as the underlying credit risk changes in the contract's life, there is a positive value for one of the parties and a negative value for the other – by the same amount.

Gross notional values reached nearly US$60 trillion in the second semester of 2007 and first semester of 2008, then it subsided. Market value rose significantly in second half of 2007, to about US$2 trillion, increased to about US$3.5 trillion in first half of 2008 and peaked at slightly over US$5 trillion in the second half of 2008. At that time, the market value represented 12 percent of CDSs gross notional value.

The fact that CDSs represent a cumulative intelligence of the investment community does not mean that some of the released information about their metrics may not be wrong. However, as Abraham Lincoln once observed: 'You can fool some of the people all of the time, and all of the people some of the time, but you cannot fool all of the people all of the time.' As far as a universal measure of exposure (and staying power) for market discipline is concerned, CDSs fit Lincoln's dictum. Their spreads point to an improvement or, the reverse, a deterioration in a bank's, sovereign's or other entity's condition.

CDS patterns tend to reveal what market participants think about default risk, which can be used to enforce market discipline. There is a reason why supervisory authorities have worked on a systemic risk indicator by decomposing the movements of CDS spreads of euroland's big financial institutions. In the second quarter of 2010, both the expected-loss component, representing the part of the CDS spread conditioned by pure default risk, and the risk-premium component, representing the part of the CDS spread driven by factors other than pure default risk, increased and this has contributed to higher CDS spreads in euroland's big banks. In relative terms, the increase in the expected-loss component was larger than the increase in the risk-premium component, which led to a decrease in the price of default risk – essentially the amount that is paid by credit risk protection buyers to protection sellers.

When, in August 2010, market participants' fears about the situation of some banks reemerged, which to some extent reversed the earlier improvements in the indicators observed in June and July, this was immediately reflected in the CDS spreads. By mid-November 2010, the CDS spreads of big banks had decreased substantially, and this was accompanied by the gradual recovery of the euro and of financial institutions' stock prices (particularly in euroland).

The more sophisticated models using this approach pay particular attention to the expectation of tail events, assisted by the fact that CDS returns are, up to a point, driven by risk appetites and changes in risk liquidity premiums. The downside is that an increase in measured risk may not be a result of increased physical risk but rather to a decrease in overall risk appetite.[22] The art of market discipline is far from being perfect, but CDSs have made an interesting contribution.

The Board's watch over compliance

Even the best rules will be gamed by unscrupulous individuals or institutions. Regulators have to be aware of the likelihood that this will happen under their watch, but unassisted they cannot do miracles. Each bank's top management should give a helping hand, fully appreciating that self-policing is an adjunct not an alternative to better regulation.

This need for a steady upgrade of the regulations is not only present in banking and finance; all industries are confronted by similar problems. Take, as an example, oil exploration. The loss in 1980 of the Norwegian rig Alexander Kieland, and the explosion and fire in 1988 on Britain's Piper Alpha platform, claimed between them nearly 300 lives. Following these accidents, regulators put a new responsibility on operating companies to go beyond meeting existing standards, and demonstrate that their plans had considered and minimized all relevant risks.

The most important new regulatory requirement at that time was to make a positive safety case for an engineering proposal that kept up automatically with the ever more advanced technology being used, as deepwater and ultra-deepwater drilling is developing rapidly.[23] Technology and innovation are welcome, but there are also downsides that find their parallel in banking when high-speed technical developments occur, setting standards in advance cannot be unquestionably accurate.

This is precisely why this chapter has pressed the point that some ambiguity embedded within regulations is an advisable approach. Uncertainty about the margin of error can keep both bankers and regulators alert. When senior management is so attracted by short-termism, which translates into fast bucks, it necessarily downplays the institution's longer-term survival and makes small game of regulations.

In the way that capital is no substitute for good governance, published rules of behavior are no substitute for sound working principles – if for no other reason than that even the most elaborate rules do not cover all possible events and/or are simply not being observed,. The process of controlling the observance of laws and regulations set by the central bank and supervisory authorities is known as *compliance*. Compliance is not a model of reality, but a control process exercised over the reality that unfolds. Its role is explained by the fact there is no substitute for vigilance in upholding rules and regulations, at all levels of the enterprise. This concept involves three related elements:

- compliance should have a status within the bank,
- there must be a compliance officer with overall responsibility for coordinating and monitoring compliance risk, and
- levels of supervision should have access to all information concerning observance of compliance, or deviations from it.

Napoleon Buonaparte said that the commander should not be satisfied with giving orders; he must also ensure that his orders are executed in a timely and effective manner, taking corrective action where necessary. His statement encapsulates the role of central banks and regulatory authorities, in assuring that all institutions in their jurisdiction comply with banking regulations. But it also speaks volumes of the role of the CEOs, CFOs and chairs of the bank's audit and risk committee. Compliance and auditing share procedural aspects, though the former is done steadily while the latter is periodic, and compliance and risk control are not the same, but they are characterized by a good deal of common thinking because, in both of them, *risk* is an overriding responsibility.

The compliance function should have the right to commission specific audits, and report its findings to the Audit Committee of the board.[24] To be effective in his work, the head of compliance should not be placed in a position where there is a possible conflict of interest between the responsibilities to which s/he has been assigned and any other responsibilities that attract the credit institution's attention.

Compliance with ethical values raises a bank's credibility and enhances its profile. But it may also require a change in policies and governance. Institutions would be well-advised to have in place a charter of 'best practices' to document an ongoing organizational culture of compliance, and demonstrate that they have systemic capabilities which generate continuous improvement in company-wide observance of all applicable laws and regulations – not only of the penal side but on all important issues. For example, in treating their counterparties fairly in regard to:

- transparency,
- suitability of sales,
- fair competition,
- product reviews,
- customer complaint resolution,
- disclosure standards, and more.

The spirit of compliance must be a standard in the organization. This spirit is at its best in a business culture which emphasizes standards of ethics and integrity, and in which the board of directors, CEO and senior management lead by example. Structural issues also matter a great deal. To be performed in an efficient manner, the compliance function should be independent of day-to-day operations.

Another important ingredient is *individual responsibility*. Everyone in a credit institution should perform his or her part of a company-wide compliance function. And, because accountability for compliance begins at the vertex, the bank's board is first in line for compliance reasons as well as for overseeing the management of compliance risk. The board should also approve the bank's compliance policy and regularly assess whether the institution is discharging its compliance responsibilities effectively.

No matter what the regulators might say about issues such as transparency and market discipline (Pillar 3 in the previous section), at the end of the day the bank's chief executive will decide whether accurate and timely information about capital elements will be made publicly available, or whether the institution will be lying with statistics.

6
Capital Adequacy and Liquidity: the Devil is in Their Detail

Unless we learn from this crisis, we shall repeat the same mistakes

As Martin Wolf, the *Financial Times* economist, said on February 5, 2008, 'unless we learn from this crisis, another one will put the world economy back on to the rocks in the not too distant future'. This is no time for tunnel-visioned ideologies. It is a time for pragmatism based on experience gained through the most recent and previous crises.

Monitoring systemic risk should be the No. 1 preoccupation of sovereigns and central bankers, while commercial and investment bankers must do their best to avoid it. This is not only for the public good. There is no better way to protect personal interests than to live and operate in a healthy economy. This is true in every individual country, and in the global financial market.

Another important lesson to be learned from the 2007–12 deep economic and banking crisis is that financial stability can be assured if, and only if, the economic system is examined, treated and managed as a whole. Because systemic risk has a cross-sectional dimension mitigating individual and bilateral exposures, contagion effects present global rather than just local challenges.[1] These involve players, markets, infrastructures and financial imbalances that are building over time and constitute the time dimension of systemic risk.

Back in the 1960s, Milton Friedman wrote,

> Economics deal with phenomena that are complex, varied and interdependent. An economic change may affect hundreds of millions of people and numerous economic, political and social phenomena. What happens in one place of the globe or in one segment of the economy may have its main effects not in that place or that segment, but in very different ones.[2]

For good reasons, regulators want to prevent banks from growing overly dependent on short-term borrowings, as was the case with Bear Stearns and Lehman Brothers, among others. The underlying concept is that capital alone is not enough to forestall a run on a bank that depends on overnight markets for funding. Supervisory rules should require credit institutions to operate under ratios gauging the exposure they have assumed as well as their dependence on short-term funding and their susceptibility to market shocks.

By comparing an institution's assets and liabilities to its stable sources of funding such as deposits and longer-term unsecured debt, regulators can focus their observations. Another ratio being used is comparing borrowings to easily sold assets. What it shows is how quickly a bank could unwind its positions if it lost its access to short-term market funding.

The most solid evidence on financial staying power is provided by capital buffers. Basel III promotes two types: the more classical capital adequacy and the countercyclical buffer. It also features a risk provisioning system that is forward-looking, helping to smooth losses over the economic cycle by means of dynamic provisioning, which reflects the time dimension of systemic risk.

Well-governed institutions appreciate these realities. They do not question the fact that capital ratios are important tools in shaping management decisions. But, as we have seen already (and will examine further in this chapter), in a number of cases lust and greed see to it that banks arbitrage the regulatory capital ratios.

Because each institution has its own risk profile, generally agreed ratios should be tightly knit to each bank's probability of insolvency. These must not be static measures. Today's fast moving global business environment requires a dynamic approach bringing together in a personalized manner:

- capital reserves,
- the probability of insolvency, and
- the likelihood of default.

A meaningful solution, for example, could be based on a steadily updated default point (DP), which accounts for current assets, current liabilities, long-term assets, long-term liabilities on balance sheet – as well as all of the bank's off-balance-sheet assets and liabilities, SIVs, conduits and other Trojan horses included. This sum of exposures could present a valid basis for calculating, solvency-wise, capital and liquidity, provided that it is linked to the economic cycle, market conditions and market psychology.

Nothing like that is included in Basel III, which so far looks like 'Basel II, one small step up'. Mervyn King, the governor of the Bank of England, was right when on October 25, 2010 at *The Economist*'s Buttonwood Gathering in New York, he criticized the Basel III rules for being *too soft*. He then said what he really thought, arguing that 'of all the many ways of organizing banking, the worst is the one we have today'.[3] Possible remedies proposed by King included breaking up banks that are too big to be saved, and eliminating fractional reserve banking.[4]

Basel III should have hit the nail on the head by outlawing the 'too big to fail' syndrome. When big global institutions are not being allowed to fail, they cause others to fail in their place. The outlawing of 'too big to fail' was not done, and regulators may well regret this in the coming years. Nor have adequate controls been put in place to restrain banks from engaging in speculative deals and high leverage.

Being rescued at the eleventh hour by a *deus ex machina* is a process feeding upon itself. As Henry Kaufman noted in an article in *The Times*:

> The assets of failing firms will end up in the hands of federal agencies or too-big-to-fail institutions. Growth in financial concentration via these paths will reduce competition enormously ... The large, dominant institution will, among other things press also to be the investment banker, lender, pension portfolio fund manager, and deposit provider.[5]

Kaufman is right. Neither the Dodd–Frank Act (FINREG) in America (see Chapter 1) nor Basel III have paid proper attention (beyond capital adequacy and liquidity requirements) to the big getting bigger via its own faults. Nor did they confront the need to eliminate financial gambling and (ironically) the fire brigade approach by sovereigns and regulators which is fed by public money, even if so many global banks today are too big to be saved.

It is not for nothing that a number of countries are considering a punitive capital surcharge for the largest firms. In November 2010, a report from the Bank of England suggested various ways of doing this. For example, it could vary by financial sector, allowing regulators to influence the marginal cost of lending to the highly risky parts of the economy. Alternatively, it could reflect the lender's contribution to systemic risk, based on the company's size, complexity, leverage and the extent of its connections to other financial entities.

Switzerland provides a good example of how much farther national regulators can go to safeguard the financial staying power of big banks. To rebuild its reputation as a financial fortress, it is not only beefing up the capital of its biggest banks but also introduces new guidelines: the new equity buffers of up to 10 percent to 13 percent of risk-weighted assets are increased by another 6 percent to 9 percent of convertible capital, and with regard to the country's two big global banks, Swiss regulators are going far beyond Basel III as well as keeping a watchful eye to make sure that financial institutions do not offset higher capital costs by making larger bets in investment banking.[6]

Quite correctly, and unlike their colleagues in some other countries, Swiss regulators have been proactive with their measures. In early October 2010, a committee of experts especially appointed by the government said that Crédit Suisse and UBS must raise their capital to 19 percent of assets. While Basel III requires banks to carry a trivial core capital of risk-adjusted assets, the Swiss banks will need 10 percent. On top of this they will have to carry of contingent-capital bonds worth another 9 percentage points that can be converted into equity if core capital ratios fall too far.

The all-important Tier 1 capital

When the first international agreement on minimum bank capital was reached in 1988, under the auspices of the Basel Committee, regulatory capital was expressed as a lump sum at 8 percent for international banks and 4 percent for national banks. Distinctions like hybrid capital instruments, such as preferred stock and fixed-maturity subordinated debt, came later. They were massively used by the banking industry to bypass the more sophisticated Basel II rules.

The original concept has been that, to be eligible, regulatory capital had to adhere to supervisory rules concerning its characteristics. Basel II introduced tiers of eligible instruments which decreased in quality and thereby affected the loss-absorbing capacity of capital. Common stock, which has always been a publicly quoted company's core capital, was considered to be the safest, and indeed, it is so. If necessary, the board can defer or cancel altogether the payment of dividends – while loans have to continue being serviced, unless the bank files for bankruptcy or is taken over by regulators.

Core capital was defined by Basel II as Tier 1 (T1). Over time, however, core capital and Tier 1 diverged because different hybrids were added to the latter, whose characteristics are closer to debt than to equity yet could still be used for up to 15 percent of total Tier 1 capital. Other T1 hybrids under Basel II have been minority interests and even Mickey Mouse money, like DTAs (see Chapter 4). That is wrong; Tier 1 assets should consist of the most secure type of capital, but under pressure from big global banks this notion has been watered down. And Hybrid T1 is as useful as feathers on a fish. Under Basel II in the USA, DTAs could be up to 10 percent of T1, and in Japan up to 90 percent, which is plainly ridiculous.

In contrast to Tier 1, Basel II introduced the so-called Tier 2 (T2) capital, which is even weaker, consisting of revaluation reserves (and possibly undisclosed reserves), general provisions and loan loss reserves. Nor does T2 benefit from a unique worldwide definition.

The European Central Bank (ECB) defined Tier 2 capital as consisting of assets that are of particular importance for national financial markets, and for which eligibility criteria are established by euroland's national central banks (NCBs) in line with minimum eligibility criteria within the Euro system. These specific national eligibility criteria for Tier 2 assets, which must be approved by the ECB, may be:

- equities,
- marketable debt instruments, or
- non-marketable debt instruments.

Theoretically, Tier 2 assets which are marketable debt instruments abide by uniform eligibility criteria. In practice, however, such criteria are of variable geometry made up within each jurisdiction. For example, T2 assets can be general government securities (such as those issued by central, state and local governments and social security funds); and Pfandbrief-style securities issued by credit institutions and backed by residential mortgages or by public-sector debt.

The reader should know that general government and Pfandbrief-style securities form an abundant but not easily controllable source of eligible assets. Other T2 types are bonds issued by corporations, and asset-backed securities other than the Pfandbrief type. The 2007–12 crisis has demonstrated that even AAA securitized mortgages, as well as other issues, can have feet of clay.

Examples of non-marketable instruments covered by the ECB's Tier 2 definitions are bank loans, trade bills and mortgage-backed promissory notes.[7] Other jurisdictions – for example, Japan and its bank supervisors – have added other similar instruments to T2, some of which are very dubious. For example, paper profits representing unrealized gains on securities, which can turn from assets to liabilities overnight.

The most ridiculous thing of all has been the asymmetric treatment of paper profits as regulatory bank capital. While paper profits are included in the assets, the huge unrealized losses with securities have not been added to the liabilities. This is *creative accounting* as practiced by Japanese regulators. It would have been at least correct to subtract the paper losses from capital. No foreigner really knows what is going on in the sovereign accounting practices of any country.

Nor has the Japanese Financial Services Agency (FSA) taken firm action to restore a balance and apply penalties when a bank has major capital distortions in its balance sheet. Resona, one of the largest and most badly damaged Japanese banks, provides the evidence. On May 17, 2003, its capital ratio fell to 2 percent from the 5 percent it had reported on March 31 of that same year. As mentioned in Chapter 4, Resona has become Japan's fifth-largest bank – the result of a merger between the Asahi and Daiwa banks, but it has feet of clay. With a straight face, Japanese regulators ensured that Resona's capital 'inadequacy' was made up by DTAs – 'Mickey Mouse' money.

There is no evidence that any regulatory authority objected to that practice. No wonder, therefore, that under Basel II there was a significant amount of jockeying both by commercial/investment bankers and by regulators. These references also document the divergence prevailing in the classification of certain capital instruments as well as a lack of precise, indispensable boundaries between different capital components. The main reasons were:

- the inconsistent definition of each capital class, including T1 and T2,
- regulatory adjustments made ad hoc in each jurisdiction to address individual problems, and
- a regrettable lack of transparency of the regulatory capital bases, which has made their fair value questionable.

In addition to this, the amount of protection most regulators provided for the banks under their control as well as the banks' own inclination to game the regulatory capital system, the global economic and financial structure was filled with banks whose capital base lacked dependability, quality and detail.

To correct this regrettable situation, Basel III began by addressing core Tier 1 capital which, at least in theory, should be composed only of common shares and retained earnings. The statement has also been made that regulatory capital adjustments will be harmonized, and generally taken from common equity. No sooner was this said than horse-trading biased (and damaged) the final T1 definition. Under Tier 1, Basel III now permits:

- common equity,
- retained earnings,
- some portions of minority interests,
- all existing deductions (largely abused under Basel II), and
- additional deductions such as deferred tax assets, which in practice means taxpayers' money.

Other portions of minority interests are excluded, while preference shares and silent partnerships are 'generally' excluded, which means that they have been taken out by the door but are coming back through the windows left open to exceptions – all that based on the discretion of national regulators under Basel III.[8] In all, it looks like an economic and financial accord not too different than the political accord at Yalta.[9]

Given this ill-advised imprecision, which is presented as 'flexibility', it does not seem to me that, under Basel III, Tier 1 capital is any better than it was under Basel II[10] – though it is higher, having gone from 2 percent to 4.5 percent (see also Chapter4). Basel III also features an additional Tier 1 with a capital weight of 1.5 percent (compared to 2 percent for Basel II), its component parts being 'some' preference shares and portions of minority interests.

Hybrids with 'innovative features' (read *creative accounting*) are to be no longer accepted. Capital instruments eligible for additional T1 will need to be loss absorbent on a going concern basis. Hence such instruments should be subordinated, have discretionary noncumulative dividends or coupons, and not have a maturity date or redemption incentive. An example of financial instruments with a redemption incentive are those with step-up clauses issued with the objective of generating lower-cost Tier 1 capital (with Basel II they are permitted up to 15 percent of T1).

Basel III did not alter the definition of Tier 2 capital established by Basel II – or its content – in any significant way. However, this definition has been simplified by removing the distinction between 'upper' and 'lower'. In addition, its weight was reduced from 4 percent to 2 percent.

A positive initiative of Basel III is the institution of a capital charge connected to the deterioration of a counterparty's creditworthiness. This complements the charge associated with default risk. Weaknesses related to correlations within the financial system and lack of transparency of the over-the-counter (OTC) derivatives markets are addressed through increased risk weights and incentives aimed at standardizing market instruments.

Higher trading book capital requirements are also being introduced, the after-effect of significant trading book losses in recent years. A developing concept is that, up to the recent crisis, the riskiness of the assets held in the trading book was not measured adequately – let alone compensated through capital and reserves – and this needs to be corrected.

Another reason for capital requirements for the trading book is that the hypothesis suggesting higher rates of turnover make the realization of substantial price losses less likely, does not hold water. Also the assumption of permanent high market liquidity proved to be an illusion. With Basel III, at least in theory, banks with expensive trading activity will need higher capital backing. But will these new rules be observed by everybody?

Capital buffers for countercyclical events and credit bubbles

The issue of countercyclical capital buffers had its origins in Spain, when Jaime Caruana, the president of the Bank for International Settlements (BIS) was governor of the Bank of Spain. In terms of capital resources, the idea is brilliant, but accountants hate the practice because they say it creates a nightmare in bookkeeping.

In a nutshell, with a countercyclical policy, banks will have to put capital aside in good times to cover losses in bad times. Countercyclical provisioning is a sound precaution. Instead of only building reserves for expected losses over the life of loans, bank treasurers must also account for the ups and down in the business cycle.

As a concept, though not in this sense of a capital buffer, procyclicality is well known in the financial system and the economy, and it has been a source of concern for many regulators. In economic downturns, credit risk rises, and it is normal to expect that capital requirements would also increase – thus building in provision for unexpected losses. Banks face higher capital needs at a time when write-offs on defaulted loans reduce their profits and impair their capacity to build up reserves.

When that happens, the intrabank market retracts, and raising capital becomes more expensive because investors are not inclined to lend when credit risk rises – or they demand an extra premium. There is often a dual effect of a general depreciation of assets and an increasing aggregate demand for capital. The opposite is true during an economic upswing, therefore making capital available for a special reserve is a sound practice.

In fact, aside from cyclicality, well-managed banks tend to hold capital buffers for reasons such as greater operational efficiency, the wish to avoid the costs associated with having to issue fresh equity at short notice, an aversion to over-indebtedness; or as a signal to the market. Also as a precaution, in upturns banks may accumulate capital in excess of regulatory capital levels, since such money plays a crucial role in mitigating the volatility in capital requirements. Not every institution is, however, doing this, and there is a difference between voluntary measures taken by banks and the requirements mandated by regulators.

Banks opposed to procyclical buffers say that cyclical effects are benign in normal times. This is true only when the banking system is generally well-capitalized. Moreover, cyclical effects can be most significant in difficult times. Hence, Basel III's initiative to strengthen the system by ensuring that banks are adequately provisioned to cope with a financial crisis. In their negative reaction, the banks forget that taking into account procyclicality offers them important advantages.

The Basel Committee has pointed these advantages out. A recent document suggests, 'Mapping the impact of the higher capital requirements on lending rates requires estimates of the cost of various sources of funding.' This includes the cost of equity and the cost of liabilities, the latter based on short-term and long-term wholesale debt, and calibrated to match the historical ratio of interest expense to total assets observed for each country.[11]

Nor is the issue of capital buffers to confront procyclicality a theoretical diatribe. An experiment done by Basel has shown that part of the fall in return on equity (ROE) is offset by the smaller amount of debt outstanding, which reduces the bank's interest expense. 'Profits' calculations which take no account of the risks associated with indebtedness are what is produced by the incapable and the greedy.

Combined with high leverage, procyclicality is also one of the reasons that bubbles build up. Regulators are concerned that risk-sensitive events can have procyclical effects on undercapitalized banks. Also at the aggregate level, the extent of procyclical effects depends on the degree of undercapitalization of the banking industry, making a strong case for countercyclical capital buffers.

Lobbying aside, not all regulators look favorably on their institution. The same is true of capital requirements for credit bubbles, and the decision taken in December 2010 (announced on January 10, 2011) came as a surprise to many observers. On that day, regulators took a major step by agreeing to raise worldwide capital requirements whenever an individual country confronts a credit bubble. The notion of countercyclical capital buffers changes the way that national banking regulators seek to moderate the economic cycle, and makes headway in protecting the health of the entire financial system, not only individual banks.

According to several analysts, this has been a turning point for the Basel Committee's authority because previously its decisions were largely *ex-ante* cooperation to make banks safer. They did not involve a great deal of reciprocity, but this is beginning to change with the latest agreement – which, in a way, crosses the line between regulation and economic policy.

Among other reasons, this agreement has been important because of the trust implied by reciprocity. If, for example, the USA imposes a surcharge, then the UK, Germany and France will be honor-bound to do the same to the US businesses of their own banks. The reader should, however, appreciate that such a deal works only if overseas banks entering a market have a similar increase in capital requirements – a condition that has not been spelled out clearly.

In addition, because details – particularly those connected to disciplinary action – have not yet been provided, it is not clear who will have the power to impose the corresponding capital buffers. Some people think that, when decision day comes, some countries may not be that willing to place additional capital requirements on their home-based banks.

A different way of putting this is that, to become generally enforceable, the deal must directly include the relevant regulatory variables, as well as penalties for not applying higher capital and liquidity requirements. Also important is to define the precise mapping between higher capital levels and stricter liquidity standards on the one hand, and the reduction in the probability of crises on the other (which, critics suggest, is in no way certain).

In conclusion, what the aforementioned agreement essentially says is that, based on the ratio of credit to GDP, national regulators can require banks within their jurisdiction to hold extra capital against potential losses. The breakthrough is that regulators in all other countries would have to follow suit and impose a proportional surcharge on their own banks, based on the size of those institutions facing a bubble.

By contrast, if after exposure to a bubble, the bubble blows, regulators could reduce or remove the capital buffer, permitting banks to use the extra capital to absorb losses. All 27 members of the Basel Committee on Banking

Supervision signed up to this agreement, the importance of which can hardly be underestimated, but still has to be confirmed by legislation.

Assuring greater liquidity than is available at present: LCR and NSFR

Theoretically, but only theoretically, prior to the 2007–12 crisis the financial industry was characterized by ample liquidity. In practice, two trends had affected liquidity in a negative way: the growing reliance on capital markets for funding, and the irrational dependence on short-term maturity funding instruments.

The after-effects of these trends was reinforced by a concurrent build-up of contingent liquidity claims, particularly from off-balance-sheet vehicles and instruments as well as marginal requirements linked to derivatives transactions. When the crisis hit, many banks faced a surge in demand for liquidity, which was a major risk that they dealt with mainly through elementary management practices. Supervisory standards were unable to keep up with the challenges posed by a global liquidity squeeze.

The best way to explain the issues raised by a liquidity crisis, and underline their importance, is to sum up a document by the Basel Committee, which proposed an international framework for liquidity risk.[12] As will be recalled, during the first year of the severe 2007–12 economic and financial crisis, it was generally believed that the main reason for it was a lack of liquidity. Only after Fannie Mae, Freddie Mac, AIG and (most particularly) Lehman Brothers collapsed, it was admitted that insolvency was the most important trigger, and lack of liquidity took the No. 2 spot as well as being the qualification of the downturn's trigger.

The Basel Committee document mentioned above initially identifies the need for a *Liquidity Coverage Ratio* (LCR), which addresses the non-pledged (unencumbered) high-quality liquid assets held by a financial institution. These can be used to offset net cash outflow typically encountered in the aftermath of a crisis, to answer requests by supervisors to increase the bank's liquidity, and confront specific shocks, such as:

- a downgrade by several notches in a credit rating,
- the beginning of a run on deposits,
- derivative collateral calls and non-balance-sheet exposure, and
- reputational risk which closes down the interbank market.

The liquidity coverage ratio extends over a time horizon of 30 days and measures a bank's stock of highly liquid assets in relation to its net payment obligations under a stress scenario. This metric makes sense, but because of pressure from several governments it will be introduced on January 1, 2015,[13] which will be far too late.

In a globalized financial environment, this LCR must be unique (in a worldwide sense), understood and appreciated, as well as being used by all banks and their supervisors. This is a sound policy that contrasts with present-day practices – which include significant differences in quantitative metrics employed in connection with liquidity risk profiles. (An early 2009 Basel study identified 25 different concepts and measures.) The LCR algorithm is:

$$\frac{\textit{Stock of high quality liquid assets}}{\textit{Net cash outflows over a 30-day period}} > 100\% \qquad (1)$$

This Liquidity Coverage Ratio is a short-term measure, establishing a minimum level of high-quality liquid assets whose existence will enable the bank to withstand, for about a month, a scenario of acute stress on its liquidity. (The longer-term measure is the Net Stable Funding Ratio (NSFR); more on this later.)

Banks have provided commentaries to which I am not privy. To my mind, however, simply stating that the LCR should be greater than 100 percent is not enough. Based on what Neil Jacoby and Louis Sorel taught their students at UCLA, I would think that a ratio of greater than 200 percent would be much better, taking into account the fact that, in Equation (1):

- the numerator has two qualitative expressions: 'high quality' and 'liquid assets' which at best are fuzzy, and
- the denominator indicates a '30-day period' over which the pattern of net cash outflow would vary widely from one bank to the next.

The opinion of experts whom I asked has been that 'high quality assets' is a vague statement open to many different interpretations. Even if an AAA credit rating is specified for these assets, as the securitized subprimes scams have shown, this triple-A can be faked, thus providing banks with the freedom to turn the tables on the regulators.

In the denominator, the term 'net cash outflows' does not have this weakness, but cash bleeding as a result of a severe bank hit by a drop in creditworthiness may be unstoppable.[14] It is therefore wise to simulate the long leg of the cash bleeding distribution to see what it produces for each individual bank under different scenarios of liquidity stress.

The Financial Stability Review of the European Central Bank had this to say with regard to the LCR:

> As central bank funding obtained through open market operations or lending facilities is recognized as liquid assets within the LCR measure, the liquidity rules could affect the demand and the variation in demand for central bank liquidity ... [Moreover] opposing effects may come into

play, given the rollover assumption on secured central bank funding against collateral which is not considered in the regulatory definition of liquid assets within the LCR.[15]

For global big banks there is also a currency risk to be accounted for in terms of its effects on both the numerator and denominator of the LCR algorithm. This is important for all four components constituting liquid assets: cash; central bank reserves; marketable securities; and government or central bank debt issued in domestic currencies. Other effects emanate from factors which, according to Basel, suggest the need for greater liquidity of financial institutions:

- the aforementioned downgrade triggers,
- market valuation changes, particularly on derivative transactions,
- market valuation changes on posted collateral,
- loss of funding on asset-backed commercial paper (ABCP), conduits and the like,
- loss of funding on term asset-backed securities (ABSs) and other structured instruments,
- drawdowns on commercial credit and liquidity facilities, and
- loss of funding on contractual and non-contractual obligations.

Overall, Basel's liquidity proposals can be seen as dividing into two parts: one requires banks to have enough liquid assets on hand to survive a potential 30-day crisis, while the other promotes stable long-term funding, favoring deposits and disfavoring wholesale sources that might suddenly be cut off.

Only time will tell how well foresight has been supported by hindsight, but there appears to be controversy ahead. Following criticisms by banks acting on conflicts of interest, Basel watered down or delayed some of its most controversial proposals. This includes the longer-term liquidity rule known as the NSFR, introduced above, which would have required banks to match more closely the duration of their assets and liabilities.

The NSFR measures the number of long-term, stable sources of funding used by a financial institution relative to the liquidity profiles of the assets funded and the potential for contingent calls on funding liquidity. The latter may arise from both on-balance-sheet and off-balance-sheet obligations and commitments. (*Inter alia*, the net stable funding ratio was intended to address complaints that the rule favored investment banks over those with large retail operations, which is not necessarily true.)

In its original definition, the NSFR required a minimum amount of funding expected to be stable over a one-year horizon. This had to be based on liquidity risk factors assigned to assets and off-balance-sheet liquidity exposures. A negative response is hard to accept, because all banks should be able to provide that, and retail banks should also not engage in off-balance-sheet trades. Moreover, all banks should be keen to promote longer-term structural funding of both their on-balance-sheet and off-balance-sheet deals.

Last but not least, the one-year timeframe implied by NSFR is by no means 'long term'. Rather, it is short-term, though longer than the LCR's 30 days. (Some jurisdictions consider the short term to be up to six months, while others take it to be equal to one year.)

If banks object to an NSFR's time horizon of one year, then they have something to hide. The best way to confront this is to remind the objectors that, because of credit rating and other financial problems, they may have cash bleeding for six months or more. On its own, any liquidity measure that is limited to only 30 days is nearly worthless.

It is time to face the music: the banks have to raise cash

Bankers and those protecting their interests should understand that rules governing their core capital, other financial reserves and the all-important liquidity of the institution, both at present and in the future, are not an option; they are an obligation. Capitalism will not survive repeated deep economic and banking crises with ruined banks and overindebted sovereigns. At last it is time to face the music.

Against a background of excessive leverage in banking and in other industry sectors, which had become the rule prior to the onset of the financial crisis, the Basel Committee had no alternative but to take a firm stand and develop measures which reflect risk-based capital requirements. But it is not enough to involve only what is written on balance sheets.

Basel's initiative to convert off-balance-sheet items into on-balance-sheet ones by means of *uniform credit conversion factors* (CCFs) is welcome. It is also subject to further review to assure that, based on historical experience and on new events, the CCFs are sound enough.

As we have already seen, however, there are different views with regard to the implementation of regulatory measures stricter than those that brought the 2007–12 descent into the abyss. Another negative is the lack of transparency because of the use of difficult to value (in terms of risk and return) derivative instruments, as well as the blanket of secrecy prevailing in offshore financial centers.

The Cayman Islands, a well-known example of an offshore, ranks in the top division of world banking centers, holding a huge amount of money. Over 90 percent of the world's 50 largest banks carry out business from the Caymans (though some have nothing more than a brass plate for identification). This stable includes all the big names from North America, Europe and Japan. Most are minimal operations, but several banks have a physical presence on the islands, and all of them offer international investors a range of private banking, asset management and trust services characterized by opaque financing and accounting.

The offshores are attractive precisely because of this opaqueness. One of the main reasons that the Cayman Islands took off as a financial center in the late 1960s was its expertise in setting up trusts hidden from supervisory scrutiny. Among the offshores, the opaque trust business remains one of the pillars of their success, with a broad choice that can deal with inquiries from residents in any part of the world.

Tax avoidance is rumored to be legion. Tax issues aside, these invisible huge accounts that can be moved at a moment's notice from one offshore to another through secret networks have a systemic importance, and therefore present regulators with special challenges. Many systemically important banks are hiding behind opaque books and accounts; the losses in their books allegedly make small game of their capital; and yet, they benefit from lavish implicit government guarantees, which assure their continuing existence.

Optimists say that both capital/liquidity norms and dedicated bank insolvency legislation enabling timely intervention by supervisors are part of the coming years' prudential rules and control methods. They are promoted by supervisors as a way of avoiding insolvency surprises because of overexposure, and as a means of assuring the orderly market exit of an institution.

Pessimists answer that, without sanctions, this is not going to work. Also, the regulators' authority to close down global banks is most critical, because the opacity discussed above ensures that the weaknesses of individual financial institutions remain a carefully guarded secret up to the point of crisis. As for the often discussed internal control and market discipline mechanisms (see Chapter 5), the truth is that generally they have failed.

Glaring deficiencies have also been revealed in internal risk management, most particularly with structured products. This speaks volumes about the market players' responsibility to critically examine their management function – from capital management to risk control in a way that enables them to confront extreme events and crises, not merely to handle routine events in normal times.

The crisis of 2007–12 has furthermore demonstrated that the strategies used by banks to increase their capital have to be rethought and reevaluated. After the introduction of Basel II, an institution that targeted specific credit ratings, such as AA or AA+, had different strategies for capital management based on:

- equity,
- hybrid Tier 1,
- Tier 2,
- assets sales, and
- securitizations (see the following section).

However, most banks still have preferred debt over equity, commenting that the downside of an equity-based approach was multifaced. Namely, raising new equity depends on the response of the markets; raising equity can be dilutive, particularly given executives' and traders' bonuses and options; and, on the bottom line, raising capital through equities may be an expensive solution compared to the alternatives.

These arguments, however, have not convinced all central bankers and regulators, whose credo has now become 'Better capital, more capital', while the debate about how much capital banks should hold against unexpected losses has attracted a great deal of attention. The counterargument to what bankers say about the expense of core capital is that the best sort of capital to assure a stable banking system is equity, because it absorbs losses directly, and can cushion against systemic shocks.

Another change that followed in the footsteps of the 2007–12 economic and financial crisis is that regulators began to resist the banks' capital dilution with cheap fillers, such as 'hybrid capital' and other questionable instruments which paid tax-deductible fixed interest. It has finally become clear that fancy deals such as 'Hybrid Tier 1' have *not* behaved quite as expected.

Where banks have been compelled to halt interest payments as a condition of receiving state bailouts, a well-known situation across the USA and the European Union, they have sometimes been unable to do this with hybrids. Payments on hybrid securities have often been mandatory. Rescued by British taxpayers' money, the Royal Bank of Scotland was able to suspend interest payments only to some of its hybrids.[16]

A similar case can be made for Tier 2 capital, which was a compromise with Basel II aimed at letting some banks off the capital hook. Several cases suggest that many of the securities introduced into a bank's capital structure had to be reexamined. Far from being based on brilliant innovations that satisfy regulatory capital rules as well as investors, in many cases such instruments seemed to represent the worst of all possible solutions.

All this is highly relevant to the existence of a banking industry able to sustain itself in the free market. Banks unable to raise capital commensurate with the amount of risk they are assuming – as measured by risk-weighted assets that are marked to market – become a millstone around the neck of taxpayers. Overindebted entities cannot afford to repeat recent experiences where politicians poured public money into the bottomless pit of private banks, and inadvertently engaged citizens in a whirlwind of moral hazard.

Insolvent banks should be broken up, and only the deposit-taking part restructured, and even that says a lot about the risk assumed by taxpayers as well as about moral hazard. The gambling aspects of failing banks should definitely be allowed to become bankrupt. 'Band-aid' solutions are no more appealing. It's time to face the music in a serious way.

In 2009, William Poole, former president of the Federal Reserve Bank of St. Louis suggested that, as a condition of their license, banks should be obliged to issue 10-year paper equal to 10 percent of their liabilities. This would be highly subordinated debt, equity included. Every year a tenth of that issue – or 1 percent of the institution's total liabilities -- would have to be rolled over into the market. A rise in the yield would tell the bank's management that danger was around the corner. Or if, even worse, the bank found it difficult to roll over this 1 percent of its liabilities, it would have to shrink its balance sheet significantly.

Paul Tucker of the Bank of England suggests another approach to the special resolution process, in which a failing bank is taken over by the regulator. Creditors of the bank would be subjected to a flat haircut, preferably in the form of a debt–equity swap. The problem with this is that, because of the (most likely) banks' high leverage, converting debt into equity would have an impact on its balance sheet, ironically by strengthening it – and with that the failing bank would be hit by a golden ax.

Another alternative was suggested by Julie Dickson, the director of financial supervision in Canada.[17] In her opinion, banks should issue securities with an embedded convertible clause to be triggered if the regulator takes control. However, this solution would also strengthen the failing bank's balance sheet and might set a trend.

It goes without saying that none of the solutions offer only advantages, and none offer a firm solution for dealing *ex-ante* with the bank's toxic waste. Basel III will be an empty shell to be kicked around. In addition, in a globalized economy, the method to be adopted must have a worldwide application and command international respect, otherwise its footprint would be very limited.

Solvency, liquidity and the effects of massive securitization

On January 21, 2012, the Bank of America recorded US$4.1 billion in fourth-quarter 2010 costs for current and future mortgage-repurchase claims. (This included those from its US$2.6 billion settlement with Fannie Mae and Freddie Mac over claims that its Countrywide Financial unit sold loans based on faulty information.)[18]

The largest US bank also set aside an additional US$1.5 billion in litigation reserves and took a US$2 billion goodwill charge on the declining value of its home-loan business. While these have been losses connected to the cleaning up of the mess left by the crisis, their magnitude suggests that they have dominated the big global bank's quarterly results. They also overshadowed any sign that the Bank of America had started to benefit from a slowly improving US economy.

This is an excellent example on the point made earlier in this chapter that liquidity problems are not '30-day affairs', no matter what the big banks' lobbyists say. Nor are these examples the only ones that could drain a bank's liquidity and put its solvency into question.

Merrill Lynch, now part of the Bank of America, had many doubtful securities which, when marked-to-market, lost 19 percent of their book value. According to some estimates, Merrill would have needed a core capital ratio of 27 percent to avoid falling through the 8 percent floor for international banks. UBS lost 13 percent, implying that it would have required a ratio of 21 percent. Research by the Bank of England focusing on other crises reached a similar conclusion.[19]

By the end of 2009, a little more than a year after the lowest point of the 2007–12 economic and banking crisis, *loss severity* estimates for the Bank of America and Merrill Lynch over the 2009–10 timeframe had gone through the roof. They amounted to the following percentages of loans outstanding:

Subprimes/Second Lien	23%
Credit cards	16%
Consumer loans	11%
Alt-As	11%
Commercial real estate	10%
Residential real estate	8.6%[20]

Two-digit numbers in the severity of loss are a danger signal. Many people in the banking industry have either not learned or are trying to forget that under stress complex instruments rarely work as intended. As recent events have documented, in a crisis the degree of uncertainty regarding liquidity requirements and worst-case losses can turn into a legend – particularly when mistrust of banks becomes widespread, and counterparties run after any, even minor, admission of trouble.

No better evidence can be provided than the after-effect of the massive securitization of doubtful loans in real estate in 2005–7.[21] When practiced in a measured way, using creditworthy loans as raw material, the process of securitization has merits, but it is its massive use of securitization based on questionable paper that pushes it into a strange financial netherworld, a situation that banks neither need nor can afford – if for no other reason than because of reputational risk.

Earlier in the chapter, different ways were presented that could be used to raise cash. Banks can proceed with asset sales, if they have assets that investors wish to buy. For example, a profitable subsidiary or sought-after real estate. These, however, are the assets that go first, and often what remains does not attract premium prices. Most of the 'assets' in the bank's portfolio are largely other people's debts in the form of all kinds of loans, mortgages and receivables. Securitization is then the solution and at the same time the poison pill.

If, and only if, securitization is done in a measured way with full attention being paid to the exposure of both originating banks and investors who buy these instruments, then there is nothing inherently wrong with it. In fact, it can be a valuable tool for raising capital and spreading risk. The downside is that the large-scale transfer of lightly assumed credit risk poses serious problems of moral and financial hazard. Loans are originated with little or no attention being paid to the creditworthiness of borrowers, and the loan underwriting process moves farther and farther away from the original holder of default risk, creating a vicious cycle.

To bend the curve of moral hazard that rocketed in the first decade of the twenty-first century, there must be increased transparency and risk control for securitization so that originating banks, underwriters, credit rating agencies, bond insurers and investors can measure and understand the actual exposure that has gone into securitized instruments. For their part, regulators must be endowed with skilled specialists who are able to analyze the way that sophisticated risk transfer mechanisms work.

Without this, toxic waste accumulates in trading books and portfolios, and its negative effects spread far and wide. According to reliable estimates, direct subprime mortgage losses were originally only somewhere around US$500 billion, but they ignited a process that went out of control. A short time after the Lehman bankruptcy its costs were estimated to stand at US$8 trillion.[22]

Here is an example on how accelerating exposure hit one of the best-known banks. Ordered by the Swiss Federal Banking Commission, an internal investigation into US$38 billion of mortgage losses at UBS blamed the disaster on a push for growth in the bank's fixed income business. This amassed vast tranches of collateralized debt obligations (CDOs), which paid more interest but ultimately bled white the bank and several of its clients. At its peak, UBS's CDO desk employed about 40 people and accounted for US$12 billion of writedowns in 2007 alone.[23]

Neither the bank's top management nor its risk controllers were in charge of that overwhelming exposure. The irony is that when this mountain of debt rose and was parceled out, UBS employed 3,400 risk managers whose efforts were either misdirected or ineffectual. Commercial banks became highly imprudent in their issue of credit because new loans turned into a rich source of raw material for securitization, and they knew that these loans would not be in their books. Loans banking any credit worthiness which underlay securitizations in the early years of the twenty-first century created untrustworthy instruments that might have qualified for a B- credit rating, but with the collusion of rating agencies these were turned into pristine AAAs till all hell broke loose.[24]

Even certified public accountants (CPAs) have allegedly been tainted. Andrew Cuomo, formerly New York's attorney-general (and now the state governor), has filed a suit against Ernst & Young, Lehman's auditors, in connection with Repo 105, a creative accounting practice used by Lehman. Toward the end of each quarter, through Repo 105 Lehman temporarily swapped some of its assets for cash with another counterparty but booked this as if it were a permanent sale of assets. The maneuver helped the bank to appear less indebted and more trustworthy with regard to its financial results.[25]

In conclusion, laws and rules made by legislators and regulators which lack depth and are deprived of detail are easily gamed. Runaway securitizations are just one example. After a bubble bursts and the economy turns on its head, even massive amounts of money thrown at the problem, accompanied by the loose monetary policy of the central bank, cannot offset the after-effects of the bubble. When business confidence collapses, even the most sophisticated instruments aren't able to provide a miracle solution.

7
Home–Host Issues Haunt Bankers and Regulators

Home–host issues defined

Charles Goodhart, the British economist, once described banks as international in life, but national in death. This is true of every institution that operates in the global market for financial services, and most particularly for the larger ones engaging in cross-border wholesale and investment banking. The home country of a bank is where it was originally instituted and, in the majority of cases, quoted on the stock exchange.

But as we shall see in this and subsequent sections, some big global banks are quoted on more than one exchange, therefore the definition that was valid in the past will not necessarily continue to be so in the future. Other relevant criteria of a home origin are: where the bank's board sits; how its revenue stream is distributed; and where it has its most significant operations, particularly in deposit-taking. A credit institution, or any other financial company, may operate in one or several host countries which are different jurisdictions.

The size of its operations and their nature can vary from one host country to the next. No foreign operation is an exact clone of its parent. Legal, cultural, product line and supervisory types of differences add to the complexity of the home–host problem. The administration and regulation of the national/international life of sprawling financial institutions are full of thorny issues that cannot easily be solved by occasional meetings between regulators, or simply by giving them more power. Nor can cross-border dealings be dismembered into country-sized components.

In the course of a meeting on home–host issues in which I participated, one of those present said that if one of the mammoth global institutions were to fail, then national regulators might be tempted to take over the assets they were able to get their hands on to protect the deposits of their own citizens. Others, however, commented that entire asset classes could not be subjected to such a procedure. Legally obtaining, valuing and managing them in conjunction with the collapsing institution's assumed liabilities makes sense only through a holistic approach and in respect of commitments, as well as procedures, outlined well ahead of such an event.

A holistic approach will be impossible as long as the current lack of transparency continues to prevail. National regulators are greatly concerned about toxic waste in the 'assets' of foreign banks operating in their jurisdiction, which are opaque both to them and to the home country supervisory authorities of these banks.

As the 2007–12 economic and banking crisis has demonstrated (particularly in terms of exposures in the European Union), British and German banks had crippling potential losses to Ireland; French and German banks to Greece; Spanish banks to Portugal; and all of them to businesses (including financial entities) whose activities spread all over euroland. If one of the weak EU peripheral countries defaulted, there would be a contagious banking crisis that would overwhelm the ability of some governments to cope.

In July 2011, the Basel Committee on Banking Supervision published *Resolution Policies and Frameworks – Progress So Far*. This well-written study brings to the reader's attention the fact that the orderly resolution of a global financial institution requires effective cooperation and coordination among the relevant home and host supervisory authorities. Such cooperation should:

- begin in the planning phase,
- pay a good deal of attention to information sharing, and
- extend into actions associated with implementation and resolution.

According to the Basel document, while there has been much international cooperation since the recent financial crisis, constraints remain in the sharing of information among relevant authorities – particularly is in connection with those more recent techniques designed to ensure continuity of critical functions (e.g. bridging loans, transfer powers, bail-in powers).'[1]

The point is further made that, so far, only a limited number of jurisdictions have entered into home–host agreements dealing specifically with cooperation and coordination in managing and resolving the cross-border after-effects of a financial crisis. Those that do exist are mainly bilateral or multilateral, focusing on enhanced cooperation in resolution contingency planning, as well as on analyses and simulation aimed at improving the authorities' preparations for resolving cross-border banking crises. The downside of these agreements is that they are usually non-binding.

Legal and regulatory differences amplify home–host problems by adding background problems relating to the globalization and regulation of banking. These include the heterogeneity of legal mandates and the fact that the lion's share of supervisory duties (along with the associated authority to act) are kept within the home country's national jurisdiction.

Like Basel II, Basel III fits best the banking supervision associated with the home country; not the hosts'. In addition, host supervisors are more interested from the viewpoint of depositor protection, which they try to ensure by involving their governments, but the home–host challenges are much wider.

The narrower view mentioned in the preceding paragraph has been demonstrated by the British and Dutch governments which, having paid deposit insurance for their citizens unwary enough to invest in IceSave and other similar instruments, obliged the Icelandic government and its taxpayers to pay for the fallen banks' dues (more on this later in the chapter). Prescriptiveness accentuates sovereignty issues, which are multiplied by the large number of hosts where a big global bank is present:

- Citibank operates in 101 countries,
- the Royal Bank of Scotland in 80 countries,
- the former ABN Amro operated in 60 countries and had three hosts: the Netherlands, the USA and Brazil, and
- Crédit Suisse is present in nearly 100 countries and it also has three hosts: Switzerland, the USA and the UK.

With 'host' becoming multiple 'hosts' as big global banks continue to expand, problems being brought to the reader's attention become magnified. Any transborder regulatory solution with a reasonable hope of success must address six questions pertinent to a home–host definition:

1. How is the second, third and so on home country ascertained:
   - Being listed on the exchange?
   - Having a large operation? How large?
   - Taking deposits?
   - Which other conditions should be fulfilled?
2. If a bank has two, three or more home countries, and is listed on different exchanges:
   - How will its core capital be viewed?
   - Will it include equity from different exchanges?
   - What about minority interests?
   - Supplementary Tier 2 capital?
   - Hybrids?
3. Which *credit risk* issues should be treated in the same way globally? And which differently by jurisdiction? The same question is valid for market risk, operational risk and business risk.
4. Will one set of correlation coefficients (see Chapter 8) and one value of risk-weighted assets be implemented in the home country and another in the hosts? If not, what are the criteria for differentiation? Are they rational?
5. How will market discipline (Pillar 3) work by jurisdiction? Will the home and host national supervisors enhance the transparency of each bank's

financial statements globally? If not, how will market discipline be promoted?

6. How often should home and host regulators meet to discuss the risks assumed by, and financial staying power of, each global bank operating in their domains? Will they address risks homogeneously in global manner or make way for jurisdictional differences?

Behind each of these questions lie the precise issues on which regulators should focus their undivided attention. These questions are not academic and all of them have to be answered, even if the home–host issue is still in the early stages of being addressed. What was said above is also the opinion of a European regulator, who added that, to date, different supervisory authorities have taken heterogeneous individual initiatives.

An executive of Sweden's Finansinspektionen, for example, said during our meeting, 'We have started discussing it with German and Scandinavian supervisors, eventually leading to a written document stipulating which authority will have responsibility for which part of the bank's book.' This regional transborder effort also examined the internal rating-based (IRB) models of Basel II and operational risk models, which is a good initiative, but not an approach that is universally followed.

The principle guiding the hand of Scandinavian regulators has been one of shared responsibility. For example, for the Norwegian operations of a Swedish bank, Swedish supervisors will rely on Norwegian authorities for inspection purposes. If, however, the models and method (M&M) used by the bank's Norwegian subsidiary have been developed in Sweden, then this M&M becomes the responsibility of the Swedish supervisors, though they will invite their Norwegian colleagues to the bank's M&M examination. Indeed, one of Basel III's failures is that it defines neither the accountability of regulators engaged in shared responsibility, nor its mechanics. Yet, individually, supervisory authorities see the need for a joint effort. At the time of writing, this by necessity is based on bilateral agreements which vary from one case to the next.

The Basel Committee's *Publication 100*, of August 2003, recognized the need for cooperation and coordination between home and host country supervisors, but in the years that have elapsed since then no firm standards have been set that are to be followed by all regulatory authorities. In the absence of global standards there is the risk that the supervisory authorities will steps on each others' toes.

In conclusion, heterogeneity in regulation and the lack of a standard framework of regulatory supervision weaken the supervisory tasks. The trust placed in the supervisory authorities, as well as the banks' reputation, can quickly be challenged.

* * *

Readers in the European Union might say that the new European Banking Authority (EBA) will do what is necessary to close the gaps in home–host supervision. True enough, the EBA has not only taken over from the Committee of European Bank Supervisors (CEBS) existing responsibilities but it has also been given more powers, ranging from improving the coherence of banking supervision to strengthening home–host collaboration, to be carried out in cooperation with national supervisors.

There are two reasons why, in this book, the EBA's projected tasks have not been given more emphasis. The new agency began its work on January 1, 2011, therefore no results can be discussed before 2013 or 2014, say. The second reason is that the remit of the ESA is European banking, while the questions raised in this and the other sections of this chapter address global banking's home–host challenges, which for the time being remain an orphan (in spite of G20, or perhaps because of it).

Financial globalization is no bed of roses

When people talk of financial globalization and its benefits to the world's economy, they typically consider only the upside. Over-optimism, however, is capable of doing more damage than pessimism, since caution is thrown aside, and this is exactly what caused the industrial globalization drama: over-optimism that things will 'go right' on their own led heads of state and plenty of others to let down the defenses that should have been in place to ensure that:

- globalization provided a level playing field,
- limits were set to cushion the inevitable downside, and
- there were no loopholes that might be enlarged and exploited to the point that globalization eventually became a train wreck.[2]

Sloppy work and disaster are linked. Promises oblige only those who listen to them, says Charles Pasqua, a French politician. Without a definition of economic justification and the setting of practical limits, the mammoth sized economic and financial organizations begin to do as they like – and the deeper becomes the drop in confidence as well as the disregard of good sense.

In addition, vague promises to business partners at the G20 level and ill-defined rights make the resolution of 'who owes what to whom' more complex in the sequel to a big global bank's bankruptcy. An interesting example on home–host regulatory responsibilities is that of Lehman's so-called 'minibonds' sold through local banks to Hong Kong citizens. For retail investors in particular, this case underlined the risks of having securities held by people in one jurisdiction that were sold by financial institutions operating in another jurisdiction, which may have assets in yet another and come under multiple regulators. In Hong Kong alone, thousands of residents held these 'minibonds' that were structured by Lehman, provided a guarantee through a swap, and were dragged into the investment bank's bankruptcy.[3]

The absence of globally implemented rules and regulations has provided the financial industry with an unprecedented degree of freedom. The failure of G20 to establish practical limits to wheeling and dealing has given oxygen to speculation. As in the past in Calumet City, south east of Chicago,[4] the easy way to avoid police action is to move back and forth cross-border – as the judiciary and law enforcement industry are not allowed to cross jurisdictional lines.

Global transnational companies with assets much greater than many independent sovereigns pose unprecedented home–host problems to regulation and supervision. If anyone thinks that globalization is a bed of roses, s/he is mistaken. Global banks are not only rich but also politically powerful. If governments decide to regulate their cross-border operations in ways they dislike, they know which levers to move: they call in the lobbyists (see Chapter 2), put in motion their connections, and threaten to move elsewhere, which is no empty threat.

Other countries would welcome their jobs and tax revenues. In addition, as with other multinationals, big global banks have also been agents for the transfer of know-how and technology. While making money is their first priority, they do contribute to the host country. The challenge is one of regulating them effectively so that the laws of the land are observed, antitrust being one example, and host country taxpayers don't have to pick up the bill for clearing up the mess.

The dissonance resulting from the lack of coordination in home–host issues ensures that even laws specifically voted to guarantee personal accountability, eliminate insider trading and avoid price fixing are made small game. To take just one example, antitrust laws vary from one jurisdiction to the next, and the absence of legally binding home–host rules presents plenty of opportunities to bypass the rules of the system.

In January 2011, the cross-border bypassing of antitrust was one of the themes discussed at the Davos World Economic Forum, as the heads of the world's most important global banks met behind closed doors to coordinate their strategies on how to oppose, if not to bend altogether, Basel III's rules. Eventually, on January 29, 2011 they were given an antitrust reminder for their behind-closed-doors gatherings.[5]

Another example of strategies adopted by steadily expanding cross-border business, and therefore involving home–host challenges, is under-the-counter deals. The news on March 21, 2010 was that American banks faced fresh scrutiny on lending from their supervisors because they had allegedly given clients below-market rates on loans in an attempt to secure further business. In the future, this will have to be disclosed to the supervisory authorities under rules being studied by US accounting regulators.

Looking at all the evidence, lucrative business in the global financial market has been instrumental in accentuating the practice known as *relationship lending*, which is now coming under scrutiny. According to published information, the proposed change could lay bare cases in which larger lenders use their balance sheets to secure lucrative investment banking contracts – a long-standing bone of contention between big global commercial banks such as Citigroup and J.P. Morgan, and big global investment banks such as Goldman Sachs and Morgan Stanley.

In a letter in 2010 to the Financial Accounting Standards Board (FASB), Goldman Sachs[6] called for fair value accounting, arguing that 'current rules are deficient when lending and investment banking are linked'.[7] The commercial banks responded. saying that determining a market price for such loans is difficult because they are rarely, if ever, sold.[8]

Still another practice that has bloomed with globalization and cross-border banking is the so-called *rowing boat*. Particularly subject to it are the illiquid and almost illiquid asset classes. A couple of years after the 2007 slaughter in the aftermath of a global herd effect, mortgage-backed securities with subprimes and Alt-As became hot property. Their price rose sharply, then market sentiment changed and every speculator rushed to get out of these 'assets'. The boat capsized. Can home–host supervision prevent the global spread of speculations like this? It is far from certain. There is no regulation of speculation that is conceivable or possible, but there should be regulation of the accumulation of toxic assets by banks, including central banks.

Toxic assets continue to accumulate cross-border in the big global banks' portfolios. The way Martin Wolf put it: 'Given the number of agents and the wealth of information asymmetries, it is astounding how little went wrong.'[9] In other words, the unmitigated economic and financial disaster experienced in 2007–12 might have been much worse and the world should be feeling lucky. True enough, as long as the 'good times' lasted, not only big global institutions but also big global financial centers prospered. Britain, for example, was home to:

- 67 percent of the world's top asset managers,
- 55 percent of international initial public offerings,
- offices of about 50 percent of the world's top 100 banks,
- 46 percent of the world's top 100 insurers,
- 40 percent of trades in over-the-counter (OTC) derivatives, and
- 33 percent of global foreign exchange turnover[10] – a huge sum.

Much of London's attraction as top financial center has been the skilled manpower that can be found there, and Prime Minister Margaret Thatcher's switch of the British economy from manufacturing to finance during her time in office. Critics, however, say that an equally important role has been played by the policy of the Financial Services Authority (FSA), the UK's financial watchdog, to turn a blind eye to what banks were doing under its watch.

Critics also add that among the major FSA failures was the lack of coordination with supervisory authorities in other countries on home–host issues emanating from, or associated with, the big global banks operating in London. The lack of transparency was paramount and nobody bothered to sanction it.

'The prime minister of Great Britain has nothing to hide from the president of the United States,' said a witty Winston Churchill to an embarrassed Franklin D. Roosevelt when the latter was wheeled in for an early morning conference into Churchill's quarters at the White House – just as Churchill was emerging, naked and dripping, from his bath.[11] The former prime minister of Britain might not, but global big banks operating out of London (as well as out of New York and other big financial centers) have much to hide – and there were no questions asked.

Regulators were not prepared, and sometimes not even willing, to confront the challenges presented by financial globalization. As an example of the preparation needed to remain ahead of the curve, Bernard Baruch (a well-known investor and consultant to three US presidents: Woodrow Wilson, Franklin D. Roosevelt and Harry S. Truman) tells of Meyer Guggenheim who, prior to switching out of the lace and embroidery business (a field in which he was well in control but did not feel had much of a future), he set about learning the mining business and ordered his seven sons to do the same.

Learning not only the basics but also the tricks involved in global financial and industrial business is a fundamental ingredient of success in supervision. This is true for all regulatory authorities – both those under whose jurisdiction the leviathan enterprises originated, the home agencies; and those under whose jurisdiction (among others) they operate, hence the hosts.

Are the home criteria applicable to the long list of hosts?

As long as home operations represented the large share of a bank's business, the basis for decisions concerning home–host issues was the home criterion. This essentially meant the country of incorporation of the bank or holding company. The home country may change, however. Take HSBC as an example. After the purchase of the Midland Bank, its country of incorporation became the UK, though it still has very important operations in Asia. Standard Chartered is another example, with the majority of its business being outside its home country.

It is unavoidable that host jurisdiction regulations are concerned about banks with significant operations in their country, particularly so if a foreign institution has large branches and is taking deposits in that host. Nor is the absence of strong home–host supervision in a globalized business environment good for the financial markets. Particularly in cases of deposit taking and the securities business, markets require a stable regulatory framework whose remit ranges: from consumer protection to investor protection and the avoidance of over-leveraging as well as of illiquidity.

It comes therefore as no surprise that, while several shortcomings exist with respect to the resolution of a banking group in a cross-border context, current interests (and associated reforms) are largely focused on deposit-taking banks. The recent deep economic and banking crisis has led regulators toward a more international viewpoint, with deposits topping the list of their preoccupations. As the Basel Committee document quoted earlier points out: 'The current reform discussion in the European Union addresses the interaction of resolution regimes in a group-context, the manner in which intra-group relations should be resolved and how intra-group transfers of assets should be handled in a resolution, in particular in the case of integrated group structures.'[12]

Cross-border resolution regimes are complicated by the fact that no jurisdiction mandates contractual *bail-ins*, in which the power (or obligation) to write down or convert debt into equity derives from a contract. Some jurisdictions nevertheless have rules setting out under what conditions contingent convertible instruments can be taken into account in calculations of capital requirements (see Chapter 4 on Cocos).

In terms of consumer and investor protection, one of the striking examples of failure in home–host supervision has been the IceSave scandal. Depositors in the European Union flocked to take advantage of its 5 percent interest rates, when the going rate for deposits at the time was less than 3 percent, without considering the risks they were taking. For deposits at or below the level guaranteed by deposit insurance, taxpayers' were relied on to pay for the damage after the bust.

The three Icelandic banks that expanded their operations to the UK and continental Europe, particularly the Netherlands, gambled with derivatives using the depositors' money. On becoming bankrupt they left behind them, on the shoulders of all stakeholders, a heavy legacy – and the Icelandic people were asked to supply hefty amounts of money to pay for the damage.

The case was put for a public decision to referendums in Iceland; it was rejected but still came back in modified forms. Had the Icelandic people voted 'yes', they would have had to pay for 35 years for the debts this small economy's big banks (now bankrupt) had contracted. That was money advanced in deposit insurance by the UK and the Netherlands on behalf of their citizens, trusting the three Icelandic institutions with their money.

For the UK alone this amounted to some £2 billion (US$3.24 billion; €2.28 billion) and another €1.71 billion (US$2.43 billion) for the Netherlands – a total of US$5.67 billion. The reimbursement of this sum is an almost impossible task for a small economy. The Icelandic citizens' pain aside, the big question this has raised is which country's regulatory authorities were responsible: the Icelandic authority which allegedly let the country's banks run wild abroad, or the British and Dutch regulators, who did not exercise due diligence in controlling the wheeling and dealing of deposit-taking foreign banks operating in their jurisdictions.

This question of regulatory responsibilities should have been the first to have been examined, before asking a country's citizens to pay for other people's faults. The globalization of financial games that eventually end in some kind of fraud is absolutely unacceptable. Associated with the necessary discipline (as well as disciplinary action) is chiefly the identification of home–host regulatory responsibilities.

Certainly, the legal and regulatory integration of the global banking and securities markets is a difficult undertaking. But the principle of minimal harmonization with mutual recognition – something like the European passport with its country of origin principle – is able only theoretically to avoid the duplication of regulatory and supervisory activities. Not only it does not do so in practical terms, but also its efficiency is questionable. Minimal harmonization means that cross-border financial market players still have to deal with different regulations and a good deal of paperwork, but, in contrast, full harmonization should guarantee that national legislators from country of origin to host countries have a unique set of rules to observe and apply – and so do the banks.

This will benefit the markets and their players, because the same guidelines, financial reporting practices and information will be available to all participants. In addition, pricing will depend on the intrinsic value of financial instruments and not, for example, on the place of issue or custody. Eventually this will most likely lead to an integration of the so far segmented global financial markets.

Supervisory authorities are well aware that by harmonizing the regulatory framework they can deepen the integration of financial markets. According to some opinions, harmonization will increase market liquidity, particularly in securities, and have positive developments regarding trading costs. But at the same time it is proper to appreciate that such harmonization will not take place overnight, and will require some minor miracles to come into effect.

Therefore, in my judgment and that of some of the people who participated in the research – but by no means including everyone's opinion – the control of big global banks and holding companies by the home supervisor alone is not an adequate solution. One example, but only one, of this situation is provided by the trend toward financial intermediation beyond a bank's balance sheet, promoted by technological developments – including models, which so far have been a no man's land regarding their supervision.

During one of the meetings I attended I was told that Australian banks have a greater derivatives exposure in New York than in their home offices.

And New York is precisely where they need the more sophisticated models for trading, investing and risk management. Are Australian supervisors supposed to control models written and used by their home-based banks in the USA?

The able supervision of technological advances and of the way these are employed to increase risk-taking is one of the key problems connected with effective home–host coordination. The other side of the coin is that joint approval of credit and market models can take a long time, because if many supervisory authorities are involved, and not all of them employ first-class experts, there will be unacceptable delays and less accuracy in exercising their discretion.

This modeling audit and control reference is valid not only for Pillar 1 and Pillar 2, but also for Pillar 3, given the nature of information (and its dependability) that should be made available for reasons of market discipline. Even if the model is considered to be a black box and only its input/output is scrutinized, the approval of the model requires considerable ingenuity and effort, since a sound examination will have to consider:

- assumptions,
- correlations (see Chapter 8),
- the probability of default calculations, and
- the model's mechanics if the input/output protocol (the black box) leaves a good deal to be desired.

A similar reference is valid with regard to credit risk ratings. 'When we rate a bank,' said Charles Prescott, managing director of London-based Fitch Ratings, in the course of our meeting, 'we rate a legal entity [and] we look not only at numbers but also at the wider picture.' If the entity being rated is subsidiary of a larger group and the group has more than one treasury, rating agencies may ask the parent company (or holding) for a letter of commitment. This has an impact on the rating and also proves that there is no standard answer regarding the values that come into the model, particularly so when the latter is supposed to serve in different jurisdictions.

In addition, while quantitative measures are important, as the discussion on correlation coefficients (see Chapter 8) will document, by themselves they are not enough to guarantee the home–host supervision of a bank. There also exist important qualitative information requirements to be fulfilled – and because a qualitative analysis necessarily includes rather subjective opinion, they tend to vary quite significantly between jurisdictions.

Precisely in recognition of this fact, since the end of the 1990s auditors have been required by regulators to make both quantitative and qualitative analyses of audited firms. According to many of the Group of Eight regulators, on-site audits can be divided into classes. The one is the classical auditing of the books; while the other is an eligibility review of each bank's internal procedures, connected to measuring and managing credit, market and operational risk.

In addition, while today's audits already address qualitative aspects connected to the above reference, the expectation is that in future there will also be a qualitative analysis of risk management systems, procedures and personnel. If the auditing of the lines of risk control authority is included to these requirements it will provide a vital common background for the supervisory authorities.

The 'ifs', however, should lead the reader to caution. The problems outlined in the preceding paragraphs help partly to explain why regulators so far have been unable to agree on a convincing mechanism for integral home–host solutions, leaving gaping holes in the regulatory armory when financial conglomerates run into cross-border problems.

By adding to these bank-to-bank reasons the complexities derived from novel financial instruments and OTC derivatives trading (see also later in this chapter), one can see why to date no one has come close to a global charter of the kind that applies to other industries such as insurance. Until there is a global agreement on a home–host approach to the resolution of serious problems associated with all crucial aspects of big global banks and their business, the different go-it-alone national approaches will continue. 'Home' rules will remain because they are not necessarily applicable to global banks, and agreements on how to establish and activate dependable home–host(s) solutions will still be elusive, though concepts such as living wills and a special resolution authority might eventually lead in the right direction.

Because time is a precious resource, and the next banking crisis is probably just around the corner,[13] in the opinion of many experts the work being done under the Basel Committee and Financial Stability Board must be speeded up. The effort to harmonize rules that at present are in conflict in a home–host setting, particularly in terms of prudential supervision, cannot continue to be delayed because of disagreements among governments. In the work that lies ahead, regulators will have to balance two conflicting interests: ensuring fair competition among local, national and foreign banks, and taking care that excessive risk-taking does not end in another king-sized salvage operation at taxpayers' expense.

Short of setting up a global home–host framework that covers the prerequisites discussed in this and preceding sections, a way to make the banking industry more stable is to simplify the problems of cross-border supervision by breaking up the huge conglomerates into much smaller and better-managed entities. This so-called *option of breaking up* the mammoth global banks is causing considerable anxiety among senior bankers but it remains on the radar if other methods fail.

It is a basic principle in effective management decisions that one should focus on what one is trying to achieve, rather than beating around the bush. Both at the level of individual institutions and of the global financial system, the greater the amount of indecision, the higher the probability of failure. Neither should it be forgotten that an able approach to home–host issues is at the heart of financial integration, which for the present is more myth than reality.

Home–host issues are at the heart of financial integration

The ideal case of financial integration can be defined as a situation with no friction – therefore of no *agency costs* and no discrimination between economic agents in their access to capital and the investment of capital. Ideal situations, of course, do not exist and therefore both agency problems and discrimination (for nationalistic or other reasons) are present in varying degrees. Even so, interest in financial integration comes from the fact that the more participants that are active in a particular market, the more benefits it tends to bring to its users.

Such benefits include greater depth and liquidity, reduced transaction costs, and opportunities for better balanced risk management, provided that market players both take care to keep their exposure under close observation and have the skill and technology necessary to do so. On the other hand, coordination problems require enhanced home–host supervision, and able solutions to outstanding issues (see the earlier sections of this chapter) are part of it.

A global market for banking and financial services is not moving toward greater economic convergence without appropriate guidance. It does so if, and only if, the interests and obligations of market participants are properly aligned and each of them appreciates that this is the case, which is far from happening with the G20, for example. The right sort of financial market integration is characterized by the reciprocal opening-up of the national financial markets, and free movement of capital, which might also lead to the structural convergence of national economic goals.

A basic feature of integrated financial markets is that similar financial products – from interest rates to fees – are reasonably well aligned. These conditions promote convergence if economic agents are able to make decisions and enter deals without violating supervisory rules in the home and host countries in which they operate. According to the European Central Bank (ECB), in a given area, the *law of one price* is the strongest implication of financial integration.[14] This law states that assets with similar *risk characteristics* should have a similar expected return, and this should hold regardless of the location or identity of the issuers or holders of assets; and thus regardless of jurisdiction.

In principle, in an integrated financial market, assets that are comparable and available for trading should generate identical cash flows, and trade at the same price in all countries. If they do not do so it is because of friction, discrimination and (most important) exploitation of home–host loopholes, thus providing advantages to some of the financial entities. Ineffectual home–host regulation is the basic reason why the test of financial globalization has failed.

When, in one or more of the countries in which they are players, big global banks are confronted by inadequate or poorly implemented home–host rules, they tend to take advantage of the loopholes by creating regulatory arbitrage opportunities. This can be corrected by bold and forward-looking regulatory approaches rather than attempting compromises.

Supervisory authorities which try to 'protect' their national banking industry by allowing (or even promoting) the use of fake capital such as DTAs (see Chapter 4) and hybrids are doing a great disservice to the economy and to the banks themselves. Money of the mind increases their appetite for risk and therefore the probability of gambling leading to ruin, as events in the Japanese, American and British economies document.

What the preceding paragraphs have brought to the reader's attention applies to the regulatory process of all major countries and financial institutions under its authority – in the West as well as in the East. The excuse that, for some magic reason, a given country's financial industry is immune to major exposures that might wipe out its capital, is not acceptable. Take China and its banking industry as an example:

- in 2006, loans made abroad by major Chinese banks stood at US$180 billion,
- in 2007 they rose by 25 percent to US$225 billion,
- in 2008 they jumped a mighty 48 percent to over US$330 billion, and
- in 2009, they reached US$480 billion; another massive 45 percent increase.

The numbers grew further in 2010 in connection with loans issued both abroad and within China, and by early 2011 the talk was about the danger of a Chinese hard landing – characterized by some experts as the most underpriced risk in the financial markets. This was also the conclusion reached by a survey of more than 1,000 institutional investors carried out by Barclays Capital.[15]

A rapid increase in global exposure through a bubble or a hard landing of a major economy's financial system inevitably leads to structural changes that imply a global redistribution of risk and an increase in channels of contagion. This is yet another reason why central banks and supervisory authorities must establish mechanisms that allow the monitoring of home–host issues, and timely analysis of changes in risk profiles.

In a globalized economy, both lack of global regulation and heterogeneity in its rules and directives as a result of important differences from one jurisdiction to the next, makes the management of systemic risk nearly impossible. The big banks themselves would not feel comfortable because instant communications and heightened media interest mean that their reputations can easily and quickly be tarnished.

This is written in full appreciation of the fact that with financial globalization the opportunities for misbehavior have increased. According to a joint study by Belgium's Center for Research on the Epidemiology of Disasters and the consulting firm A.T. Kearney, growing globalization brought with it an increased frequency of both man-made and natural disasters. This happens for a number of reasons, which range from a fast-growing world population and associated climatic changes to greater sophistication of instruments and machines, as well as wide and instantaneous media coverage. On the other hand, our knowledge of how to handle complex transborder situations and massive deviations created by the herd behavior of key players, has not been increased proportionally. And there is an old axiom which states that a little knowledge is a dangerous thing.

Though an effort is being made at coordination and transborder regulation of the global financial industry, the people selected for key positions are not the best. For example, politicians who have twice quit the government have been assigned the sensitive task of trade negotiations and other critical missions, which speaks volumes about their credentials as well as of those who placed them in those jobs.

Untangling the complex situation of homogeneous regulatory rules and directives – which involves plenty of conflicts of interest, including 'national' ones – requires character, foresight and steady vigilance. Moreover, no law or regulation can protect a person or a company from its own errors. A successful solution is, first and foremost, a structure resting on self-discipline, reasoning powers and an objective analysis of the value of things one needs to give up in order to enjoy other things.

National markets have their own coordinated arrangements and externalities. But these are not what a global market requires. Of course, giving up what one considers to be one's acquired right is not easy. A lack of the political will to do so is slowing down the transformation from a juxtaposition of national systems, to a genuinely integrated financial landscape in which the global banking industry can operate.

It would be illusory to aim for an ideal regulatory environment or an absolutely stable global financial market, but compromises are never bold enough to provide a new departure. The thought that today's society lives in a dream of comfort and certainty is a chimera, and there is no purpose in trying to replicate it in the business world.

In fact, a truly effective global regulatory system should be characterized by a fair degree of uncertainty, keeping the financial agents guessing. A solution that is too prescriptive would create new and major arbitrage opportunities, eventually leading to another crisis. A better solution is that of establishing a system of stochastic control.

After-effects of innovation, derivatives trades and deregulation

The philosopher, Immanuel Kant, wrote that in moral judgments the only absolute value is goodwill which consists, and can only consist, of one's willingness to accomplish one's duty. This poses the interesting questions of what is duty, and to whom is this duty owed?

The way an old American saying has it, one's duty is to do an honest day's work. If to this is added 'in accordance with prevailing ethical values', then the first part of the question, 'What is duty?' is being answered. What remain to define are the ethical values of the society in which we live, which have made small game of Moses' Ten Commandments. As for the second part of the question, the best answer to the query 'to whom' is to oneself, one's profession, and society at large (in that order).

Theoretically, ethics and the letter of the law should work in unison, but in practice this is never the case. According to Voltaire, what renders the laws of dubious standards inconsistent, if not outright erroneous, is that they are nearly always established on past realities and needs. They resemble medicines administered stochastically, in that they restore to health some ill people, but at the same time railroad many others into the cemetery.

The first four sections of this chapter concentrated on the home–host problems created by the globalization of financial services. Innovation, derivative instruments and deregulation are also the forerunners – albeit the more recent ones – of home–host problems currently confronting sovereigns and regulators.

The era of modern finance began with the 1971 Smithsonian Agreement, which unleashed a torrent of novelties regarding the way that financial products are designed, peddled and traded, as well as new forms of risk. Much has happened in banking and finance without paying due attention to potholes and crevasses on the road to the new economy.

The 1970s were a take-off period characterized by relatively low-profile events (apart from the two oil shocks and stagflation), and. In the 1980s, the Zero fighter[16] pilots (to use an analogy from the Second World War), were the managers of Japanese banks. At that time, American and European bankers resembled the pilots of commercial airliners, prudent in the way they were taking off, flying and landing.

Things changed in the 1990s, however, as the Zero fighters disappeared, derivative financial instruments became the prominent gateway to profitable trading, and exposure carried the day. As Richard Feynman, the physicist, once wrote, innovation is a very difficult thing in the real world,[17] and because of the rapid pace of innovation that characterized the financial industry, even the experts had difficulty in understanding exactly where and how much risk was embedded in the new instruments.

The nationality of the pilots also changed. Those manning the Zero fighters today are American and European bankers over-leveraging their institutions and their clients with toxic waste through novel derivative, largely custom-made financial instruments. Both bankers and hedge fund managers are roaming the globalized financial market to make a kill, quite aware that in terms of home–host regulation, the bankers are subject to a very light supervision, and the hedge fund manager is faced with no regulatory rules at all, neither cross-border nor (in the majority of cases) in their home base of operations.

It is not for nothing that Josef Ackermann, the CEO of Deutsche Bank, said that without regulatory oversight hedge funds pose systemic risk.[18] Ackermann did not specify precisely *why*, but one assumes it has much to do with derivatives, gearing and innovation in financial instruments. This is creating an explosive mix, particularly so in the absence of strong regulation and steady supervision.

Some, but not all, regulatory authorities try to correct the current pitfalls. In mid-December 2010, American regulators produced the first version of rules that will determine how derivatives will be traded in the future. From interest rate swaps used to hedge interest rate to credit derivatives – trading will have to be done in a more public way.[19] The US regulators want to see:

- many derivatives trades being settled through clearing houses,
- the reporting of information being done in a way that ensures greater transparency, and
- originators, traders and users of derivatives being subject to more stringent capital requirements.

Experts say that the new rules around trading have the potential to shake up the derivatives market, but will other jurisdictions follow? The problem in a home–host sense is that other countries have not adopted similar legislation, and this leaves open the possibility that big global banks will have plenty of opportunities to play the system.

For example, with the new US regulations, derivatives deals that are cleared will have to be traded on newly created *swap execution facilities* (SEFs). Big global banks, however, can use their subsidiaries in the UK, Germany, Australia or Japan to bypass the regulator and ensure that the status quo is retained as far as *their* business is concerned.

Not only banks are gearing up to leave the new US rules in the dust but also manufacturing companies such as Caterpillar and Ford.[20] The latter have been meeting regulators to express their concerns about whether they will have to post billions of dollars in cash as collateral against margin requirements connected to derivatives trades. (Currently in deals struck directly between banks and companies, many companies do not have to put up cash against trades.) The answer to such unwarranted reactions by firms that want to have their cake and eat it too, is very simple: if they don't want to post capital to cover risk associated to margins, then they don't need to do the derivatives deals in the first place.

It is no secret that many of the so-called *end users* in derivatives deals mismanage their hedges and find themselves on the lose–lose side of the equation. Competition is king, but cutting corners, increasing the risk and reducing the quality of deliverables is highly unwise. This has reached the point that many today blame deregulation (at least in part) for the ongoing misery of so much toxic waste collected in the banks' – including the central banks' – vaults.

In a way, the situation resembles deregulation of the air transport industry,[21] which has been turned on its head as far as customer comfort and satisfaction is concerned. In banking, deregulation has been used to arbitrage regulatory rules and, through bonuses, to overpay bank bosses and their inner circles. On January 27, 2011 it was announced that the CEO of Goldman Sachs was tripling his salary. Other chief executives, too, such as the CEO of Crédit Agricole, also tripled their salaries right after the bank under their watch had the worst-ever losses in its history.

Superficially, it might seem that the themes treated in this section have little or nothing to do with home–host circumstances. In reality, however, they have a great deal in common. Systemic risk, consumer protection and sound governance of financial institutions is influenced greatly by the after-effects of innovation, derivatives, deregulation, risk and greed.

If this short list of factors that amplify risk-taking is omitted from the subjects to be settled through home–host negotiations, laws and regulations, then little will be accomplished by way of systemic risk solutions. Globalization has many secret sides which get into the spotlight only after a court decision. For example, in mid-January 2011, a Paris court found Jean-Marie Messier and Edgar Bronfman Jr. guilty of criminal charges relating to the period when they went on a hectic acquisition spree at Vivendi Universal and turned a French utility company into a go–go global media group.[22]

Global risk capital and home–host supervision

The risk being assumed transborder by big global banks, and therefore the building blocks of home–host relationships and collaborations, must be viewed from a multiple standpoint: that of regulators, shareholders, bondholders, employees and the general public whom credit institutions are supposed to serve.

Before the First World War, a bank's capital buffers were in very large measure *equity capital*. This is the most stable financial asset, and therefore able to support the company's future, because shareholders receive dividends at the discretion of directors and their investment is first in line in case of trouble. Among a company's stakeholders, shareholders have a much higher risk of losing their investment, because they are the owners of the firm. Bondholders have a relatively lower risk, though they may be called upon to share in the pain of a bankruptcy. However, less appreciated is the fact that the risk taken by employees is multidimensional: in a bankruptcy they may lose their jobs, their pensions and the equity they might have put into their company by buying its stock.

Theoretically, all the equity of a financial institution is available to cover risks. In practice, however, if all the equity was actually to be depleted because of financial losses, this would result in liquidation. In addition, there exist legal equity requirements which stipulate that part of the equity is essential to continue the current profile and volume of a bank's business.

It follows that, from an operational standpoint, only part of a financial institution's equity may be employed to cover risks into which management has intentionally entered as well as those resulting from unexpected or miscalculated consequences. The part of the equity and of retained earnings that can be seen as having been set aside to cover exposure, across all risk classes, is *risk capital*. To this may be added other capital such as special reserves.[23]

The notion of risk capital is neither fully appreciated not does it have a legal basis across jurisdictions. This complicates home–host issues. Risk capital is proactive, allocated to potential risks for solvency reasons. In contrast, accounting loss is post-mortem. Because of being a proactive risk, capital essentially defines the level of acceptable potential loss in economic terms, and addresses many events that are not relevant from an accounting perspective prior to their occurrence.

Examples of exposures to be confronted *ex-ante* through risk capital range from mismatch risk between loans and deposits to guarantees provided by the bank to its clients, bridge loans, credit default swaps, structured products, securitized products of which the bank retains the lower quality tranche(s) and a horde of other derivative financial instruments. In this sense, risk capital must be distinguished from the part of equity that constitutes legal, regulatory or residual requirements, and while no bank may want to lose its funds earmarked as risk capital, it should be understood that without entrepreneurial risk nothing significant can be gained.

The amount of risk capital connected to a specific transaction is a projection of its future price and its impact. Contrary to regulatory capital, risk capital is not a common denominator but a function of a bank's risk appetite based on past behavior and an explicitly stated management intent for the year ahead. Evidence of the latter is provided by established risk limits, thereby making risk capital a quantitative expression which can serve home–host supervision.

When regulators meet to discuss problems associated with global banks under a home–host perspective the link that exists between solvency, liquidity, assumed exposure and set aside risk capital should be given due weight.

Marking to market the bank's portfolio is a good practice (if there is a market for the portfolio's contents) but by the time this is done it represents, so to speak, yesterday's reality. What is just as important is the future price and the risk incorporated in it.

In my book *Risk Pricing*[24] I have described a method for future pricing with assumed exposure in mind. It is based on quantum electrodynamics and is particularly applicable to the higher-order risks which are being assumed increasingly by the global banking industry. As such it can be of assistance to bankers and regulators when, among other projects, a bank's exposure in a host country associated with deposits, loans, transactions and investments is being examined.

Taking the *projected* evolution of prices into account in estimating risk capital is important, since the latter is connected directly to expected return. Any transaction into which the bank enters has, or at least should have, an expected return. This conditions the assumption of risks to two basic factors:

- potential profits and losses over the life of the instrument or transaction, and
- How much risk capital must be set aside to cover losses in a case-by-case situation, allowing at least five standard deviations from the mean (expected value).

The best way to compute risk capital requirements is as the difference between expected loss level and potential loss level. Stress test scenarios provide estimates of future risk potential.[25] Five standard deviations is far from being a worst-case scenario. The latter should assume at least 15 standard deviations from the expected value.

Worst-case scenarios serve to convert risk capital into the highest limit for each risk category. In each risk category, limits are usually calculated on the basis of both quantitative evidence and experience. This is the basis of the Delphi method. When risk factors are based on a worst-case scenario, they help to produce estimates reflecting a conservative policy that takes into account adversity well beyond expected risk. As a senior executive of one of the money center banks put it:

- the total distribution of risk capital is subject to limits to concentration,
- senior management looks carefully at big names and major exposures, and
- trading desks and loans officers are required to stress test positions with major counterparties across instrument classes.

The majority of financial institutions, however, lack such policies and there is an unfortunate tendency among regulators to try to protect poorly managed banks – both in exercising home supervision and in negotiations with host country supervisors. As a result, many home–host problems confronting supervisory authorities are far from being handled objectively in terms of expected value and unexpected value resulting from outliers or extreme events.

As the careful reader will recall, the worst case will be at the long leg of the risk distribution, towards its extremity. How much at the tail of the distribution should be taken into account in home–host and host–host negotiations depends on the *level of confidence* that is chosen: the 'four nines' (99.99 percent) is best, but 99.9 percent is acceptable. The sense of a level of confidence is the assurance it provides that the real risk will be within the estimated limits – for example, the 99.9 percent level of significance.

In conclusion, whether or not it is being called *risk capital,* the extra financial resources enable a bank to enhance its staying power. When it boasts of having, for example, 12 percent capital adequacy which is by 4 percent above the 8 percent regulatory capital, that difference is made up by risk capital seen as a necessary buffer given assumed exposure. One of the significant challenges associated with this higher capital level is the way in which exposures are aggregated across principal risk types (see Chapter 7) and business units.

Because, as we shall see in Chapter 8, the computation of and work with correlation coefficients is more an art than a science, this extra capital can be compared to a life saver. It is a very helpful 'on demand' liquid financial resource that also helps regulators when they become negotiators trying to establish a reliable capital basis that is considered to be fair in home–host deals.

Part IV
Risk Management Needs a New Culture

8
The Concept of Risk Management Must Be Thoroughly Revamped

Personal accountability

Aeschylus, the first of the three great dramatic authors of ancient Greece, wrote the *Oresteia*, three plays about the House of Atreides. *Agamemnon*, the first of the trilogy, shows why and how the glorious victor of Troy (1180–1170BC) was assassinated by his wife Clytemnestra on the very day of his return from the 10-year war. Was this murder a divine jealousy?

At stake was the freedom of men to do as they pleased. Agamemnon had strangled with his own hands Iphigenia, his daughter, obeying an oracle which said the gods demanded the sacrifice. While the question of whether this was justice or injustice on the part of the gods was not settled, it demanded *nemesis*. In his play, Aeschylus acknowledged that Agamemnon paid not only for his own misdeeds but also for those of his father Atreus, declaring the belief in jealous gods to be false and saying that our own errors are our hecatomb, and man makes his own destiny.

There is no better way of explaining the principle of personal accountability than these sentiments expressed by Aeschylus about Agamemnon. But the tragedy does not end with Agamemnon's disappearance. It is followed by two other dramatic plays. In Choephores (*The Libation Bearers*), Agamemnon's son, Orestes, incited by the god Apollo, his advisor, kills his mother Clytemnestra to avenge his father. At the end of *The Libation Bearers*, followed by the Erinyes (Furies), the old divinities of vengeance, Orestes is driven out of Argos.

In the third play of *Oresteia*, however, Aeschylus brings Orestes back to reason. Apollo accomplishes this miracle and Agamemnon's son finds refuge near the old statue of the goddess Athena in the Acropolis of Athens. There he prays to the goddess to save him from the Furies who revindicate his life and his blood. To protect him, Athena creates in her city the first tribunal ever made to judge such crimes: the Areios Pagos (Areopagos).

Presided over by Athena, this was a tribunal for the people and the judges were the Athenian citizens. Apollo defended Orestes who was eventually acquitted – but in the process gods and people provided evidence of personal accountability, and the gods gave advice on its importance by underlining that accountability is most precious in the troubled times in which we live.

While responsibility for future events is typically identified by words such as 'anticipate', 'intend', 'forecast', 'expect', 'target' and 'plan' which suggest uncertainty with regard to future outcomes, current decisions, and actions representing tangible commitments. Their after-effects can be measured and assigned to the person who did, or failed to do, what was expected from him or her given his status and position.

Managing the risk created by their decisions and actions is the duty of everyone working in an organization. The preceding chapters have already brought this fact to the reader's attention in connection with the bank's top executives. Excuses such as 'risk involves unknowns and is amplified by uncertainties' are not acceptable. A core mission of every professional is that of weighting uncertainties. Catastrophes happen when we ignore evidence and use a vague style of risk assessment. The comment by Richard Feynman, the physicist, on the space shuttle *Challenger* tragedy in 1986 makes the point:

> A kind of Russian roulette ...
> [The shuttle] flies [with O-ring erosion] and nothing happens.
> Then it is suggested ... that the risk is no longer so high for the next flight.
> We can lower our standards a little bit because we got away with it last time ...
> You got away with it, but it should not be done over and over again like that.

Science has tools for attacking problems of uncertainty, but most people do not use them. Risk is not always seen as the stochastic part of a complex situation which somewhere down the line would end in major disruption or catastrophe. This is the wrong way of looking at a problem, but it is widespread.

In any financial organization, the absence of risk targets and risk limits leads to lack of direction and to the impossibility of choosing a course of action with an acceptable level of confidence, for attainment of the desired goal. If the level of exposure that could be assumed is not evident, then the goal was not set clearly in the first place. Lewis Carroll expresses this notion in his book, *Alice in Wonderland*:

> 'Would you tell me, please, which way I ought to go from here?' said Alice.
> 'That depends a good deal on where you want to get,' said the cat.
> 'I don't care much where...,' said Alice.
> 'Then it doesn't matter which way you go,' said the cat.[1]

Knowing where we are and where we want to get to, what we want to reach, and how far we are ready to go is *not* a challenge that presents itself just once in a lifetime, or even once a year or once a month. It's a daily challenge for which we are accountable – and it is our duty to appreciate it for what it is, not for what 'it should be'.

The best risk management policy is that every day we question what could be wrong with every asset we own, or over which we exercise a responsibility. To be in control we must express, both qualitatively *and* quantitatively, assumed exposure over our responsibility's time horizon. For speculators this is a matter of following their gut feeling. In contrast, entrepreneurial activity requires the projection of expected benefits, calculating probabilities as well as the impact of risk events, and deciding whether 'the play is worth the candle', as an old Italian saying has it.[2]

The time horizon is important, because time transforms risk as new events arise and (often) have the power to alter previously established measures or conditions. The entity for which one works may also raise the stakes in response to policies or moves of its opponents; not every change, for better or worse, is exogenous.

General James Burns is said to have answered President Harry S. Truman, in response to his query about the hydrogen bomb project: it's a fundamental law of defense that you always have to use the most powerful weapons you can produce. The challenge is how to control these most powerful weapons, and this is a matter of *personal accountability*.

In the financial world, for example, deregulation has created many opportunities for excess. Developments in risk control, however, have not been commensurate in sophistication to the novel instruments and trades, and this discrepancy has hit the global economy and global finance like a hammer.

The frequency of high profile cases has also changed. In the second half of the twentieth century, high profile cases were one a decade. The year 1995, for example, saw the bankruptcy of Barings Bank engineered by mismanagement in London and by Nick Leeson, who resorted to a hidden account to cover his losses and show him up as a win–win performer. For some time, this allowed him to save his trading independence, but when that scheme went awry Barings went bust, selling itself for £1 to ING, the Dutch bancassurance (which a dozen years later also went became bankrupt). In both cases, and in many others, good management sense disappeared, governance became substandard, and there was no supervisory control worth talking about.

Personal accountability is often found to be wanting at all levels of the organization. The trader who in January 2008 single-handedly lost for Société Générale €4.9 billion (US$6.8 billion) through his deals, stated in his defense that his bosses knew exactly what he was doing. The aim was to win money for the bank, he said in a public statement. Winning big money through gambling meant, and still means, a great deal in terms of bonuses and promotion.

All these happenings speak volumes about personal accountability, and its absence. To paraphrase an old real estate property maxim, the three most important things in characterizing a company's quality of governance are management, management and management – with evidence provided by the quality of membership of the board of directors as well as of the firm's chief executive officer (CEO).

In the light of many corporate collapses, it would be rewarding to prove that a given company has independent-minded, non-executive directors who are both qualified and respected in their field. And for the whole board it is good to know which of its members have reputations for integrity, honesty and business acumen (as well as those who do not).

An old investment rule is to beware of boards that are overly large – more than a dozen members; or too small – fewer than six members. As a strategy-making body, a small board is probably missing some crucial skills. But too many directors turn board meetings into little parliaments with interminable arguments rather than concentrating on making focused, debated and documented decisions.

Moreover, *personal accountability* – which, as we have just seen, is a most critical factor in effective management – tends to diminish with large boards as it becomes quite difficult to trace responsibilities directly, whether these are related to unwarranted risks or to other factors such as allowing the company's competitiveness to decline. Events which 'by default' damage the franchise of the firm or increase its exposure, end by bringing it down.

Principal risks

If policy-makers, traders, loans officers, investment managers and other professionals are personally accountable for the risks they deal with, then a prerequisite is to properly appreciate what risk is all about. Etymologically, the word *risk* derives from the Italian *rischiare*, which means to dare. Risk is a choice, not a fate, but it can also become a fate by default.

The risk being assumed may be related to the volatility of the future value of an asset – be it a commodity or a position – as a result of market changes and, more generally, to uncertain events and outliers. Generally speaking, the notion of risk tends to be associated with a chance of injury, damage, loss or a hazard. This narrow definition, however, forgets that at the same time risk-taking is the most vital ingredient of opportunity. The doors of risk and return are adjacent, and indistinguishable, and finance is a game of risk. No policy or design, let alone wishful thinking, can eliminate the likelihood of risk.

It is s/he who uses the opportunities that risks provide but simultaneously keeps a close eye on exposure and takes timely corrective action who wins. As noted in the first section of this chapter, personal accountability ultimately relates to timely corrective action. The physicist, Max Planck, once said that without occasional ventures, or risk, no genuine invention could be accomplished, even in the most exact sciences. But he never stated that assumed exposure should be left unattended.

In finance, risk is often defined in terms of changes in values between two dates. This fits well with market risk and can be extended to credit risk with default as trigger. But it is not fully applicable with the broader concepts of counterparty risk and of operational risk – nor does it apply in other domains, such as engineering, which are not related to market changes of an *uncertain* nature.

What particularly interests us in this section is the (brief) identification of *principal risk*, from which other risks can be derived and with which are associated important risk factors (see the third section of this chapter). The following list presents (in alphabetic order) a snapshot of the principal financial risks pertinent to a bank's portfolio. It has been a deliberate choice to take only one major domain of exposure and look at it in detail, rather than trying to cover in a summary manner all the risks confronted by a financial institution.

- *Asset class.* Some equity classes in the bank's securities portfolio may under-perform in comparison to other asset classes or a general securities index. All classes, however, whether industrials, pharmaceuticals, technology, utilities and so on, are subject to rotation.
- *Bond securities.* The value of fixed income instruments rises when interest rates fall, but falls when interest rates rise or inflation raises its head. The same reference is valid in connection to fixed interest rate loans.
- *Concentration.* To the extent that investments are concentrated in a particular industry sector, country, market or asset class, the portfolio will be susceptible to loss because of adverse occurrences affecting the sector of choice.
- *Credit.* There is always the likelihood that the counterparty will not perform. Credit risk is one of the major exposures facing the loans book, as well as investments and trends such as the rush toward emerging markets.
- *Currency.* Since the 1971 Smithsonian Agreement there have been no fixed exchange rates for hard currencies (soft currencies never enjoyed that luxury). This forex risk affects either positively or negatively the bank's portfolio when marked-to-market.

Also, for global banks, part of their currency risk lies in the fact that some of their subsidiaries conduct at least a portion of their operations in the local currency of the country in which they operate. Financial institutions attempt to minimize their currency exchange risk by seeking international contracts payable in local currency in amounts equal to their estimated local currency deposits – and operating costs payable in local currency with the balance of the contract payable in base currency.[3] But it is not always feasible. To continue with the list:

- *Derivatives.* As derivative financial instruments are becoming increasingly sophisticated and complex, their pricing becomes less certain. Many OTC-traded derivatives have a market only when they are issued and when they expire. In the absence of an active market, they are sometimes marked to myth rather than to model.
- *Emerging markets risks.* Investments in emerging markets may be subject to a greater risk of loss than investments in established Western markets. But they are made in the expectation of higher returns and for diversification reasons.
- *Equity securities.* Equities, more than other asset classes, are subject to volatile changes in value. However, it is generally considered that in the longer run they provide a better return than bonds.
- *Interest rates.* See bond securities.
- *Industry sector risk.* Some industry sectors, such as telecommunications, are characterized by increasing competition and by a great deal of regulation. Also companies in some industry sectors may experience distressed cash flows because of the need to commit substantial capital to meet increasing competition.
- *Issuer(s) risk.* A portfolio's performance depends on the performance of the individual entities in which the bank invests. Changes to the financial condition or prospects of any of the issuer companies may have a negative effect on the value of their securities.
- *Legal risk.* Legal exposures are not connected solely to wrongdoing. They may relate to corporate governance, stockholders' rights, and directors' fiduciary duties and liabilities, as well as to markets in which the fund invests that have different laws and rules than its principal market.
- *Leveraging debt* is a double-edged sword. In good times, profits are boosted through gearing, but the risks mount in bad times. It is a truism that banks are becoming more sophisticated at managing their leveraging. In reality, leveraging amplifies their other financial risks.

In addition, the leveraging of the bank's clients can have a boomerang effect on the credit institution. As borrowers default, the bank's losses erode its thin layer of capital. 'Banks are leveraged and property is leveraged, so there is double leverage,' says Brian Robertson, who runs HSBC's British and continental European operations and used to be the bank's chief risk officer. 'That is why a property crash is a problem for the banks.'[4] The list continues:

- *Management.* The bank is subject to the risk that its strategic direction is ill-conceived; also that its loans policy, as well as its investment management strategy, do not produce the intended results. When this happens, the quality of management is questionable.

- *Market risk*. Market volatility can ensure that the portfolio's asset value declines over some periods because of short-term price movements, and over longer periods during market downturns. This sort of risk is widespread in a free market.
- *Passive investment*. Typically, bank portfolios are not actively managed; and neither are they always hedged. In addition, aspects and liabilities (A&L) executives do not always take up defensive positions in declining markets and this increases the amount of exposure.
- *Small capitalization*. Equity prices of small-capitalization companies can be more volatile[5] than those of larger companies, and therefore the portfolio's net worth may increase or decrease by a greater percentage than if funds were invested solely in stocks issued by larger capitalization firms.
- *Social unrest*. The economies in which the bank invests may be subject to considerable degrees not only of economic but also of political and social instability, all of which have adverse effects on market risk, and sometimes on credit risk.
- *Technology*. Innovation is a boost to company profits and market share but also requires major expenses in research and development (R&D) for new developments in products and services. Moreover, technological innovations may make obsolete the products and services of companies in which investments have been made.
- *Valuation*. The value of the securities in the bank's portfolio may change in ways that make fair value estimates difficult, either because there is no market for some of its positions or because of new conditions affecting the purchase or sale of some of the securities.

If the bank's investment portfolio uses indexes, then there are also index risks to watch out for. *Representative sampling* is the indexing strategy of investing in a sample of securities that collectively have an investment profile similar to the underlying index. Based on return variability and yield, these securities are expected to have, in the aggregate index, characteristics such as market capitalization, industry weightings and liquidity measures similar to those of the index – but it may well not be so, because of poor attention being paid to indexing, or the absence of control.

Tracking error is another exposure relating to the fact that an index is a theoretical financial calculation while the bank's portfolio is an actual investment vehicle. Therefore its performance, and that of its underlying index, may vary as a result of transaction costs, foreign currency volatility, asset valuations, unfortunate corporate actions and more. (Tracking error is the difference between the performance of the portfolio and that of its underlying index, which, experts say, should not exceed 5 percent.)

The principal risk connected to a portfolio's exposure may be worsened by weak accounting; perverse disclosure and reporting practices; lower levels of market efficiency; an exceptional securities price volatility; unexpected exchange rate fluctuations; lack of public information about issuers; an imposition of restrictions on the expatriation of funds or other assets; higher transaction and custody costs; difficulties in enforcing contractual obligations; delays in settlement procedures; too low or too high levels of regulation of the securities market; and so on.

Risk factors

If the definition of risk is nearly universal,[6] and many of the principal risks listed above are transferable from one sector of operations to the next, this is not true of *risk factors*. The focus of the latter is that of greater detail in answering questions beginning with 'what' and 'why'; thereby focusing attention on the nature of exposure specific to a given instrument or sector of activity by identifying some outstanding characteristics.

It has been a deliberate choice that most examples included in this section are not from banking and finance but from oil, gas and pharmaceuticals. This broader range of references enlarges the reader's understanding that every business is exposed to risks; it also helps to better explain what risk factors are and are not. Challenges are universal; finance does not have the monopoly of them.

For the oil industry, a major risk factor is the price per barrel. Market volatility as well as general political and economic conditions such as recessions, wars, invasions, regime changes, interest rate or currency rate fluctuations, and other reasons may play havoc with the market price of oil. Also, by extension, of oil companies' stocks.

It goes without saying that downturns in the demand for oil and gas have a negative effect on the sales and profitability of oil companies. Negative short-term and longer-term trends in prices also affect the level of oil firms' activity. Other factors that contribute to the volatility of oil and gas prices include:

- the political environment of oil-producing regions,
- policies of various governments regarding exploration and development of oil and gas reserves,
- technological advances in exploration and extraction of oil and gas,[7]
- new reserves discovered in oil and gas which may create a glut in the market, and
- the ability of the Organization of Petroleum Exporting Countries (OPEC) to set and maintain production levels and pricing.

The revenues of oil firms as well as of oil service companies may be negatively affected for a variety of reasons. Service firms, for example, are often negatively affected by contract termination or renegotiation.[8] In this industry it is customary for contracts to provide either for automatic termination or termination at the option of the counterparty if the drilling unit presents environmental problems, with the result that drilling operations are suspended for a period of time when events are beyond the control of the service firm.

This offers only a glimpse of risk factors in oil firms, because the oil industry is also exposed to significant and numerous operating hazards such as fire, explosion, blowouts, loss of well control and oil spills. (What has happened with Halliburton, Transocean and BP in the Gulf of Mexico in 2010 is just one example.) The occurrence of any of these events can cause:

- personal injury or loss of life,
- severe environmental damage,
- damage to property and equipment, and
- delays to or suspension of operations.

Other risk factors are machinery breakdowns, abnormal drilling conditions, failure of subcontractors to perform adequately or to supply goods and services, shortages in personnel and perils peculiar to marine operations. The latter include the capsizing of drilling rigs or other equipment, grounding, as well as collision and loss or damage from severe weather. It may also be that insurance and indemnification agreements may not provide complete coverage against the full list of losses.

There also exist business risk factors. For example, oil companies operate in a highly competitive and cyclical industry, with numerous participants and intense price competition. During periods of slower growth or in a depressed market, oil exploration companies lower the price of oil and this represents lower revenues. Moreover, the market for services provided by oil firms is conditioned by risk factors, such as:

- customers' drilling budgets,
- the ability of oil and gas companies to raise capital,
- the development and exploitation of alternative fuels,
- changes in government permits and tax policies,
- the rate of decline of existing oil and gas reserves,
- available pipeline and other oil and gas transportation capacity, and
- weather conditions connected to exploration projects.

Other risk factors revolve around legal risk (see the second section above), which is one of the important principal risks faced by oil companies. Examples are changes in laws, and adverse outcomes resulting from governments contesting companies' tax returns. Tax laws and regulations are highly complex and subject to various interpretations and disputes, which exposes companies conducting worldwide operations through various subsidiaries and operating structures to litigation in a number of different jurisdictions.

Risk factors leading to litigation include, among other things, contract disputes, personal injury claims, environmental claims or proceedings, asbestos and other toxic tort claims, employment issues and so on. Also, public health threats such as outbreaks of highly communicable diseases, which occur periodically in various parts of the world, the quarantine of personnel, and similar situations resulting in the inability to access offices or rigs.

One of the risk factors confronted cross-industry, for example, by both the pharmaceutical industry and the oil industry, is *intense competition*. Typically, a pharmaceutical firm competes with a large number of multinational pharmaceutical, biotechnology and generic pharmaceutical companies. To do so successfully, it must continue to deliver to the market innovative, cost-effective products that meet important medical needs. In such an environment, its product sales can be affected adversely by the introduction by competitors of branded products that are perceived to be superior by the marketplace, generic versions of its branded products, and generic versions of other products in the same therapeutic class as its branded products.

To deal with these challenges, a pharmaceutical firm depends on patent-protected products for most of its revenues, as well as its cash flow and earnings. But it also knows in advance that, with patent protection laws varying widely between jurisdictions, it may lose effective intellectual property protection for many of them in the next few years. The answer is to be ahead of the curve through intensive R&D, which is not only very costly but also uncertain in terms of deliverables.

There are many risk factors inherent not only in R&D but also in obtaining licenses and in the introduction of new products to the market. Taken together, these challenges guarantee that there is a high rate of failure inherent in new drug discoveries as well as in the transition from the discovery phase to the market, which typically takes a decade or more.

Failure can occur at any point in the process, including at a point after substantial investment has been made. As a result, most funds invested in research programs will not generate financial returns. Among the key risk factors associated with new products that appear promising in development are their:

- failure to reach the market because the drugs administration does not license them,
- after being licensed, having only a limited commercial success because of efficacy or safety concerns,

- after evidence is accumulated that they only have a limited range of approved uses, this makes them excessively costly to manufacture, or
- there is an unexpected infringement of the patents or intellectual property rights of other drugs firms, leading to very costly litigation.

Other risk factors are delays and uncertainties in the approval process in host countries (after getting approval at home), which can result in lost market opportunities. (In recent years, approval times have increased substantially and fewer new drugs are being approved, so sales growth rates are also difficult to predict.)

Yet another risk factor is that, as drugs become increasingly sophisticated and complex, their effects on some patients tend to become unpredictable. There are cases of new pharmaceuticals that have helped a large number of sick people, but have also led to the deaths of others. This concept of bifurcation of results on treated populations has not yet been properly studied by drug administrations and the medical profession. The outcome of this failure is that drugs are taken off the market while they are still valuable to many people.

Last but not least, there is an important financial risk factor confronting the pharmaceutical companies. The development of new drugs development is tremendously expensive and to recover their costs pharmaceuticals have to be global. Product pricing, however, has a dual focus. In industrial countries, governments try to keep prices low because the social security and health care coffers of the State Supermarket are virtually empty. At the same time, many developing countries simply do not have the money to pay for drugs and thus press the global pharmaceuticals to let them obtain the licenses for low cost to make the drugs locally, which the pharmaceutical companies simply cannot afford to do.

Independence of opinion and transparency

Henry Wallich (a Federal Reserve governor in the Carter years) commented:

> It is not an easy thing to vote against the President's wishes. 'But what are we appointed for? Why are we given these long terms in office? Presumably, it is that not only the present but the past and the future have some weight in our decisions. In the end, it may be helpful to remind the President that it is not only his present concerns that matter.[9]

Independence of opinion is both ethical behavior's alter ego and the best way to confront crises before they reach the point of no return. This principle applies equally to families, companies and states. 'The individual family member,' says Antonio Ferreira, 'may know, and often does, that much of the family image is false and represents nothing more than a sort of official party line',[10] but when this 'party line' leads to high indebtedness or other ills, every family member has to express his/her doubts and ask for a change of course.

Precisely the same concept should prevail in a financial organization or any other enterprise. Following the 'party line' blindfold without having the courage to express an opposing opinion, eventually leads the entity itself and its stakeholders to the edge of the precipice. Plenty of examples come from the most recent economic and financial crisis.

Investment advisors and other property valuers in America, Britain and Dubai, who advised their clients 'to buy' were the parties appreciated most willingly by speculators. In contrast, the opinions of those who pressed the point that the market was overheating were ignored. Whistleblowers inside banks were disregarded or even dismissed from their posts. Opposing opinions were not welcome. Their warnings were shouted down by salespeople, who argued that if they priced for credit risk they would sell nothing.

As these and plenty of other cases recorded during the go-go years in the middle of the twentieth century's first decade demonstrate, not everybody appreciates the importance of opposing opinion as an effective tool for management control – and, most important, also for the control of risk. This is true not of just one but of a list of critical risk factors associated with financial stability. Examples include:

- lack of sustainability of public finances,
- the impact of public deficits on economic growth,
- the financial industry's contribution to global imbalances, and
- the systemic risk of disorderly unwinding of overleveraged positions when the market turns sour.

The acceptance and, even more so, the importance and impact of such factors is often hidden by creative accounting aimed at keeping reported figures positive – and ending by misleading common citizens and experts, bank managers and the governments' own top brass.

True transparency means not only releasing accurate and timely information, but also structuring that information in such a way that everyone: from prime ministers, regulators, board members, and risk controllers to the general public, can understand it. Because transparency facilitates the process of holding all financial institutions – including central banks – accountable for their actions, the European Central Bank (ECB) regards it as a crucial component of its monetary policy framework.

The ECB says that an integral part of a transparency policy is that central banks explain clearly how they interpret and implement their mandates. This helps the public to monitor and evaluate a central bank's performance, as well as its effect on the state of the economy, and to understand the economic rationale behind changes that have to be made in monetary policy.

A central bank's transparency is enhanced strongly by a publicly announced monetary policy strategy. A comparable criterion of transparency for a commercial bank would be public announcement to all stakeholders of the level of risk the institution is willing to assume, including:

- leveraging,
- loans,
- investments,
- derivatives trades, and
- trades other than derivatives.

When a company wishes to access private capital through the credit markets, it must accept and fulfill certain obligations necessary to attract investors and protect their interests. One of the most basic is the full and fair public disclosure of reliable corporate information, including financial conditions and results. Not only is the company's management responsible for the accuracy of financial statements, but also the US Supreme Court has recognized that when independent public accountants express an opinion on a public company's financial statements, they assume a *public responsibility* that transcends the contractual relationship with their clients. The independent public accountant's responsibility extends to the corporation's employees, stockholders, creditors, customers and the rest of the investing public, and the regulations and standards for auditing public companies must be clear and unambiguous to safeguard that public trust. Not only must auditors adhere to standards but also be responsible if they are violated.

Absolute transparency is the No. 1 requirement in the management of a crisis says James Burke, CEO of Johnson & Johnson. Offering more insight might help fund managers to lock in capital, and overall, the mutual funds industry could be more candid about fund conditions and management, concludes Laura Lutton of Morningstar.[11]

In contrast, when opaqueness dominates, the dispersion of estimates is elevated, suggesting that there is uncertainty about data made available as well as other concerns. The opinions expressed by analysts covering stocks are destabilized by opacity and by a decrease in companies' guidance. While general economic conditions may be the primary driver for this lack of visibility, opaqueness makes matters worse.

Transparency is not only a better way to support independence of opinion, it is the only way beyond the courage to go against the mainstream which might well be heading in the wrong direction. Areas where such independence of opinion may be the most critical to the longer-term survival of a financial enterprise include:

- evidence of high leverage,
- pockets of vulnerability,

- increased correlations,
- balance sheets items which don't add up,
- reasons for low profitability, and
- background events making financing conditions difficult.

Another domain where independence of opinion is most valuable is that of macroeconomic risk factors. Every economy has special factors which may be strictly its own or a variation of more general ones. For example, after the economic crisis that hit Greece, Ireland and Portugal, euroland's risk factors included:

- concern about the sustainability of public finances in profligate member states,*
- strains on the financial system because of heightened funding vulnerabilities for other member states,
- vulnerabilities of financial institutions associated with concentrations of lending exposures to sovereigns and to commercial property,
- the likelihood that macroeconomics would fail to live up to market expectations, and
- greater than normal financial market volatility, promoted by a lack of transparency about some national economies.

Concerns about the fiscal gap cause negative financial market reactions and lead to significantly higher financing costs for sovereigns.[12] This increases the probability of an unsustainable debt spiral – which is itself a risk factor. Higher public sector financing requirements increase bank funding costs through greater competition for funds from bond investors. This used to be a major risk factor in less developed countries, but emerging economies such as China, India and Brazil are off the sick list with their places in hospital care being taken up by Western countries.

On both sides of the Atlantic the consequences have been the creation of conditions for adverse feedback loops, resulting in downward spirals affecting economic growth, as well as fiscal imbalances and funding vulnerabilities in the financial industry. The after-effects of such risk factors is contagion. Country-specific disturbances can spread more widely in the global financial system.

Event risk

Event risk is that of an unexpected exposure resulting from specific shocks. A major adverse event can develop into principal risk (see the second section

* A friend who read this text asked, 'Are Greece, Ireland and Portugal considered to be profligate?' I answered 'Yes! And Spain, Italy, France, the UK and the USA too.' Any nation, company, family or individual living beyond its means is profligate.

of this chapter). For debt instruments, for example, an event risk is the downgrading of the credit rating, which becomes the principal risk in the aftermath of successive downgrades. For equities, an event risk can be an after-effect of intense rumors – for example, about an acquisition for which the acquiring company pays well above what the market considers a reasonable price, or overleverages itself with debt.

Lenders are fearful of event risks that in one stroke may reduce the credit quality of corporate borrowers (or the value of their fixed income securities). Downgrades are credit events. A broad definition of a *credit event* is any happening that has adverse effects on the solvency of a borrower or securities issuer, thereby damaging its credibility. Often, though not always, the credit event has an impact on the entity which it puts under stress, its equity price and its bonds.

Stock and bond investors do not necessarily suffer at the same time because of event risk. With RJR Nabisco's mammoth leveraged buyout (LBO), stock investors profited, but for bond investors Nabisco's overgearing was a disaster. Since then, the markets have appreciated that virtually no blue-chip company is safe from a debt meltdown. The easy availability of junk financing encourages entrepreneurs to overpay, and this is causing bid premia to soar to unprecedented levels.

In RJR Nabisco's case, high-credit bonds were converted into junk bonds overnight. Many investors thought that management had a duty to all constituents of the enterprise's business, including bondholders. Metropolitan Life Insurance sued RJR in a New York State court, charging that its LBO plan enriched a handful of executives at the direct expense of debt holders. The insurer wanted its money back.[13]

In cases of event risk there have been several incidents of bond-investor expropriation without representation. Another example that comes to mind is Federated Department Stores senior debt, which also went from AA to B after Robert Campeau's debt-financed takeover. This and other sharp changes in credit rating reflect the fact that credit markets are based first and foremost on *trust*. Because of event risk, in their exasperation many fixed income investors have been shunning industrial company debt, and instead they focused on government bonds and other issues thought to be far less vulnerable to restructuring, until the governments themselves became over-indebted and investors returned to the corporates.

For a government, an event risk can be the revelation of high interest payments as a proportion of government revenues (according to experts, when this gets beyond 10 percent, the government faces important difficulties). Another event risk is the sudden jump of public debt to GDP, because of large budget deficits which persist, making a downgrade inevitable.

In Portugal, there was an event risk in mid-February 2011, when the yields of its government bonds rose above 7 percent and continued to rise until, in early April 2011, the country asked for an EU/IMF lifesaver to the tune

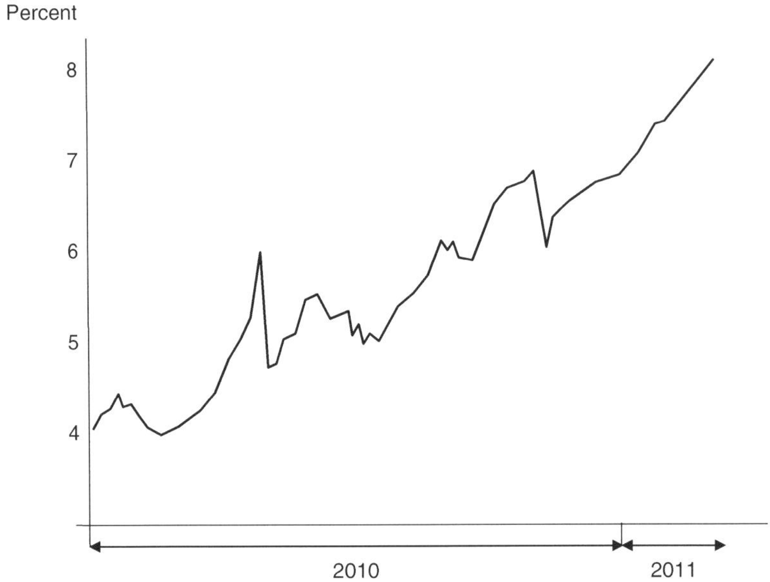

Figure 8.1 Trend of interest rates in 10-year Portuguese government bond yields, percent

of €90 billion. Figure 8.1 shows this trend curving steeply toward 8 percent, the mark at which Portuguese officials had a priori said that the country's borrowing costs would be unsustainable.[14]

For Ireland, the event risk came the day the country had to admit that its budget deficit would hit 32 percent in 2010, because of the huge amount of public money it (unwisely) poured into the coffers of its self-wounded banks. Just keeping this mess from spilling all over has cost the country as much as a seventh of its national income and caused a ballooning sovereign debt. Investors know that the current bail-outs are not sustainable, and event risk has had a disastrous effect on Irish government bonds.

The nature and magnitude of a credit event's impact can also be triggered through covenants attached to a transaction, thus altering its credit terms. Or it may be a result of the economic nature of a financial institution's product(s), its guarantees and other seller circumstances, as well as its cash position. With securitized instruments, the ratio of sub to senior spreads is often viewed as a reflection of relative losses at different seniorities following a credit event – but not every happening has the same impact: a simple credit event can be arrears in paying some major bills, and complex credit events can have a lasting impact on financing.

Fear of loss or harm is often, but by no means always, proportional, not merely to the size and impact of a projected loss, but also to the probability of a given event taking place. The problem is that, with 'unknown unknowns' such probabilities are pure guesswork. Suddenly, a spike shows that what was considered to be a most improbable event becomes a reality which hits like a hammer. Many such happenings are hard to predict because they are not always related to the fundamental credit quality of a debt instrument's issuer.

Event risk can be dangerous to financial stability, and particularly so in connection to high-frequency trading, as its effect may be magnified for speculative reasons. Regulatory authorities are also concerned about its effect from a macroprudential perspective, hence they care about its timely identification, assessment and monitoring. Appropriate trading contributes to the sustenance of the global financial system.

The follow-up of an event risk's trajectory is made so much more difficult when the definition of the boundaries of the system under consideration is missing. Another challenge is defining the boundaries and gaps of global regulation, whose remit is never really defined in a straightforward way.

A systematic approach must take into account event risks generated by all sources that are capable of causing material financial system damage – either on their own or as a group. The work to be done is significantly increased by the fact that full coverage requires that unregulated firms must also fall under the supervisory umbrella. As for the regulated financial institutions, these may be monitored by different regulatory agencies – and more likely than not they are subject to the home–host problems discussed in Chapter 7.

Regulatory authorities monitoring event risks affecting the financial system as a whole pay attention to shocks in economic variables that may potentially lead to financial instability. These include inflation, recession, significant interest rate changes, asset bubbles, terrorism and sovereign defaults. Also important are correlations of exposures across credit institutions (see Chapter 9), poorly calibrated risk controls, and issues relative to a panic caused by collective negative behavior.

The long tail of risk distribution

Those versed in statistics have been trained to understand and use normal distribution, which is largely theoretical. This is a reflection of the fact that their teachers were also trained in the same way, as research in the 1920s and 1930s – which established the science of statistics – produced some terrific all-weather statistical tables based on the bell-shaped (normal) distribution of measurements and events.

It is no less true, nevertheless, that events in life rarely obey normal distribution. The same statement is valid of all sort of risks and prices. Benoit Mandelbrot, the mathematician turned economist, calculated that if the Dow Jones Industrial Average followed the pattern of a normal distribution, then:

- between 1916 and 2003 it should have moved by more than 3.4 percent on 58 days, when in reality it did so on 1,001 days,
- it should have moved by more than 4.5 percent on six days, when it did so on 366 days, and
- it should have moved by more than 7 percent only once in every 300,000 years, when in the twentieth century it did so on 48 days.

There is no evidence that measurements connected to, and the after-effects of, principal risks and risk factors are normally distributed. In fact, existing evidence points towards a skew or leptokurtotic distribution – not a bell-shaped one. Based on Mandelbrot's and other calculations, one is led to the conclusion that, as far as the financial markets are concerned, working along normal distribution leads to erroneous conclusions. Even so, economists continue to work in that way.

This leads to a conceptual shortcoming. With more than 99 percent of events under the normal curve within ±3 standard deviations from the mean, the analyst or economist cannot observe what happens at the tails. Yet, as noted in the previous section, that is precisely where they have to study the frequency and impact of extreme events.

Analysts also have to deduce significant trends regarding the amplitude and frequency of extreme events and their impact, which cannot be achieved by studying average expected values. While concepts underpinning normal distribution are vital and useful (and so are its statistical tables), in a mathematical analysis sense the bell shape and the pattern of real-life events are for practical purposes decoupled. Failing to estimate the tail beyond the 99 percent level of confidence would omit some reasonably common but devastating losses, and it is very short-sighted to focus on average day-to-day events falling in the center of the distribution; economists must definitely take stock of and analyze the potentially severe losses that are much rarer.

A different way of making this statement is that the last couple of decades of the twentieth century produced a rapidly growing body of evidence that the concept underpinning normal distribution is not able to reveal what happens at its tails. In contrast, in banking, as well as in engineering, the tails are the areas where most of the risks, of gains or losses, lie.

Extreme values hidden in a distribution's long tail have been a relatively recent preoccupation in financial analysis. Because outliers may have a high impact, even if they are of low frequency, analysts are now paying greater attention to the shape of the underlying risk distribution, in particular under extreme market conditions. One of the tools is *extreme value theory* (EVT), which provides a way of estimating the potential for extreme market moves that are outliers. (Theoretically, extreme value theory can be applied to single instruments calculating, for example, a portfolio's margin by reflecting on distributions based on a large number of positions. In practical terms, however, this may present several difficulties, one of these being that, if every player focuses on the higher initial margin implied by EVT, this could have adverse effects on market liquidity.)[15]

Instead of considering the entire distribution, EVT focuses only on the parts that provide information about the extreme behavior found in the tails. The message the reader should retain from this discussion is that in a market where 10 standard deviations (10s) events occur with an increased frequency, traditional approaches to risk management are utterly inadequate. New tools are necessary for the study of *extreme events* along with a methodology able to model information asymmetries, behavioral biases, and uncertainties in inference about risk and return.

Risk events which find themselves in the tail are those about which analysts, investors, bankers and regulatory authorities should worry the most. The October 1987, Black Monday was a 14.5 standard deviations event. Twenty years later, in 2007, David Vinair, chief financial officer of Goldman Sachs, told the *Financial Times* that the bank had seen *25 standard deviation* moves for several days in a row.[16]

Between these two references there were other events that put individual institutions and economies under stress, and found themselves at the tail of the risk distribution. The better known are Japan's crash in 1990–1; the bond market and Orange County's descent into the abyss in 1994; Barings' bankruptcy in 1995; the East Asia and South Korea crisis in 1997; Russia's bankruptcy and LTCM's near bankruptcy in 1998; the dot-coms and telecoms crash in 2000; and more – all the way to the 2007–12 economic and banking crisis.

With this in mind it could be stated that what has classically been considered extreme events are gradually becoming rather 'normal' as their frequency continues to increase.[17] It is as if the markets have moved toward the tails of risk distribution. Therefore, models based on normal distribution, such as VAR, do not even begin to predict what the tails might be doing. People are at risk of being greatly misguided by focusing on the central values of a risk distribution. As Figure 8.2 shows, the real exposure does not lie at the expected value but in the long, long tail.

In everyday parlance, *tail risk* is technically defined as a higher than expected exposure of a loan investment, derivative instrument or other transaction moving more than three standard deviations away from the mean. I would think that this reference to three is trivial. Rather, analysis should focus on 5, 10, 15 and more standard deviations (see also the next section, 'Stress testing').

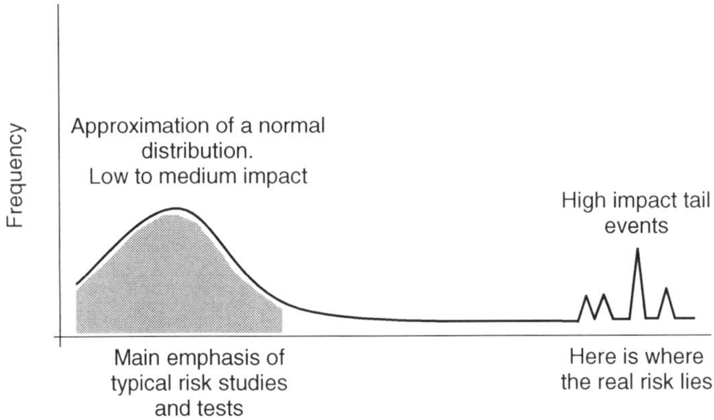

Figure 8.2 Currently, minor attention is paid to tail events, when major attention is needed

This stratified reference has come to signify any big downward movement in a portfolio's value. There are no solid theoretical approaches regarding how to hedge such risk. A dubious one is to create a basket of derivatives that may perform poorly during normal market conditions but soar when markets plunge. These include options on a variety of asset classes such as equity indices and credit-default-swap indices; however, if anyone tells the reader that this is a 'sure thing', then s/he is lying, because payoffs are asymmetric and subject to many surprises.

We shall examine the reasons and effects of asymmetries in Chapter 10. Because of these, hedges have a nasty habit of turning on their head, particularly those hedges involving derivative instruments and designed to be sold to clients who do not understand what they are buying. Investors must not let themselves be carried away by such garbage even if it has had a favorable mass effect in the past.

Another error often made in risk analysis is of forgetting that much of it focuses on unknown risks. In real life there are plenty of unknowns, and these can be divided into two major classes: 'known unknowns' and 'unknown unknowns'. Donald Rumsfeld made the distinction between so-called 'unknown risks', whose nature is more-or-less known, but not their frequency or magnitude. The other class is the real unknowns, about which no one has a clue. Specifically, these are the things that we do not know that we do not know, and where uncertainty is king regarding their nature, evolution, frequency and impact.

The way to bet is that unknown unknowns will tend to populate the risk distribution's tail, and this suggests that a great amount of attention should be paid to their study and modeling. One of the problems in this connection is that mathematicians know too little about finance and the great majority of financial people know next to nothing about mathematics. As a result, they cannot explore, let alone properly model, the expanding frontier of financial risk.

Yet another challenge adding itself to what the preceding paragraphs have stated, is that the risk and return of a financial instrument, transaction or investment may be changing from symmetric to asymmetric and vice versa. Market players behave differently as market psychology changes, with important after-effects on market risk and counterparty risk, as well as in regard to expected frequency and amplitude in the after-effect of a crisis. For example, in an upswing, over-confident bankers, traders or investors take on bets that they later find themselves unable to discharge, and this inventorying of what becomes dubious assets amplifies the outstanding features of a crisis.

Last but not least, tail effects are promoted by the mammoth size of big global banks and their reach, as they repeat similar bets in different markets where they are present. In addition, big banks have a handicap that relates to timely and effective risk control, which means that the financial dimension of risk is often overlooked.

Stress testing

Stress testing is a generic term that does not necessarily mean the same thing to different people. In the general case, in the financial industry it describes various techniques and conditions used to gauge the potential vulnerability of a bank's capital adequacy and financial staying power. A portfolio is stress tested by simulating the ramifications of large market swings and credit events. The stress test's parameters are exceptional or unexpected but plausible. Such a test can be made through:

- scenario writing,
- sensitivity analysis,
- statistical inference under extreme conditions, or
- drills for a meltdown, which essentially means worst-case scenarios.[18]

Periodically, central banks and supervisory authorities ask the credit institutions under their watch to conduct a stress test.[19] In the background of this policy lies the fact that most often markets are better than the banks' managements in reading the writing on the wall, especially when the message is written in their language. Stress tests capitalize on simulated exceptional conditions to provide an early warning, in appreciation of the fact that crises don't run to a fixed timetable, but the aftermath can be tested and studied experimentally and, helped by experimentation, forecasting is a powerful weapon because it provides a lead time for measures that need to be implemented.

In late January 2011, for example, American regulators warned that banks needed to sharpen up their management of interest-rate risk in readiness for a rise in short-term rates. Having studied the possible effects of rate hikes on the banking industry, they urged credit institutions to account, in their stress tests, for a sudden rise of up to four percentage points.[20]

Depending on their nature and objectives, stress tests make available a capacity analysis of risk bearing – whether principal risks, risk factors or the likelihood and of extreme events are being tested. Typically, what are being sought are the risks on the long leg of the risk distribution. All of these have been covered in this chapter.

Stress tests require clearly defined goals as well as skills, a methodology and tools to implement a system solution. Just calling any test a stress test will not provide any benefit. Figure 8.3 provides a snapshot of the growing testing sophisticating which is necessary, including the stepping stones of analytics and of the design of experiments.

Experiments using stress tests are instrumental in detecting a credit institution's vulnerability to losses under unfavorable or extreme circumstances. This is an important help with regard to risk analysis, since it represents a reflection of a plausible reality, reflecting interdependencies and enriched through expert assumptions.

In stress testing, the risk manager selects a set of likely but rather extreme moves for the key market parameters under study. These may be connected to the trading book, banking book or a portfolio whose risk profile is being examined. Depending on the severity of the test, we use events at 5, 10, 15 or more standard deviations from the mean, and measure the simulated

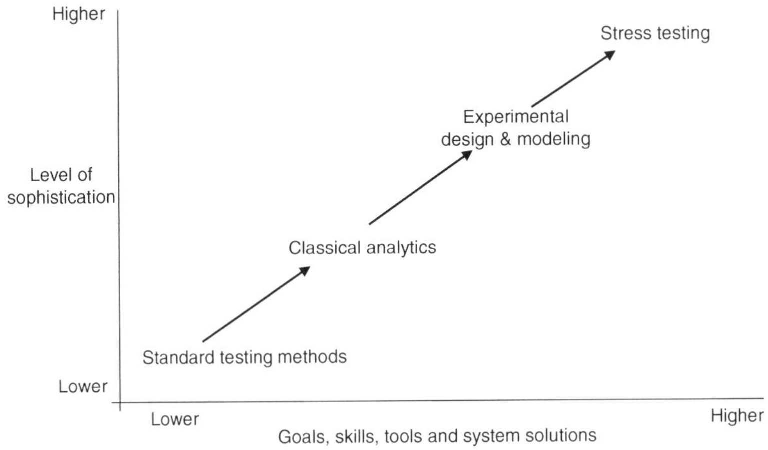

Figure 8.3 Capacity analysis of bearing risks at different levels of sophistication

change in, say, portfolio value. To perform this job effectively, however, we must fulfill the prerequisites of stress testing, which involve finding the drivers of risk: principal, risk factors, extreme events or other critical criteria, and estimating for each of these drivers the origin, causes, background conditions, projected frequency, most probable impact, and likely correlation(s) – now and as volatility rises.

A careful examination of correlations between drivers and after-effects is most important, as we shall see in Chapter 9. For example, when short-term rates rise, banks may face simultaneous problems of dearer funding and less profitable assets. Correlations can put upward pressure on a bank's funding costs even if monetary policy remains unaltered.

Another basic prerequisite is deciding on the level of confidence to be used: 99 percent, or even better, 99.9 percent. A stress test should be done with the chosen level of significance in mind – which is true all the way from defining risk values based on plausibility hypotheses to interpreting obtained results. Stress tests are meaningful only when the level of confidence is high.

Only by developing realistic stress tests at high levels of confidence can banks increase their sensitivity to situations that could be critical, and improving their risk management systems greatly. Testing past historical developments against the hypothesis of their repetition provides alerts that might otherwise go undetected. For example, after periods of stability, stress tests based on past crises help to make management aware of trend reversals, or of what might happen if stability ends abruptly.

The reader should, however, notice that what stress tests reveal depends a great deal on the skill with which they are carried out, not only on the level of stress. The latter is often, though not always, set by regulators. In March 2010, Britain's Financial Services Authority (FSA) published new stress-test benchmarks for banks that assume tougher economic conditions, such as an unemployment rate of 13.3 percent. Such a benchmark provides a guide to banks regarding how much capital they should hold during a severe downturn. If worsening market conditions are not reflected appropriately in a stress test, then the term 'stress' is used inappropriately and the results will be unreliable.

In late February 2011, Timothy Geithner, the US Treasury secretary, asked all American banks to make a stress test assuming recession and 11 percent unemployment. Critics pointed out that this was not really a stress test, but rather a normal test under projected likely conditions. A stress test would have assumed unemployment at 15 percent (from the level at that time of 9.1 percent), and a more severe situation with unemployment at 20 percent (which is the case in Spain at the time of writing).

Along a similar line of reference, a bank stress-testing market risk would project a steepening of the yield curve by 50, 100, 150, 200 or more basis points, along with changes in interest spreads, swaps spreads, an increase in volatility by 20 percent of prevailing levels, an increase (or decrease) in currency exchange values against other major currencies by 10 percent and 20 percent, and similar change in the equity index. Equally important is stress testing the *synergy* of increases and decreases in currency exchange and equity index volatilities, and in liquidity and volatility changes by a significant amount.

Time and again, hypotheses made for and underpinning stress tests do not go far enough, with the result that the outcome does not reflect extreme situations. The way an article in *The Economist* put it, Morgan Stanley has been reviewing its stress-testing procedures and criteria because the worst-case scenario, if envisaged, turned out to be less than half as bad as the circumstances that did arise in the markets.

Similarly, J.P. Morgan Chase's debt-market stress tests foresaw a 40 percent increase in corporate spreads, but high-yield spreads in 2007–9 increased many times over.[21] It is not unusual that stress-test hypotheses (and therefore obtained results) fall short, because they are frequently based on assumptions that the future will look positively on the bank much more than in the past,[22] but in reality it turns out to be much more severe.

In conclusion, in the background of a successful stress testing policy is a sophisticated approach to experimentation and financial modeling based on clear goals; factual and documented assumptions on market behavior; the proper definition of principal risks and risk factors; the ability to project extreme events; and a plan of action. The latter should outline concrete steps for corrective action, if the stress test points to a potentially dangerous situation for the institution.

9
Correlation Risk Overwhelms the Global Banking Industry

The correlation coefficient

Banks don't need to wait until the Basel Committee tells them what they should do in terms of risk control decisions, tests and procedures. That would be a poor policy because, typically, what is included in new rules and directives is the common denominator. Well-governed institutions would want to do much more to be ahead of the curve. A policy which can pay dividends is to pay attention to correlation coefficients, and use them for both experimentation on latent or hidden exposures and for effective risk management.

Correlations have the uncanny ability to show up in the most unexpected portfolio positions and transactions. For example, both in convergence and in divergence in operations among financial firms; mergers, acquisitions, consolidation and downsizing activities; capital adequacy and capital allocation; asset lending and financial guarantees; banking and the bank-related activities of insurance companies; the effects of product diversification; as well as structural and regulatory changes.

Other areas of financial activities where correlations may be significant are securitizations; collateralized debt obligations (CDOs); credit default swaps (CDSs); industry loss warranties; and maturity mismatches between funding sources and loans, investments or trades. Correlations play an important role with derivatives, and in convergence in the scope of activities of financial firms. They are promoted strongly by the effects of crises on the financial industry, both at the level of the firm and industry-wide.

Other fertile domains for correlations are those of bail-outs and general funding by sovereigns attempting to salvage a badly wounded bank. The analysis of implications from new regulations, the design of new financial instruments, particularly derivatives, as well as other activities, often reveal correlations that have so far escaped attention. Systemic risk is also a vast correlations domain and the same is true of shock transmission across the financial industry, including contagion.

All told, the deep economic and financial crisis of 2007–12 revealed most significant interrelationships within and between the different branches of the banking industry which contributed significantly to the magnitude of the crisis. It also underlined the need for additional research on correlations, including the risks and opportunities they may present to market players, as well as inflection points that may be associated with those risks.

Because the reader might not be familiar with the concept underpinning correlation coefficients as well as good practices and malpractices associated with them, let alone their computation and use, it has been a deliberate choice to start this chapter with two sections that can provide a basic background to the topic – though, also deliberately, mathematical equations have not been included, except as endnotes.

The *correlation coefficient*, usually denoted by *r*, is a statistic computed from samples of measurements, or time series, related to events. For example, events 'A' and 'B'[1] might be connected to each other by common factors; or they might influence one another. If they correlate positively, then an increase in 'A' leads to an increase in 'B' (though not necessarily proportionally). If they are negatively correlated, then when 'A' increases, 'B' decreases and vice versa. In economics and finance, we are particularly interested not only in the correlations of time series but also in their impact.

The statistic *r* is an estimate of the parameter ρ the population correlation coefficient of 'A' and 'B' which is unknown.[2] Both *r* and ρ vary between –1 and +1. From –1 to 0, 'A' and 'B' are negatively correlated. Between 0 and +1 they correlate positively. As with so many other models, tools and tables in statistics, an assumption underpinning correlations is that the sets of measurements 'A' and 'B' (or, more precisely, the events behind them) are normally distributed. For skew or other non-normally distributed populations, the value of the correlation coefficient is questionable.

Theoretically, the higher is the coefficient of correlation – for example, if its value is 0.7 to 0.9 – the closer is the relationship between the time series under study, or any other two groups of data in samples 'A' and 'B'. In practice, this is not always true. Two sets of data (or time series) might show a high correlation and yet be completely unrelated. This is a good example of a principle underpinning scientific investigation: in science, we are more certain when we reject a hypothesis than when we accept it. If we find that groups 'A' and B' are uncorrelated, we are more certain of this outcome than if the result of our calculations was that 'A' and 'B' correlate.

Therefore, when we actively search for correlations we should do both a quantitative and a qualitative analysis. An integral part of sound analytics is first to establish whether the relationship between sets 'A' and 'B' happens randomly or has a cause-and-effect basis. The latter is far from being self-evident.

One of the mistakes often made in the evaluation of correlation coefficients is that of mixing the stochastic with the causal interdependence.

In most analytical projects, and economic analysis is a case in point, our foremost objective is that of unearthing the causal correlation of 'A' and 'B'.[3]

Another frequently encountered mistake in analytical studies is that both the analysts themselves, the managers they are working for and the end users of the results of experimentation, are searching for what I call *phony precision*. This is endemic, because people fail to realize the difference between accuracy and precision; and do not always appreciate that, in analytical studies, from engineering to other sciences as well as in economics and finance, by far the No. 1 criterion and guide is *accuracy*.

The problem of searching for precision to the 7th or 8th significant digit, when up to the 3rd (or even 2nd) digit most often suffices, is that one loses track of accuracy. When this happens, the results being obtained are not dependable.

Yet another problem with analytical finance is that few people pay attention to margins of error. This means that even differences that are too small to be statistically significant are used to rank something. Therefore, unsurprisingly, correlations and rankings may change with every minor revision – making the results unstable.

In financial statements, and the accounting practices associated with them, there exists the concept of *materiality*, of which it is wise to take notice. A difference in the accounts of, say, US$10,000 is immaterial to a large corporation such as IBM, but quite material to the corner drugstore which might do business worth US$300,000 per year.

A similar principle exists with risk. To judge its materiality, exposure should be examined in relation to the *core capital* (Tier 1 equity) of the bank assuming it. The other side of this argument, however, is that, because quite frequently risks are given different ranks despite fairly similar correlations between underlying factors, relatively small data changes can send them shooting up or down, thereby altering their materiality. There also exist conflicts of interest, and creative accounting is used to reduce the correlation coefficient.

Other things being equal, the lower the correlations between critical factors of exposure, the less is assumed to be the exposure and therefore the corresponding capital requirements. This leads the management of many banks to lower correlation coefficients artificially 'on command', which created one of the major problems with Basel II, and which will surely infiltrate Basel III. In some banks the board has decided that the correlation is no higher than 0.25, doing so without any documentation or supporting evidence.[4]

This understates badly the risk(s) being assumed. It also biases management thinking right down the line. The board of a financial institution has many important decisions to make, but what the correlation is between key risk factors (in contrast to what should be the limit) is not one of them.

Wishful thinking about levels of risk assumed in the bank's daily operations, or low intensity risk embedded in novel financial instruments, resemble the policy of Soviet planners on managing the economy. Sitting comfortably in the armchairs of Gosplan,[5] they used to decide that 'so many millions of a given product' would be manufactured during a given 5-year plan – including how much raw material and how many semi-manufactured goods had to be set aside, and what would be the final price of the product. The price was subsidized by the Soviet state without regard to the real cost of production and distribution. Commodities which were cheap, such as energy, in the Soviet Union, were squandered, leading to material shortages, and eventually the planners' balances were faked as 'how to lie with statistics' became common currency until the Soviet system crashed. Remember this next time when you think that correlation coefficients 'on command' and the massaging of other critical numbers does no harm. An argument I have heard put forward by board members and their underlings is, 'It helps the bank beef up its profits.' It does until the institution crashes Soviet-style.

Low quality management which condones, and even worse, instigates, *quantitative vandalism* is not the only problem. Sometimes the statisticians themselves tend to round correlation coefficients to stylized levels such as 1.0, 0.75, 0.50, 0.25 or 0.0. That's nonsense; while two significant digits might do, these must be fully documented. Structured answers are meaningless.

Some other initiatives, however, make more sense. While they deviate from statistical theory they account for qualitative uncertainty surrounding an analytical study. Some statisticians say never use $r = 0$, because 'You don't know if there is a hidden correlation'. Rather, they use $\rho = 0.15$ as proxy. Merging quantitative and qualitative aspects of their work, the most prudent analysts, when in doubt use an up to 100 percent correlation, and choose the upper range of r computed through analytics.

They also regularly revalidate the values of r, as market conditions change and so do the assets and liabilities in the bank's portfolio. Correlation coefficients are dynamic and they have to be steadily (as well as properly) recalculated in order to be of help to their users. Correlations that are not steadily recalibrated at best become meaningless and at worse destructive.

Working with correlations

The previous section presented the reader with some fundamental notions about correlation coefficients, their 'dos' and 'don'ts'. Essentially what the coefficients are revealing are analogies in the behavior of principal risks and of risk factors. The term *correlation* is preferable to that of interpretation or analogy because implicitly it contains these latter terms, while also adding to them the notion of a common relation and complementarity. In its broadest sense, correlation means *synergy*. It is the synergy between individual instruments (securities) and risk factors.

Computing correlations between sets of data (or time series of these) within a portfolio is accomplished through quantitative approaches. The true sense of correlations, however, spans far more than quantitative guidelines and concentration limits. As the previous section brought to the reader's attention, it also reflects qualitative elements such as exposure to management risk (which, strictly speaking is not quantifiable) and subjective factors prevailing in the economy or in an enterprise that impacts on the correlation.

Figure 9.1 gives a glimpse of a correlation pattern between S&P 500 and FT Europe. This clearly shows that the correlation between the two indices has significantly increased, making diversification in investments regarding these two securities markets nearly impossible. A lower correlation prevails between Western securities markets and emerging markets, but this too is increasing. There are, however, uncorrelated risks typically found in different:

- types of activities,
- business lines,
- event types, and
- geographic areas.

For example, several of the entries in Basel II's matrix for operational risks are more-or-less uncorrelated. But this also is changing, because globalized

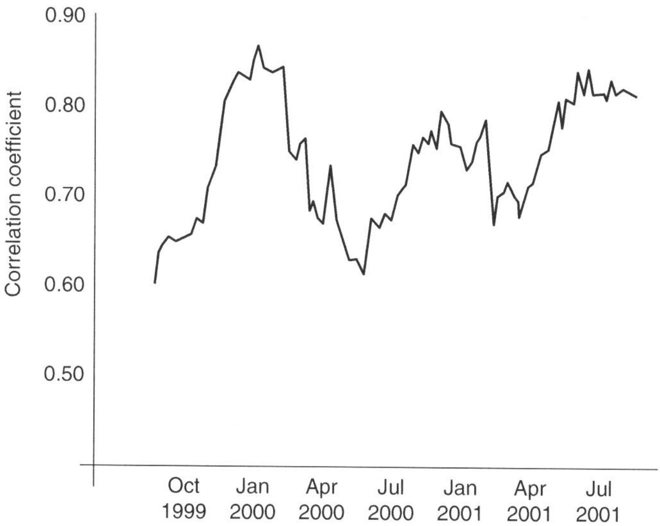

Figure 9.1 Correlation of S&P 500 and FT Europe

banking has brought about a significant correlation in credit risk around the globe, particularly within certain geographic areas. For example, the risks faced by banks and governments in the worst affected euroland countries rose simultaneously, leading to a high correlation between risk premiums for governments, and risk premiums for financial institutions.

Not all companies are affected in a similar way. There is some evidence to suggest that correlation among losses is less for smaller companies than for large ones. While small and medium enterprises (SMEs) tend to have a higher probability of default, their defaults are less concentrated in economic downturns than in the case of large firms. Another interesting case of hindsight relates to retail banking, where losses on exposures to lower-quality borrowers seem to be less dependent on the economic cycle.

Correlations change as a result of national vulnerabilities, cross-border contagion effects and other burdens. For example, unsuccessful government bond auctions in one euroland country triggered a rise in risk premiums on the bonds of governments and banks in other euroland countries. The increased uncertainty in countries whose economies correlated led to further haircuts on the markets for government bonds, and such losses in market value placed a strain on banks throughout euroland.

These examples underpin the need to depend on both quantitative and qualitative criteria when it comes to correlations, as explained in the previous section. In addition, a sound methodology is vital, and this should include exactly where to concentrate one's attention. A good piece of advice when studying correlations is to look at the figures with an inquisitive eye, trying to find the message behind 'this' or 'that' irregularity, or the periodicity in a correlation pattern.

When a correlation pattern presents inflection points, sudden rises or falls, or other aspects appear, interpreted as 'anomalies', the analyst conducting the study, as well as the end user of the correlation statistics, should ask pointed questions:

- Is there an internal contradiction?
- Are the time series really *causally* related?
- What might be the reason for such 'anomalies'?

Sometimes correlations may be an optical illusion (see also the discussion on uncorrelated events in the previous section). One of the best teachers of statistics teased his students with two series which showed $r = 1$. One of them was the annual herring catch off Newfoundland, while the other was the number of illegitimate children born that same year in North Dakota.

Indeed, some correlations *are* meaningless. 'What is the correlation between a rogue-trading event in Asia and a U.S. government action over consumer-lending policies,' asked Dr David Lawrence (formerly chief risk management officer of Citibank, for Europe) in one of his lectures, 'Or between credit card fraud in Latin America and a clerical error in a correspondent-banking transfer in Japan?' The point Lawrence was making is: 'Can you *validate* that correlation using empirical analysis?'

In addition, the fact that two time series are found to have a causal correlation, and this, for example, stands at 0.62 (or 62 percent) is only part of the analytical finding. Not everyone appreciates that $r = 0.62$ is only the mean value of r, which is up to that level only 50 percent of the time. All correlated risks must be studied through confidence levels, preferably at 99.9 percent (more on this later).

The better-managed banks now believe that *confidence intervals* provide a much more dependable measure of correlated events than the r classically used with correlations. They are also confronting the correlation's aftermath by developing policies able to differentiate between the frequency and the impact of the risks whose correlation (or lack of it) one is analyzing. Furthermore, they religiously avoid the (not uncommon) bad practice among poorly governed institutions of transferring a correlation calculated on one case to label as another case, because the two present a certain similitude (real or imagined). Correlations are unique identifiers – *they are not transferable.*

This is true both of banks, and of instruments of markets. 'There is no sharing of correlation coefficients', said a senior executive of a global bank in a meeting I had with him. 'Correlation factors must be computed in conjunction with [the subject under study] and they are very specific to an institution.' This is absolutely true.

Other bankers, too, suggested that every financial institution has its own portfolio pattern, which implies certain correlations between credit risk and interest rate risk. Some, however, said that 'while another bank's correlations may be a starting point, they are not for the long run'. I would not subscribe to this argument. Another bank's correlation might be an interesting reference – but not a starting point.

There has also been, in the course of my research, the case of a major commercial bank which even believes that correlation coefficients are transferable. When I expressed my surprise at such a statement the bank executive added that in any case correlations are only indicative, because the whole field of correlations has not yet reached maturity. This is only half true. The mathematics of correlations reached maturity long ago, and what is still in development is the qualitative–quantitative connection.

In addition, even if a certain tool or process 'has not yet reached maturity' this is no excuse for it being misused. People who make such statements don't really understand what they are talking about. Worse still, these opinions are also heard in conferences – and when this happens it indicates that the people expressing them do not have a clear mind about what correlations are and what they are not. There exists, so to speak, a certain amount of *correlation illiteracy*, which is regrettable.

It is time to close this gap in the knowledge and in understanding of correlations at senior management level in the banking industry. Some central banks and regulatory authorities try to convey that message to institutions under their watch, because they are very attentive to the correlations issue.

The Dutch central bank, for example, wants to know how the financial institutions under its jurisdiction examine correlations, not only through present statistics but also by means of forecasts and projections. This makes sense because correlations can be used as an important element of a steering mechanism in the control of exposure, particularly in conjunction with risk pricing models.

Counterparty correlation risk

Counterparty correlation risk refers to the likelihood of a correlated deterioration in the credit standing of different parties with similar characteristics with which the bank maintains business relations. A better way of looking at counterparty correlation risk, however, is as a specific case of credit deterioration hitting a given major counterparty or group of counterparties – and the underlying reference entity. The targeted measure is the correlation between counterparty, reference entity and collateral deposited by the counterparty.

One type of correlation risk apparent through analytics is the risk that a bank holds a position in a security of an amount that represents a large portion of the overall market for that security. Another type of risk identified through correlation relates to exposures associated with its transactions and portfolio positions, which work in unison. As the correlation risk increases it amplifies the bank's exposure. The rule can be expressed through '*If... then...*' hypotheses:

> *If* risks are correlated,
> *then* upward changes in some of them have a negative impact on the bank's financial staying power.
>
> *If* They are independent,
> *then* the influence of the larger one is, relatively speaking, diminished.

Correlation risk is a dynamic measure and critical factor in credit risk transfer (CRT). Many financial instruments, such as collateralized debt obligation (CDOs) and collateralized loans obligations (CLOs), are structured on the basis of assumptions about the degree of concentration and diversification of an underlying pool (see also the next section). Estimating the correlation of defaults among loans in that pool is a key input to the model being used to design and subsequently value the CDOs and CLOs.

What matters in particular for the performance of an investment and its associated exposure, is the projected development of correlation risk.

Well-managed banks experiment on worst-case correlations because they have the potential to generate the largest losses in the underlying pool. The downside of such studies are wishful thinking, which has detrimental effects on correlation estimates, and the fact that differences between average and worst-case correlations can be elusive, and they are often not taken into consideration.

Even if correlations are reasonably evaluated, it may be difficult to incorporate them into models in a way that investors and other market participants can understand. In addition, because in many cases correlations are subject to estimates that are poorly documented, pools may experience higher than expected defaults if the financial environment comes under stress. Because of this, banks should carry out stress analysis[6] of correlations, and rely much less than is current practice on third party assessment of correlation risk, which is typically an underestimate.

Time and again, reliance on third-party estimates is misplaced. Because of asset-backed securities and other structured products, opinions expressed by third parties have not been derived from empirical data. Short historical records on default histories are partly responsible for such an outcome – as documented by the underlying subprimes and other residential mortgage backed securities (RMBSs).

'The relative impact of correlations,' said a senior S&P executive in the course of our meeting, 'is that the further we look in the tail, the greater is the impact of correlations.' Unexpected financial shocks happen at the tail of risk distributions. Hence it is most valuable to look carefully for exposures associated with correlations at the tail of risk distributions, where the picture of losses includes outliers and is more representative of reality under stress conditions.

While, as we shall see in the following section, diversification helps to reduce correlations, and hence co-movement and dependency, many claims about diversification are simply hype or are based on relatively superficial studies. Or on studies that fail to document the assumptions they are using.

Another factor with a significant impact on counterparty correlation risk is the quality of assets in a pledged collateral. As Figure 9.2 shows, counterparty risk is associated with the quality of its assets, but the correlation is not high because other factors also play a part – such as the quality of management. Moreover, even collateral which, when it was pledged was of high quality, can become questionable if the assets being used come under stress.

Precisely because correlated risk is highly dynamic, regulators have introduced it in counter-party studies to make bankers aware that different risk factors underpinning a bank's exposure may move the same way. In addition, the Basel Committee insists that credit institutions validate their correlation assumptions through analysis, and provide documented evidence on the correlation coefficient they are using.

Figure 9.2 The quality of assets held by counterparties and their credit quality correlate

One of the aspects of an excessive appetite for risk in some institutions is the miscalculation of correlation risk. Errors are introduced because insufficient attention is paid to the creditworthiness of counterparties. To eliminate this problem, top management should not only decide on a correlation risk strategy but also monitor its implementation, checking constantly whether correlation risk limits are being observed.

Stress scenarios should be designed around changes in exposure embedded in portfolio positions because of correlations. A bank must represent and model credit risk appropriately, to prevent a fatal bank-run spiral from being triggered as well as heavy losses to accumulate. One of the better-known casualties of misjudging correlations has been Long Term Capital Management (LTCM). Its investments had high correlations and these moved the same way on the downside.

The pattern of LTCM correlated risks, which became known after its failure, has puzzled financial analysts. As a senior Merrill Lynch executive put it during our meeting: 'Post-mortem it was revealed that hardly anybody in LTCM knew the true correlations and they came as shock even to the hedge fund experts, because they involved extreme values.'

Are there any mathematical hints and twists which might help when dealing with ongoing changes in correlation coefficients? Speaking from personal experience, I would suggest that the best policy is to be on the lookout for nascent inflection points. The way to go about this, when looking at statistics, is to watch out for a switch somewhere between the raw figure and the conclusion.

Quite often, what is missing from the typical evaluation of a rising correlation risk is the factor that caused a change to occur. Small changes tend to go through the analyst's filter undetected until it is too late. On the other hand, a somewhat invariant time series may be misleading, as even small changes can have a major impact (the butterfly effect), but in general small changes are looked at fleetingly, or overlooked completely.

Skill and experience help in unearthing something that is not otherwise visible. A trained mind would not miss an opportunity to detect what was taking place, because it knows that any analysis worth its salt must challenge the 'obvious'. A major bank said that in one of its divisions it found a correlation of 68 percent between credit risk and market risk. A trained mind hearing that would immediately ask:

- Is this too high or too low under present market conditions?
- Is the 68 percent correlation good, or bad for the bank's business?
- Which types of risk are most exposed to such a notable level in correlation?
- How, and how fast, are such risks being confronted by senior management?

These questions should precede the query: 'What might have caused such a correlation?' because they could provide the necessary linkage on the way from effect to cause (rather than the classical cause to effect, which is frequently less than transparent). An inflection point in counterparty correlation risk, or market correlation risk, might assist in thinking outside the box – which is unconventional but often proves to be effective.

Risk concentration and the diversification hype

Risk concentration takes place at many levels, ranging from the aggregate of the banking industry to the portfolio of each financial institution and clusters of securities within each portfolio. According to the Bank for International Settlements (BIS) the share of the *five* biggest global banks in international bond underwriting, arrangements of syndicated loans and derivatives, is over 40 percent. In international equity issuance their share stands at over 50 percent. This huge and unwarranted risk concentration is the aftermath of globalization and of mergers and acquisitions.

As far as risk concentration is concerned, things are rather better in retail financial services (deposits and personal loans), but within retail banking there is a concentration in credit card issuance. Risk concentrations happen all the time and they often appear even in portfolios thought to be diversified.

The deep economic and financial crisis of 2007–12 has been in a large measure the result of the concentration of risk in structured instruments underlain by subprimes. It is important to know the weight of concentration in exposure because of its impact. A commonly used metric is the *concentration ratio* (CR), measuring the market share as a percentage of the largest three to ten credit institutions (depending on the total number of banks), relative to the total banking market.[7]

This CR for a small group of big banks should be compared to the total banking market in a given country. The lending volume, volume of deposits, balance sheet quality or, preferably, a combination of the three are taken as a proxy for market share. An algorithm can be used to account for the total number of banks and accompanying distribution of market shares.[8]

Employing a proxy, or a rough indicator[9] is an approach frequently employed when dealing with models representing a real-life situation. Though the chosen variable could conceivably be improved to reflect more accurately the market structure, it cannot describe in an accurate manner the entire national (or, even more so, global) market, because real life is so complex. Moreover, risk concentration ratios may not say much about the actual prevailing market conditions, given the dynamic nature of the banking industry whose characteristic ratios change all the time. Even with these shortcomings, however, modeling is a very helpful tool, but bankers, managers and other professionals who think that models relieve them from thinking and from making up their own minds are deceiving themselves.

This is as true of the study of concentration and diversification of risk as it is of the analyzing, planning and controlling of any other activity. Instead of relegating one's responsibilities to models it is better to think of models as useful exercises in the study of risk concentration. Its *prototyping* should be user-driven and oriented in visual thinking, thus opening the way to experimentation and the evaluation of levels of concentration exposure, as well as the risks associated with them.

One of the principles of a good diversification is that no position in the portfolio should be greater than 5 percent of total investment value, no matter how solid a given investment might look at the time the decision was made to enter into it. Another principle is to target overall risk and return using diversification to reduce assumed risk at a certain level of return, *or* to maximize return for a given level of assumed risk.[10] (A piece of advice: don't try to do both at the same time.)

Prototyping should account for the bank's history of exposure (see also the following section). Whether or not they admit it, global banks are behind the financial industry's concentration. Citigroup has operations in 54 countries, but in most of these its wholesale clients are similar. HSBC is another example of globalized retail and investment banking, serving multinational companies around the world.

There is an almost unavoidable concentration of risk in the wholesale portfolio of big global banks, while lip service is paid to diversification, everyday policies don't point to diversification but rather towards concentration. This is no reflection on the quality of management but rather on the way that business is done – and it is true all the way from global institutions to the small savings banks, which find themselves over-exposed to real estate.

As the preceding sections emphasized, for financial institutions correlated assets are nothing out of the ordinary – but they are the enemy of a bank's financial staying power. Basel II did not focus on concentration, as it should have done. With the 2007–12 crisis in the background, Basel III looks at concentration as an important dimension of credit risk (not yet enacted by Basel III) which can be expressed in the following way:

- there should be an explicit recognition of concentration risk under Pillar 1, to be accounted for in financial statements, and
- Pillar 2 should explicitly require banks to provide their supervisors with an analytical assessment of concentration (Basel II made some reference to the bank's loan portfolio, but though necessary this is not sufficient).

The result of a lack of explicit rules in reporting the concentration of all principal risks and their associated risk factors is that regulation does not go far enough in recognizing the aftermath of concentration on an institution's financial health and that of the banking industry as a whole. Proper recognition requires explicit quantitative and qualitative criteria as to what should be considered excessive risk concentration. But leaving it up to regulators, by jurisdiction, to address this risk and rethink the issue of large exposures is not what should be done in a globalized economy.

Diversification in banking is often found wanting because boards, CEOs, CFOs, loans officers and traders are not careful enough in watching over concentrations. Typically, they turn a blind eye to them if they enhance profits, promote bonuses and are not properly sanctioned by regulators. The result is that banks are not diversified enough. In its own way, each institution is concentrated in countries, industries, clients and instruments.

Studies show that geographic diversification is of a higher grade than industry diversification in the same country. As for client diversification, a bank needs a large number of names to diversify – around 100,000, say. However, even the largest banks today have about only around 10,000 big names each. Hence the concept that if 20 big banks put together their loans at risk, they might diversify, but must be responsible together for the lowest layer, whose names can be found cross-institution.

This is evidently a theoretical reference because in real life these big banks are competitors and in no situation would they reveal names and amounts involved to other banks. Only the regulators are able to have a broader view after receiving inputs from the banks under their authority. The problem with this is that global banks come under the authority of many regulators – and therefore of none.

This increases the responsibility of each bank's board to be alert to risk concentrations, as well as to what can go wrong with a diversification project. Consider the following real-life example. The president of a bank gave one of his senior traders the mission to: 'Create me a portfolio with 40 single 'A' bonds of European banks'. As far as diversification is concerned, the mission and the way it was executed, have a number of defects:

- The sample was too small. A sample of 100 would have provided a broader basis for spreading counterparty risk.
- The originators of the 40 bonds were only 17 banks. This increased the concentration even more in terms of counterparty risk, in violation of the principle of diversification.
- The portfolio is concentrated in only one industry: financials. Therefore, it is highly dependent on that one industry, its fortunes and misfortunes.
- The 17 banks were chosen from only two neighboring countries, and belong to the same economic community. This unwarranted choice further increased concentration as the two economies in the same community move more or less in unison.
- The portfolio gave equal weight to the 40 bonds regardless of their differing characteristics. The weights should have been unequal, using the attractiveness of each bond in regard to its duration, its rate, and other important factors that impact on risk and return.

This case was not an exception or outlier. Similar examples are found all over the investment landscape, both in banking and in other industries.

Default correlation

Most of the qualitative characteristics of risk correlations are not evident at first sight. Nor are the risk factors easy to distinguish in terms of their range of variation and impact. Much can be learned about them, however, through a careful study of past events, of the way they have unfolded, of the footprint they left, and of how the trajectory of given events has developed. Has the end result been a resurgence of financial staying power, or limping along for some time, and ending in default?

To acquaint bankers and analysts with the likely future ups and downs of credit and market events, movements and trends – as well as to prepare them for active life – business schools should teach financial and economic history before risk modeling. Such teaching should include plenty of case studies as well as exercises with practical, real-life examples.

Financial history, for example, shows in no uncertain manner that the loosening of the credit rules associated with deregulation and 'good times' leads to a notable reduction in credit standards. At times, modernity in financial instruments introduces questionable innovations, creating the illusion that credit risk can be reduced because of some wizardry in the instrument's design.

Financial history also provides evidence that the bankers' perception of liquidity is, quite often, too optimistic – and, as such, unrelated to real life. For example, that liquidity can be obtained not only from assets one could sell but also from liabilities that can be securitized and sold at any time to any party. This sort of thinking forgets that assets always have a market, though it might be at fire-sale prices but the market for liabilities may well dry up,[11] even at such fire-sale prices, and with liquidity disappearing the bank drives itself up against the wall.

Another lesson that financial history teaches is that the transition from the mismanagement of risk to its proper management is a long and torturous process – not a simple change over. During the transition period, the risk of default increases significantly.

The previous section also emphasized the fact that some of the prevailing hypotheses about exposure do not stand up to deeper scrutiny. Other things being equal, a portfolio spread over debt instruments traded in different markets could have a lower volatility of returns than a portfolio invested in a single government bond market. 'Other things', however, are not equal. The international bond markets, for example, are increasingly correlated (albeit not perfectly), because of the dynamics of a globalized business cycle, and the role played by monetary authorities whose policy used to differ from country to country but now (at least in the West) moves in unison.

Other factors, however, may diverge. For example, the trend of inflation may be different and the way that buyers and sellers look at the role of debt instruments may vary among markets because of local traditions, institutional forces, fiscal and other policies. All this is being reflected in correlations that change over time, increasing in precisely those periods when the benefits of diversification are most sought after – but when concentration of risk is the dominant feature.

Default correlation has an impact on the risk of corporate bond portfolios and further limits the sought-after diversification. The importance of computing default correlation comes from the fact that it identifies the strength of the default relationship, defined as the correlation between the default indicators for two counterparties. Typically, this is calculated over one year or some other chosen time interval.

By focusing on the extent to which a particular counter-party, industry sector or country contributes to the overall credit risk of the portfolio, the default correlation maps *concentration risk*. One of its primary drivers is the asset return correlation between counter-parties. Its quantitative analysis proceeds by calculating correlation coefficients for credit risk based on the counter-party default rate.

Over time, for wholesale lending and international lending, one major bank found that correlation coefficients ranged from $r = 0.70$ to $r = 0.80$, with $r = 0.75$ as the mean value. In comparison, according to the same credit institution, the correlation of real estate to all lending was only $r = 0.25$ (computed two years prior to the start of the 2007–12 economic crisis).

While these are real life examples, they should not be taken as reflecting universally valid correlations. High credit risk correlations have important after-effects on a portfolio's dependability. For example, a portfolio with 1,000 names but with an almost 100 percent default correlation, would in practice have the risk profile of a portfolio with a single name – a huge concentration.

Market players often assume that default correlations are significant for firms in the same industry, but there are also important cross-industry correlations, particularly between low-rated firms. To estimate these, some analysts rely on models that attempt to derive them from the degree to which sharp downward movements in equity prices coincide between firms.

When the quantitative information available for computation of default correlation (or other correlation coefficients) is not sufficient for dependable estimates, it is advisable to use the Delphi method.[12] Managers and analysts should keep in mind that correlations can be notoriously unreliable in cases of *data insufficiency* – and therefore estimates made by knowledgeable people by way of community intelligence might be the better bet.

Delphi helps to improve the accuracy of correlations by means of iterative queries involving known experts. It is an established methodology whose performance rests on the quality of a panel of experts who estimate independently what a given correlation 'could be'.[13] Received responses are arranged in order of magnitude, and quartiles are determined so that intervals are formed on these quartiles.

Alternatively, instead of quartiles, the three most representative values can be selected, as explained in the following example. After the first round of collecting expert opinions on the most likely value of a given default correlation, the values of these estimates are communicated to each respondent, asking them to reconsider their previous estimates.

If the new estimate lies outside the evolving interquartile range (or representative value) the expert is asked to briefly state the reason why, in his/her opinion, the answer should be lower (or higher) than the one that corresponds to the clustering of opinions expressed in the preceding round of the questionnaire. These commentaries are communicated to other experts, always preserving anonymity. The latter are asked to consider the given reasons, giving them the weight they think they deserve – and revise their own previous estimates or, alternatively, to stand by them if they choose to do so.

The results of each round are best presented as a pattern with corresponding frequencies, as shown in Figure 9.3. Generally, after each successive iteration, expert estimates will be less dispersed than in the preceding one. This process of successive iterations makes people *think* – which is the main goal not only of Delphi but also of any sound management practice.

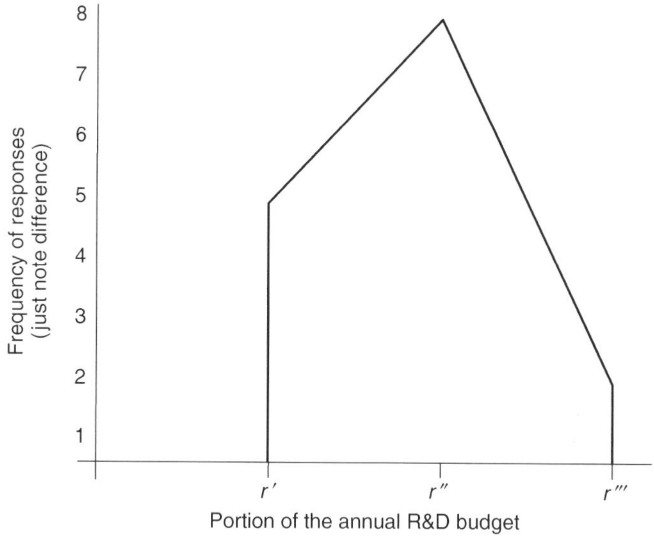

Figure 9.3 The opinions of participating experts can be presented as a pattern with corresponding frequencies

Correlations change over time, and must be revised regularly

The computation of correlation coefficients has a long history in mathematics, as well as in physics and engineering. But it is a challenge in finance, mainly because the needed data is incomplete, unreliable or both. There is also the qualitative element, discussed earlier, conditioned by fairly subjective evaluations as well as by the question: 'How conservative does *our* bank want to be?' If top management prizes longer-term survival, it should pay plenty of attention to high correlations, which is what regulators like to see. But if its risk appetite is high, it will use as an excuse for greater exposure the lower correlation coefficients, explaining them as the result of carefully planned diversification.

Because of this bifurcation, well-managed banks have been adopting a firm policy regarding the choice of correlation coefficients. In the opinion of one of the risk management officers who participated in my study, a better metric than r is the square of the correlation coefficient r^2 – as used in the KMV model whose distribution is shown in Figure 9.4.

Moody's KMV portfolio manager uses the correlation square of the correlation coefficient because it spreads the correlation effects better. It also helps to overcome one of the problems with correlations in all branches of science: the reversal of a correlation from negative to positive and vice

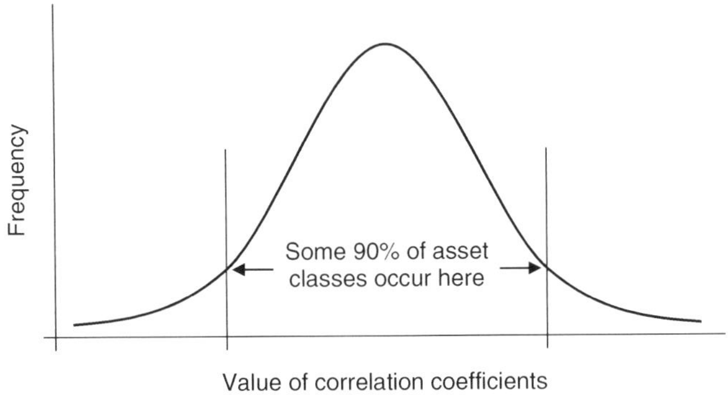

Figure 9.4 Moody's KMV correlation square of *r* spreads the correlation effect better

versa. KMV researchers have also identified the existence of some limits with correlations. For example, equity correlations are a poor proxy for asset correlations, because asset values are firm-specific. Therefore, Moody's model computes the assets to liabilities ratio with equity capitalization taken as a proxy for assets, while the bank's liabilities are assumed to be at fair value by marking to market.

Indeed, the choices made in developing and implementing Moody's algorithm provide one more piece of evidence as to why the answer to the query: 'Can banks exchange correlation coefficients?' has to be negative. Correlation factors tend to be quite different from one bank to another, because of market conditions, financial instruments, methods used to identify and measure exposure and more. If regulators really want banks to use correlations, they must produce them not only with firm guidelines but also with properly defined control procedures.

In the early years of the twenty-first century, when the Basel II debate was running high, I asked Hirotaka Hideshima, of the Basel Committee, what was the sense of allowing banks to use, practically simultaneously, both the regulators' conservative (hence higher) *r* and the commercial bank's own *r*. This, to my thinking, can only lead to huge discrepancies in risk policies, with negative after-effects on prudential supervision.

Hideshima's answer was that trying to focus too much on the individual elements behind the model underlying the risk weight function could be misleading in some cases. The derived risk weights, he said, are based on assumptions such as asset correlation, confidence interval and other assumed factors, adding that many of these parameters are not meant purely to represent what they are called, and many considerations have been embedded in those measurements and coefficients (thus making them difficult to separate).

Hideshima also pointed out that the banks' own estimation of asset correlation would not be used in minimum capital requirements, but would be reviewed by supervisors under Pillar 2, with the regulatory authorities reviewing the capital adequacy assessment procedures of banks. It is now common knowledge that in practically no jurisdiction did this happen in a consistent and critical manner before the crisis hit.

There are two reasons for bringing this fact to the reader's attention: the way to bet is that rules and regulations which leave too much leeway in terms of supervision and evaluation will be subject to arbitrage. And, if past experience counts for anything, then such practice should not be repeated with Basel III.

What Hideshima said might have been the regulators' intention with Basel II, but as the major economic crisis that followed in 2007 has proved, credit institutions have been doing a great deal of regulatory arbitrage and minimalist correlation coefficients were a big part of it. What is even worse is that this minimalist policy was not sanctioned by the regulators.

This does not mean that regulators know everything. They don't. In addition, because so much depends on strategic choices as well as on portfolio differences, no two banks have the same correlation coefficients. To be able to document the *r* they are choosing, the better-managed financial institutions are doing *reverse engineering*. They are also very careful in *updating* their correlation coefficients regularly.

A different way of making this statement is that, in a free market, correlation coefficients change all the time; therefore, they must be revised regularly. When the market is neither in an upswing nor under stress, a policy of at least annual correlation revision makes sense. In contrast, if there are substantial financial or political events, then correlations must be recalculated more frequently, including:

- data mining involving long-term and short-term time series,
- stress analysis of the correlation coefficient, particularly when something big takes place, and
- expert opinion surveys for qualitative analysis, using the Delphi method.

In further correspondence with Hideshima, I received the following answer:

> On the need for updating, please do note that my remark was related to the use of correlation estimation for internal purposes, and not for regulatory purposes. For the latter, it does not seem practical to me to update them. For the former, I agree, as mentioned in my previous e-mail, that it does make sense to update them. The determination on the frequency of doing so would probably be on a judgmental basis, and the factors listed in your slide [in my presentation] seem to be among those that should be considered.

I am under the strong impression that also under Basel III the position of regulators with regard to the policy that banks should follow with correlation coefficients is still ambiguous. 'We will monitor how other countries handle correlations; we will not establish our own,' said a senior executive of one the regulatory authorities. He nevertheless acknowledged that this presupposes increasing contact with other supervisory authorities, to

- compare how they handle the correlation challenge,
- examine what other banks do in respect to modeling, and
- establish an effective method of model supervision.

Discussions with this frame of reference have begun among the leading regulatory agencies, but there is not yet in place a system that I know of (see also in Chapter 7 the discussion on home–host challenges and the fact that not much progress has been made there either). Yet, having a supervisory policy on the computation and revision of correlation coefficients can be a booster in other domains where the Basel Committee has concentrated its attention. For example, risk weights, which are at the heart of capital requirements, and the unearthing of hidden risk factors by revealing discrepancies which show up in connection to correlations.

A thorough analysis of results obtained during revisions of correlation coefficients can lead to the identification of risk factors which had not been considered up to that point (let alone thought to be important) or were downplayed because of a lack of proper evidence. One of the major financial institutions participating in the research that led to this book said that after extensive modeling it ended up with differences in *operational risk*[14] which were not easy to explain. In an attempt to explain them, the chief risk officer asked for an analytical study aimed at identifying correlations between credit risk and operational risk. This led to some interesting findings:

- balance sheet analyses had left some fraudulent incidents undetected,
- information on missed payments which was skipped, as a result of information technology insufficiency, and
- grading procedures were not respected, resulting in the approval of loans that should not have been granted.

The reader should appreciate that these and other failures are everyday happenings. Operational risk management, after all, is about avoiding such nasty surprises, but it took an investigation on correlation coefficients to unearth problems that for many years had attracted nobody's attention.

Backtesting and benchmarking correlations

Validation is a complex and demanding process involving not only the value of coefficients but also that of the tools and methods being used to compute and update them. Other distinctions too are important. For example, for the validation of probabilities of default (PDs), we differentiate between the discriminatory power of a rating system and the calibration of the accuracy of PD quantification. There are several approaches for the assessment of discriminatory power, the most common techniques being:

- the cumulative accuracy profile (CAP),
- the accuracy ratio, which condenses CAP information into a single number, and
- portfolio-dependent confidence intervals, which allow statistical inference.

The best method for validating correlation coefficients and their calibration (as well as other critical factors), is backtesting. The downside is the scarcity of data, caused by the infrequency of targeted information, such as default events. Also, the impact of a default correlation is not always evident.

In its broader sense, the term *backtesting* identifies the use of statistical methods to compare estimates of risk, and of its component parts to realized outcomes. This differs from the narrower approach of traditional backtesting of market risk models in an important way. For market risk models, backtesting involves the model *as is*, for example VAR, and for internal credit rating systems, it concerns only the risk components or model inputs being tested.

The broader sense of backtesting provides a better perspective on how well risk estimates translate into real life. Backtesting should not be confused with *benchmarking*. The latter term stands for a comparison of internal estimates across the same industry, such as banking. It may also involve external benchmarks, such as agency ratings, vendor models or artifacts developed and used by supervisory authorities. In a way, backtesting can be viewed as *ex-post* benchmarking, and benchmarking can be seen as *ex-ante* backtesting.

Alternatively, benchmarking could be regarded more as variance analysis, useful for providing a qualitative indicator of potential differences in technologies used within a given peer group. Critical in this connection are selection of the benchmark, a process requiring prior knowledge or inference of features of the underlying model, and mapping to the benchmark, with regard to the one-to-one relationship that can be inferred between the model and its benchmark.

With regard to its use for credit risk evaluations, benchmarking is basically a comparison of internal ratings and estimates with those externally observable or provided by agencies such as S&P, Moody's and Fitch. Backtesting and benchmarking can also be viewed as part of non-parametric tests aimed at detecting potential and systematic bias in a methodology, a set of tools, and/or the execution of different tests.

Combined with statistical tools, backtesting and benchmarking permit the identification and analysis of outliers, though sometimes differences in estimates may just stem from differences in approaches or methodologies. For example, probability of default (PD) estimates may differ because of a different definition of what is involved in default.

Some of the problems associated with correlations, which were discussed in previous sections, are present with both backtesting and benchmarking. Tests based on an assumption of *independence* are too conservative, with even the generally well-behaved rating systems performing poorly. Tests should take into account a correlation between defaults to allow for the detection of cases of rating system miscalibration.

Because all backtesting methods have shortcomings, with many of them being connected to data insufficiency, statistical tests alone will not be enough to validate an internal rating system adequately. This brings into perspective the benefits from a broader benchmarking exercise, including the case of obligors who will likely be in default at some predefined time, and obligors who will not be in default during this time horizon, but may be unwilling to fulfill their obligation.

Because it is not known in advance whether an obligor belongs to the first or the second category, banks face a classification problem. They have to assess an obligor's future status based only on presently available characteristics. Since this involves subjective judgment, behavior analysis of major obligors could be improved through the Delphi method.

In this particular sense, ratings systems could be seen as classification tools, providing indications of an obligor's likely future status. The discriminatory power of a rating system, and generally of scoring, denotes the ability to discriminate *ex-ante* between borrowers prone or not prone to defaulting. Among valid statistical approaches are:

- binomial tests,
- chi-square tests,
- a traffic lights approach,
- central limit tests (normal test), and
- operating characteristics (OC) curves.

The binomial test can be applied to only one rating category at a time. This limitation might be circumvented by using chi-square tests to check several rating categories simultaneously, based on the assumption of independence and an approximation to the normal distribution.

Chi-square tests are essentially a statistical analysis of variance. In every system, the measure of dispersion, and therefore variance, is most crucial in establishing performance and quality – with small variance denoting high-quality and large variance low-quality results. The sequence of curves shown in Figure 9.5 presents an excellent example (from manufacturing engineering) of a process that goes from low to high quality results.

In contrast to the binomial and normal tests, a traffic light approach is independent of any assumption of normal distribution, as well as of constant or near-constant factors (for example, probability of default) over time. It is a multi-period back-testing tool for a single rating category, based on the assumption of cross-sectional and inter-temporal independence of default events.

Yet the distribution of the number of defaults in one year is approximated with a normal distribution. Based on quantiles of this normal distribution, the number of defaults is mapped to one of traffic lights: green, amber and red. When observed over time this mapping results in a multinomial distribution of the numbers of colors, making possible an inference about the adequacy of default probability forecasts.

The central limit theorem is an approach to dealing with dependence problems that occur in the case of the binomial and chi-square tests. The normal test is a multi-period test of correctness of a default probability forecast for a single rating category. It is applied under the assumption that default events in different years are independent, and the mean default rate does not vary by too much over time. The test motivated by the central limit theorem is based on an approximation of the normal distribution of time-averaged default rates. However, the quality of this normal approximation tends to be moderate, and it exhibits a conservative bias.

The operating characteristics (OC) curve is a power curve sensitive to sample size from two viewpoints: absolute number of values in the sample,

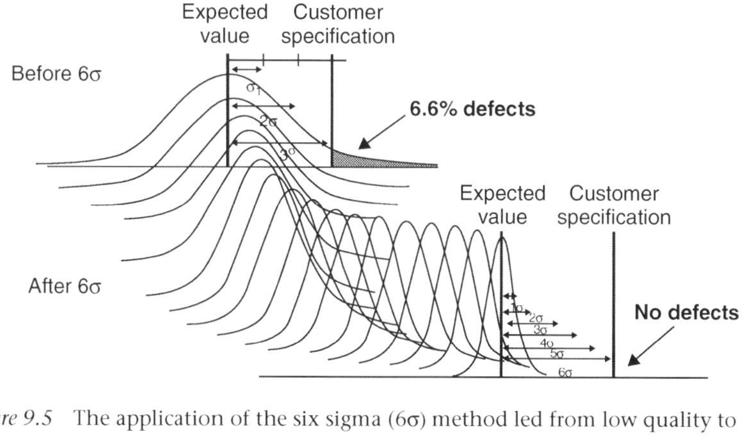

Figure 9.5 The application of the six sigma (6σ) method led from low quality to high quality results

and relative number as a percentage of the population being examined. The OC curve permits the establishment of the level of confidence (α, type I error).[15] This is also my preferred solution.

As a final observation, consistency between models being used as well as tools and methods, is a prerequisite to benchmarking and backtesting. A dynamic approach should range over time and space, taking into account the current and likely future impact of the risk factor under study. Changes in tools and in methodology can lead to results incompatible with those previously obtainable. Prudence therefore advises one to be careful with comparisons.

10
Risk Control Requires Authority, Goals and Organization

Risk control and the effect of asymmetries

When, in my seminars, I am asked about a basic prerequisite for rigorous risk management, my responses include not one but several factors, some of which are general and others specific to the enterprise. By far the most important is independence of opinion, which was discussed in Chapter 8. The person entrusted with risk control must be able to speak his/her mind, and advise top management to stop compounding the risks.

This requires the chief risk officer to have a strong personality and to fully document his objectives. Louis Pasteur, according to the great scientist's biographer, was intolerant of frivolous contradictions and vulgar objections which questioned a change in the status quo even if scientific reasons demanded such a change. But he accepted what can be called *militant skepticism*, which doubted a finding or a method, and promoted militant skepticism by sustaining a transparency.[1]

Pasteur's principle was that a researcher should not stop in the middle of a project, without deeper investigation, because of the appearance of objections, particularly when his work had started to provide evidence. This principle goes hand-in-glove with the work of risk controllers and calls attention to another important factor: *freedom from organizational pressures* that aim to bend the risk manager's will to back his position.

Still another important background factor for sound risk control is conceptual skills associated with domain knowledge. Clearly, the risk manager cannot be an expert in derivative financial instruments, loans, investment and currency exchange all at the same time. But among themselves, the members of his team must have these domain skills.

Domain knowledge is also vital in filling the requirement posed by one's ability to *challenge the 'obvious'*, which in the typical case is an established practice, a mainstream event or something set by the line of command. Challenging the obvious is so important because the discovery of what exactly overruns risk targets is not accomplished just by analyzing statistics.

The examiner and the analyst have to investigate and discover reasons or facts that are not immediately apparent, yet they have a major impact on end results. A reason frequently encountered is *asymmetries*. 'If we envisage all of nature's creations in the mineral, animal and vegetable worlds, and we also consider man-made artifacts,' said Louis Pasteur, 'we will see that they belong to two great classes: some have a sense of symmetry, while others don't.'[2] Risks belong to this second category.

Pasteur took as an example of objects exhibiting mathematical symmetry, such as the human body, a dice and a table. Then he pointed out that there are other objects and parts of objects that lack these characteristics. Taken as a whole, the human body exhibits a symmetry if a vertical plane passes through the middle of the nose, but the parts themselves, which constitute either side of such a symmetric aggregate, lack symmetry.

What is important to recall in connection with this observation is the way it applies to risk control, that the image of objects lacking symmetry is not superimposable in reality. The mirror image of a hand is not superimposable on to the hand because it is not symmetric. Minerals and man-made products present a symmetry, but in contrast, living vegetal and animal entities , are anatomically asymmetric, and their lack of symmetry is characterized by what Pasteur called the force of deviation of the polarization plan.[3]

It is indeed difficult to find a more profound separation of biological matter and inorganic substances than through this asymmetry in the world around us. Inorganic substances are symmetric. By contrast, objects under the creative influence of *becoming*,[4] have an internal asymmetry. What might be the reasons for such a difference? Pasteur maintained that they can be attached to nature's molecular forces and probably also in asymmetric or dissymmetric phenomena of the universe.[5]

As far as risk control is concerned, precious lessons can be learned from molecular biology, which has greatly benefited from Pasteur's ingenious analytics. For example, from the fact that an asymmetry in the internal arrangement of a chemical substance manifests itself in the external properties, which are capable of asymmetry.

Such a fundamental issue dividing the world of minerals and artifacts from that of living matter has not been studied in a deeper sense in the context of the economy, finance and financial instruments – let alone the nature of exposures derived from them. If the same principles hold, then hedging is far from providing investor protection since it is applies to a living market and its players and it is also by definition asymmetric, and this will show up down the line when protection from hedging proves to be an illusion.

The long leg of risk distribution detailed in Chapter 8 is a manifestation of this asymmetry in risk and return. Take residential real estate as an example: under this heading are included assets whose values moved furthest from fundamentals during the boom. They were loaded with increasing amounts of bank debt and, some time later, hedges based on symmetries turned on their heads.

Though, at the time of writing, four years have passed since the July/August 2007 subprimes bust, there is still a big gap between prices owners want and what bargain-hunters are prepared to pay. This is holding up deals, increasing the 'to sell' hangover and adding to the gap. In addition, many banks have been willing to roll loans over, ignoring breaches of loan-to-value covenants by using a strategy of *extend and pretend*. This has left the residential real estate market in limbo.

Notice that when asymmetries set in, the opposite can also be true. The way a recent Bank of America Merrill Lynch financial report put it:

> spite some investors suffering from 'black swan fatigue', weary of constantly buying insurance against a tail event which has not materialized, tail hedging remains important today as absent a tail event, unprecedented liquidity means there is risk of asset prices continuing to inflate ... [and] hiding cash is dangerous as it:
>
> - Creates cash-drag on the upside,
> - Protects no better than a good hedge[6] in a downturn, and
> - Is earning negative real yields.[7]

Asymmetries have been wreaking havoc in the vast over-the-counter (OTC) derivatives market, where even large dealing firms lack the information to determine the consequences of others failing. Asymmetries also make it hard to gauge the exposures to tail risks built up by sellers of swaps on collateralized debt obligations (CDOs), characterized by a limited upside and a low but real probability of catastrophic losses.

The now classical analytics and relatively newer tool introduced by 'rocket science'[8] are important, but even more crucial information may be provided by the hindsight imparted through risk control failures and the analysis of asymmetric results. Not all risk management efforts are successful, but investigating those that failed is more rewarding than doing so for those that succeeded.

Another basic factor behind ineffective risk control approaches is the lack of direct contact with the floor. Such direct contact provides the risk manager with information – and, most important, with *a sense of the situation* – that cannot really be extracted from reports and statistics promoted by real-time information. This sense of what is going on positions him well in the performance of his mission of weighting uncertainties.

Catastrophes happen when we ignore the evidence that exists 'between the lines' of a study, or use a vague style of risk assessment. Experience assisted by scientific analysis provides tools for attacking uncertainty problems, but most companies are not using them. Risk is not always seen at the stochastic part of a complex situation which somewhere down the line might end in major disruption or huge financial losses.

Practically everything in the financial business (and in many other industry sectors as well) is probabilistic. No matter how good one's information or judgment might be, it can prove to be wrong and one must be prepared for this. The best-looking deals can turn on their heads because of things one did not anticipate or an event risk that sneaked in at the last moment. A fundamental concept the previous chapters presented to the reader was that it is necessary to take risks, but it is important to recognize human fallibility.

From economic forecasting to investments and trades we are dealing with an imprecise science that in no way approaches mathematical certainty, even if mathematical models have entered banking in a big way. The policy mentioned above, of risk controllers being close to the floor where operations take place, satisfies the ancient Chinese proverb: 'I hear and I forget, I see and I remember, I do and I understand.'

Risk control lessons from a failure: Fannie and Freddie

The Taoist Laotse was not the only ancient philosopher who spoke of ambiguity in human affairs. Around 600 BC, in ancient Greece, the Temple of Apollo was established at Delphi, whose oracle gave its pronouncements in riddles. In the fifth century BC, Herodotus, the historian, records how, by misinterpreting the fuzzy oracle of Apollo, King Croesus of Lydia went to war against Cyrus, the founder of the Persian empire. The oracle told Croesus that if he crossed the Halys river he would destroy a mighty state. Croesus succeeded in doing so, but by failing to take into account the ambiguity embedded in the oracle's declaration, the state he destroyed was his own.

According to experts, the Apollo cult of Delphi followed the *Sophists* school, who taught that basically there is no such thing as truth. There is only opinion, backed by sensitivity to events. Among the Sophist philosophers was Protagoras (480–410 BC), a friend of Pericles. Socrates (470–399 BC) taught exactly the opposite; his method was a search for the truth through questioning.

The late Dr. Vittorio Vaccari, who was considered to be the greatest philosopher of modern Italy, once said that the civilization which we developed in the twentieth century is based on the Sophist school, not on Socrates' teachings. It is therefore inevitable that modern business is characterized by a significant amount of ambiguity, and this should be taken into account in risk control.

One of the better examples of prevailing ambiguity is in government rules and directives. In 1936, the Office of the Controller of the Currency (OCC) issued a rule prohibiting banks from buying bonds that were 'distinctly or predominantly speculative'. Today, more than 60 percent of American banks with less than US$100 million in assets have invested more than 50 percent of their capital in mortgage-backed securities (MBSs) of Fannie Mae and Freddie Mac, the mammoth US government-sponsored mortgage agencies.[9] Because of an implicit, but not explicit, government guarantee, these securities were (incorrectly) given AAA rating. However, scandals and huge derivatives exposure have rocked the two agencies' reputations, and a drop in the value of MBSs caused severe difficulties to banks inventorying them and could further trigger a credit crunch.

Over the years, both Fannie and Freddie have been in and out of trouble, but eventually risks overtook them and at the time of writing they are in government receivership. In 2003, when the Federal Home Mortgage Corporation (Freddie) came under fire for using, among other things, falsely valued derivatives, its shares price plunged, two CEOs were fired within three months of each other, the SEC initiated investigations, and Freddie said it would restate its 2000 to 2002 financial statements.

Subsequently, on June 23, 2003, the New York Times revealed that Fannie Mae made no money in 2002, despite a reported US$6.4 billion in 'core earnings', and US$4.6 billion in earnings, as measured by standard accounting rules. From all evidence, Fannie Mae had underestimated how fast interest rates would decline and homeowners would refinance their mortgages. Therefore, it did not protect itself against the risk that some of its higher-yielding mortgages would be replaced by lower-yielding ones, and this management oversight resulted in losses that showed up in its income statements over the next several years, turning black figures into red.

Since these events took place in 2003, therefore well before the crisis that began in 2007, the bonds of both Fannie Mae and Freddie Mac have come under great pressure. Selling by European and Asian investors accelerated after rumors spread on markets in July 2003 that the European Central Bank (ECB) was liquidating its holdings of US agencies debt that lacked an explicit guarantee from the US government.

The risk was commensurate to the exposure. Fannie and Freddie had bought a swarm of American mortgage debt from commercial banks. Most of it they subsequently sold, in the form of MBSs, to other banks, insurance companies, and investment funds. They also issued bonds to refinance their operations, and were engaged in multi-trillion-dollar high-risk derivatives contracts which also went wrong.

Looked at from a mounting risk point of view, by 2008 the situation had become perilous because, between them, Fannie Mae and Freddie Mac accounted for an estimated nine out of ten secondary mortgages in the USA and (according to reliable estimates) they owed guarantees of around US$5.3 trillion. At the same time, hundreds of America's banks relied on their shares to shore up their capital, and foreign central banks were big investors in their bonds; which meant that there was plenty of collateral damage both in America and abroad.

Evidence of absentee risk management was provided by the balance sheets of both federal agencies, which looked like a runaway train crash. Since the second quarter of 2007, both had been losing plenty of money, but nothing near the torrent of losses in the third quarter of 2008: US$29 billion for Fannie Mae and US$25.3 billion for Freddie Mac (see Figure 10.1). They were taken over by the US government in early September 2008.

This added greatly to the financial earthquake shaking the USA and the global economy at that time. Apart from the Fannie and Freddie equity which they held, US commercial and investment banks were exposed to paper issued by both government-sponsored agencies, which accounted for roughly

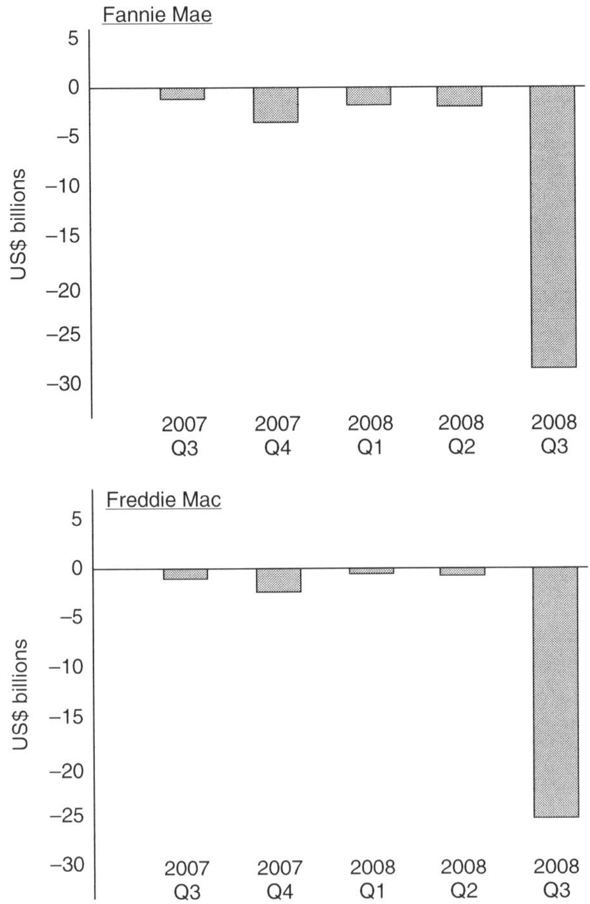

Figure 10.1 Net quarterly losses of two mismanaged mortgage agencies, Fannie Mae and Freddie Mac, in US$ billions

half of their total securities portfolio. They also owned much of the preferred stock issued by both of them, most likely attracted by the preferred shares' combination of a fake low-risk weighting and a comparatively good yield.

Compounding the risks was exposure associated with the two agencies' credit default swaps (CDSs). Contagion began to spread through the market, because poorly-managed banks had written an unprecedented amount of credit protection contracts based on Fannie's and Freddie's US$20 billion of subordinated debt, while knowing very well that it sat below senior debt in their capital structures. All this made the risk containment problem confronting the then US Treasury very complex. Hank Paulson, the Treasury secretary at that time, had to decide (a) whom to hurt, and (b) by how much.

One thing he could not allow himself to do was to enjoy the luxury of sitting still. When, in August 2008, he had permitted the Treasury to make loans to, or invest in, Freddie and Fannie, Congress made explicit what was always tacitly admitted: that Uncle Sam stood behind the two mortgage agencies, even though they had private shareholders and their executives were paid an incredible amount of money – which was both irrational and unjustified.

At the end of the day, the American taxpayer bore the losses, and there was a sea of red ink. By December 2008, three months after being taken over by the government, the two agencies had between them more than US$200 billion of debt to roll over and the market was uneasy, because the collapse of just one bond auction could send shock waves around the USA and the rest of the world. That is why a growing number of experts were suggesting that outright nationalization was the best way forward, and the only fair one to taxpayers. It could, show commitment to the stability of the mortgage market at large, and lower the two agencies' funding costs, and therefore also the mortgage rates.

The downside was that their nationalization would add, in one shot, a huge liability to the government's balance sheet. Washington's (unrealistic) hope was that, subsequently, as the market recovered, the two agencies' assets could be liquidated and/or the entities broken up and privatized. Because of the huge mismanagement of risk and political exploitation, Fannie and Freddie had outlived their usefulness, having become a very expensive form of obsolete public policy.

Poor governance and torrents of red ink continued throughout 2009 and 2010, nearly two and a half years after the 'conservatorship' provided by the government's Federal Housing Finance Agency. Finally, in mid-February 2011 the Treasury Department issued a report in which it proposed the eventual elimination of Fannie Mae and Freddie Mac. It also laid out options for reducing the role of government in mortgage financing.

This report frankly admitted that Fannie and Freddie had gone the wrong way, straying from their core business of promoting sustainable home ownership. One of the ways they had done so was by extending credit to riskier borrowers. Following such a painful experience, the US Treasury foresaw the government's role in housing being limited to robust oversight, consumer protection and targeted assistance for poor households.

It all sounds very satisfactory, but it is unclear how all this will be achieved without reigniting the risks that haunted Fanny, Freddie and the taxpayer.

Organizational and personal prerequisites for effective risk control

Feats like the unearthing of opaque extreme events, a close watch over asymmetries and the avoidance of persistent risk control failures, such as those characterizing the life of Fannie Mae and Freddie Mac, do not happen merely by asking people to work more diligently. They require a great amount of organizational effort as well as the authority to take decisive steps in bringing the company back on track to its main business.

While the market rewards profit it does not necessarily look kindly on excessive risk-taking, which weakens the financial staying power of an institution. And as we saw at the start of this chapter, different forms of risk mitigation only reward the risk-taker if s/he pays full attention to how serious is the likelihood of asymmetries, and the timely containment of their impact.

One of the better strategies for return on risk capital that I have come across is to target an 'A' or 'A+' risk rating for the entity as a whole and for each of its business units (BUs). One of the banks with which I was associated had a target of an 'A' rating for each of its operating divisions, with the hypothesis that, because of a carefully watched product line diversification, the holding's rating could stand at 'A+' or 'AA-. The risk horizon being assumed was one year, with business plans targeting capital adequacy over a 3- to 5-year period, with an 'A' rating as a minimum, and management appreciated that this 'A' rating was a simplifying assumption that needed to be tested, and indeed it *was* tested periodically.

The pillar of this whole scheme was *diversification*. No two financial institutions employ the same approach and thus have fairly similar diversification profiles, but the notion of establishing and maintaining a credit rating target is valid for everyone – provided that honest periodic tests validate it, because every organization is open to excesses, and attitudes toward risk diversification changes over time.

All this requires strong organizational commitment and personal accountability measures (see Chapter 8). Drawing on my experience with financial institutions in four different European countries, I use as guidelines seven organizational prerequisites for effective risk management. First and foremost one must establish clear objectives and a culture able to sustain the entity's reputation, profitability and financial staying power.

The second prerequisite is not to forbid risk-taking, but to identify carefully both evident and opaque risks, steadily monitoring their behavior, projecting their longer-term evolution and having in a place a statistical quality control chart down to the personal accountability level. An integral part of this policy is to price all risks, because risk is a cost (see the section below entitled 'The philosophy underpinning risk control limits').[10]

The use of statistical quality control charts is very important, because a neat risk-control organization requires exception-reporting procedures, and the best way to do so is to track every principal risk and the most important risk factors through SQCs (see the next section). They are well established and help to keep each exposure within limits spelled out by the board.[11] This system should report immediately on deviations, and those responsible should apply corrective action without delay.

The third most important prerequisite for effective risk control is to benefit from the unambiguous support of the CEO and the board. It is 'third' only in the sense that without the previously mentioned 'first' prerequisite, it is not easy to obtain a consensus, and without the 'second' one cannot demonstrate or convince others about the effectiveness of the risk-control action.

Deregulation and globalization have contributed considerable uncertainty in risk control. The same is true of the mobility of human capital, which in a positive sense fosters the ability of companies to take advantage of unanticipated opportunities, but in a negative sense decreases the formerly prevailing amount of *esprit de corps*. Promoting individualism is good, but the downside is that it goes against information sharing and co-operation. Yet, both of these qualities, along with transparency, are precisely what is needed to handle risk in an effective manner.

The fourth important prerequisite is that the chief risk officer reports to (and is judged by) seniors in the organizational structure. The best options are: the chairman of the board's risk committee, or the CEO. This is because I know of two cases where the chief risk officer reported to the chief financial officer, which led to conflicts of interest. Even worse was the case of a big global bank where the chief risk officer reported to the board's audit committee until a new chief executive bent the line of command and made him report to the trading division head – which is ridiculous. Since that day, in that particular institution, risk control has been nonexistent.

Company politics works against this senior reporting structure for the chief risk officer. Several efforts have been toward observing that principle, but frequently they do not extend much further than the initial groundwork because of opposition by embedded interests. Nor are banks creating the necessary incentives to encourage employees and managers to adopt the right attitude toward risk control. Training is inadequate, because trainees are left with contradictory objectives, and rewards for watching over risks effectively are not linked directly to financial indicators that integrate risk control performance.

The fifth prerequisite is that risk control methods, tools and models should steadily develop in sophistication and adapt to changing risk profiles and conditions. Not only the order of principal risks, their drivers and associate risk factors evolve over time, but also novel financial instruments will have different (often deeper) risk control requirements than those already known. Therefore the best policy is that the risk management organization is sensitive to all changes, proactively adapting its goals, methods and tools to them.

Typically, though by no means always, this adaptation involves two changes. One is the introduction of more powerful quantitative models; and the other is the establishment of qualitative methods. As the reader is already aware, qualitative analysis both complements and helps in interpreting quantitative results. Statistics can sometimes be widely misleading without an associated qualitative examination. Analysis gives form to the formless, and an unbiased investigation into the nature and message of numbers and tables makes them reveal their secrets.

All things have to be examined by calling them into question. This may well be done through brainstorming meetings, where every participant is prompted to think aloud, with questions and answers providing food for thought. It is a welcome practice to freely express doubts and opinions about strengths and weaknesses of quantitative results associated with the subject under discussion.

The sixth prerequisite has already been mentioned at the start of the chapter, but it is important enough to repeat the reference. Risk control should operate closely with the trading floor, and wherever else the action takes place. Remoteness means cold numbers, and this is highly ineffective in terms of risk control results.

Examined from a distance, a rapid increase in a bank's value at risk (VAR) can be an alarm signal even if VAR is a primitive model. However, when asked about it, the boss of the trading division would say that he was proud of it because derivatives are engines of business growth. To the risk controller, in contrast, a zooming in VAR is unwelcome because it speaks of much greater risk-taking, and s/he has to find out why by looking squarely into the eyes of the desk head.

The risk profile of the bank may well be changing, and if it continues to do so unabated the institution might turn into a giant hedge fund. If the risk controllers are not able to observe the nature of trades directly and to judge their changing pattern, then their boss would be left with no alternative but to accept the trading desk's argument that 'the market has picked up, and competitor banks, too, are trying to make the most of it'.

In contrast, if the risk controllers are near the floor, when there is a spike in VAR (or any other risk metrics that are being used), they will ask for a clear explanation. Is it within the board's limits? Can the bank afford it? A great deal will depend on how much more risk capital is available. If there is a shortfall, this will have to be covered. What happens next depends on the mismatch and on the chief risk officer's mandate.

The seventh prerequisite focuses on the stamina of risk controllers and of their bosses. They should train themselves to work under stress. Risk management is like pretrial preparation, and involves a broad range of issues from policies, practices, procedures, skills, independence of opinion and effectiveness in regard to deliverables – which definitely should be audited.

This brings our discussion to the vital issue of staffing the functions of risk control. At the top of the list of qualities is high ethical standards, best expressed by former US President Harry Truman's famous statement: 'The buck stops here'. In terms of the basic personality characteristics and qualifications of a risk manager, these can be expressed in three words: conceptual, analytical and directive.

A sound educational and professional background would include an aptitude for mathematical analysis, statistical experimentation, modeling, experience in research and investigation as well as the ability to tolerate uncertainty and ambiguity (to which reference has already been made).

The careful reader will recall the discussion on domain knowledge with hands-on experience in areas such as trading, loans and credit rating, investments, derivatives, financial or system analysis, and finance or engineering. Versatility in advanced technology and its implementation, including knowledge engineering, is a 'plus', and the same is true of the renewal of skills through formal training as well as the ability to learn from one's own experience and that of others.

Risk management is a metalevel of quality control

A *metalevel* is a higher level in a hierarchy of concepts, missions or functions. As such it orients the way the lower level(s) should work, and guides the hand of the professionals working on a given project or program. A branch of science known as *meta-analysis* (it was originally invented in 1948, but has become more popular in recent years) is a way of extracting statistically meaningful information from a large number of relatively small trials, and continuing to do so even if such trials had been conducted in ways that make it difficult to compare the results without a meta-analytical focus.

The conclusions of meta-analysis (which has something in common with statistical sign test runs) are only valid if negative trials are included among the positive ones. If the negative trials are omitted, the results will probably be too optimistic, as often happens with the interpretation of half-baked experimental findings.

By applying Heisenberg's Law[12] that nothing is straightforward, we can plot a band of risk values that are acceptable, while what falls outside them is an outlier. Figure 10.2 provides a graphical example. The abscissa is time

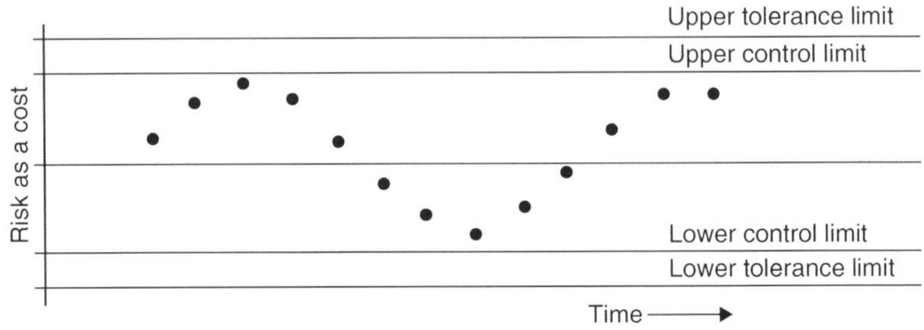

Figure 10.2 Nothing is straightforward. Risks within the band of control limits are acceptable; those outside are outliers

while the ordinate is amount of exposure, preferably expressed as a cost (see the next section).

The risk in the abscissa can be any chosen variable. For example, that assumed by a desk, integrating separate plots made for each of its traders and for its manager. Or, risk associated to loans by a branch office – to be detailed through separate charts at each loans officer level and summed up at regional and corporate levels, also in separate charts. Here again, risks within the band are acceptable, but those outside are not, and this is true both of those higher and those lower.

The question could be posed: Why should the lower risks be rejected? There was a professor at UCLA who taught his students that a loans officer who has very few bad loans is as dysfunctional as one who has too many – because s/he is rejecting plenty of business that might be profitable. (The way to deal with this is through a sequential sampling plan where the options are: Accept/Test again/Reject, and with every 'Test again' a premium is added to the loan's interest.)[13]

The plot in Figure 10.2 is a metalevel of a statistical quality control chart by variables shown in Figure 10.3. Developed during the Second World War for the manufacturing industry, and widely implemented, a system of statistical quality control charts (SQCs) can be analyzed into two main parts: the monitoring measurement subsystem, and the statistical decision and reporting subsystem.

Statistical theory ensures that between the two lies a filter, which can be thought of as passing the desired data stream for the message we are seeking, but blocking the noise. *Noise* is any unwanted or irrelevant input that alters the message. In risk management this noise may well be a psychological factor that alters the behavior of the risk controller, trader, loans officer, investment officer or other professional.

Filtering works in conjunction with the statistical decision system to sort information elements into those falling within and those outside

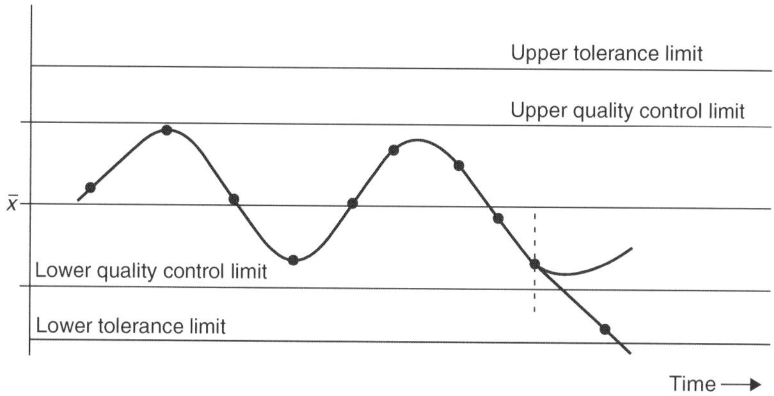

Figure 10.3 Using a statistical quality control chart to track product quality

specifications, limits or tolerances. There is an analogy to this process in information and communication theory, when several types of messages are sent simultaneously over the same channel, and then unpacked and sorted out at the receiver.

Basic notions from information theory can be applied to a substantial number of risk control problems. For example, at quality control level data streams can be analyzed to give answers to a potentially wide variety of problems involving compliance with, or alternatively, lack of observance of, tolerances. At the metalevel of reference, the principles of information theory enable the risk controller to assume the proper perspective in evaluating the performance of operating units under his/her supervision – and that of their people – in relation to compliance with risk limits or any other criteria being targeted.

At a metalayer, risk management may decide that to suppress errant impulses in the production process (trading, investments, loans or other items) more control has to be exerted in one direction or another. Notice that such an exercise can be successful if it monitors continuously the attitudes, operations, trends and positions of professionals and managers in line disciplines. This should be made in a way that keeps the risks being assumed within established tolerances, but without killing individual initiative or creating a bureaucratic culture where a person is punished for mistakes but is not rewarded for positive results. Individual initiative is welcomed. As Napoleon Buonaparte said, every soldier carries in his knapsack the possibility of a marshal's baton (a five-star general in US terms).

While a risk management training program must include all the tools that traders, loans officers, investment specialists and managers need to be prepared to handle risk, assisted by SQCs, metalevel analysis should address the human element. It can do so by providing a pattern of how people act on the ground in response to problems connected to exposure, which arise in relation to their business activities. This synergy is a valuable contribution to effective risk management.

Another contribution of patterns provided by SQC charts tracking every professional's actions and reactions, is to provide a warning about rogue traders. These are no recent invention. In the 1920s a trader in the Brussels office of Lazard Brothers made a wild bet on the collapse of the French franc. The franc recovered, ironically thanks to the advice given to the French government by Frank Altschul, the boss of Lazard's New York branch. Because of that rogue trader, however, Lazard lost US$30 million – a huge sum of money at the time.

Patterns revealed by SQC charts may also help to document whether the rogue trader's superior had taken corrective action or, on the contrary, had covered him. In early October 2010 a French judge sentenced Jerôme Kerviel, a former trader at Société Générale, to five years in prison (two of which were suspended), and told him to repay the bank €4.9 billion (US$6.7 billion) for losses it incurred as a result of his 'unauthorized trades'. But were these trades really 'unauthorized'?

According to Kerviel's arguments, the bank shared the blame for his major trading losses because it had looked the other way when his positions were profitable. According to other opinions, the bank's weak oversight allowed a relatively junior employee to place bets worth more than the bank's entire capital. A pattern based on SQC personal accountability charts would have been instrumental in terms of evidence regarding who was really to blame. This, of course, has prerequisites:

- selling the metalevel concept to senior management,
- establishing a procedure for standardizing, collecting, databasing and datamining risk control data, and
- using frequency-and-impact distributions in connection with critical variables.

The latter should be designed for comparison purposes and for determining whether assumed exposure is in control – a feat that SQC charts are well suited to accomplish. This is a positive factor promoting a bank's ability to manage risk well.

As Warren Buffet said:

> When we look at the future of business, we look at riskiness as being a sort of go/no go value. If we think that we simply don't know what is going to happen in the future, that does not mean it is risky for everyone. It means *we* don't know that it's risky for us.[14]

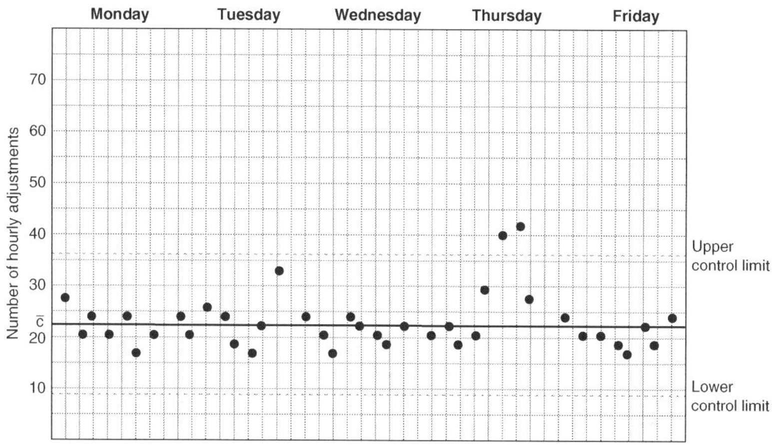

Figure 10.4 Quality control chart for number of defects per unit in a week

In risk control terms, this go/no go concept is served through statistical charts by the attributes shown in Figure 10.4, and can be extended to the test of inventoried positions in a portfolio of shares, debt or derivative financial instruments. All portfolios must be evaluated frequently in terms of recognized gains and losses, therefore of exposure, and for a factual risk evaluation it is most helpful to have a pattern that can be checked at all times and with deviations corrected before it is too late.

In conclusion, better risk management can be assured by a significant synergy between auditing, quality of service and risk control, such synergy being exploited through patterns similar to those being discussed here. Auditing identifies, through accounting evidence, defaults in accounts, and measures fraud which may lie behind them. The methods and tools of SQC provide a comprehensive visualization of variations in the bank's exposure. The notion of a risk control metalevel enriches management with the ability to carry out rigorous investigation to discover deviations and assign responsibility for these.

The philosophy underpinning risk control limits

J.P. Morgan established, and wanted to see observed, tough lending limits. 'We used to think of Morgan as a nice small bank,' remarked Guido Verbeck, then a Guarantee Trust officer. 'Because of their lending limits, when they participated in large loans they could only take a small share and they were very worried about it.'[15]

No matter what the organization and its business, risk management will not be able to fulfill its responsibilities with no philosophy underpinning its risk control policies and no system of limits. These must be set in a way that makes possible steadily monitoring – for example, through statistical quality control charts. Limits must be established for all principal risks. Three examples are credit risk, market risk and liquidity risk.

Far from being an abstract business practice, limits are one of the most powerful tools for keeping a close watch on exposure and for management control in general. This is particularly true when they have been expanded in the full knowledge of risk positions, following a study of how well these fit the bank's type of business. Other prerequisites are an analysis of all instruments and trades, a good knowledge of counterparties, and an appreciation of the amount of risk capital the bank can afford to put on the table.

Limits are like traffic lights. Their presence is crucial in many industries, processes and products that have to be under steady control. They have an impact even when they have not been properly examined in terms of their bearing. Basically, however, business and industrial enterprises cannot be managed without thoroughly studied limits. In engineering design, limits are often expressed as tolerances, but in trading, limits indicate the amount of exposure an institution is able or unwilling to assume. Other examples where limits exist are the tax burden a community can bear, the type and depth of social services it can provide, the number of immigrants it can assimilate, and plenty of other social issues. A life without limits is something no person or organization can afford.

Not all limits are, or could be, of the same nature, however. A great deal depends on the activity they are expected to contain, and on the likelihood of overruns. There should be a different level of limits for instruments that are very volatile than for those exhibiting a lower volatility (and a smaller number of unknowns). This can be explained better by using a metaphor from the animal kingdom. Limits and associated organizational controls are analogous to designing the enclosures for different animal species at a zoo: deer and gazelles, which are good at jumping, need well-reinforced high walls, whereas elephants and other animals that are poor jumpers can be confined by relatively low walls and narrow moats.

In either case, however, the limits must be clear and unambiguous. Limits that are vague are rarely, if ever, observed. 'Reasonableness', a kind of limit often set by law, is highly ambiguous; 'for adults only' the limit on the access to literature and films by citizens, is clearer, but still involves uncertainty. Some limits are fictions, such as the speed limits for motorways that almost no one obeys. But other limits are real, hard and enforced, thereby defining the extent of individual freedom, and delineating the intrusive powers of the government.

'Your freedom of action ends where the nose of your neighbor begins,' said a judge in Los Angeles to a defendant who claimed freedom of action for what he had done but was brought to justice. The government should not eavesdrop on its citizens is an often heard truism, but it is not a real-life limit.

Setting limits is an art, not a science, even in engineering, and it has much to do with the product as well as with the process used to manufacture that product and the quality history of the factory. A basic rule for limit-making is that the burden of its design should fall on those who create the changed process or product, and the choice being made should be based on experimentation. By contrast, the burden of proof that limits have been violated falls on the shoulders of the controllers. If done in a light way, lowering or raising limits can have unexpected consequences, boundaries set for normal operations would not be able to handle exceptional circumstances, and limits that are not observed soon become a joke.

This is true in engineering and is also valid in finance; in fact, even more so in finance because the unknowns are greater. An often 'unforeseen' event with a major impact on limits is the correlation between risk factors (see Chapter 8) which in the past were controlled individually, but are now integral parts of a system.

One of the erroneous policies often encountered is that limits are set through compromises. This is a doubtful way to proceed, but common among those who do not really understand the problem. A good way to explain to senior bankers the importance of carefully studying the limits is to emphasize that risk is a cost. It's integral part of a risk control philosophy that we must stop talking of risk as being balanced by return. Risk is the cost:

- of today and of yesterday, when the commitment was made,
- of inventorying the instrument over its lifespan and marking it to market, and
- of tomorrow, further out at the transaction's maturity, when the profit or loss is accounted for.

The contribution of *risk cost accounting* can be appreciated through analogical thinking to energy cost accounting – a concept discussed by Paul Roberts in his seminal book, *The End of Oil*.[16] According to Roberts, every gallon of gasoline or ton of coal being burned imposes an *economic cost*, which is currently not included in the price paid for our energy – but which is real, heavy and can be measured from the time the oil is produced and refined to the moment it is burned in the internal combustion engine.

This requires a *well-to-wheels* analysis, supplemented by medical expenses, sick days, and other costs coming along with them. Full energy cost accounting should also integrate external costs from flood damage to crop losses because of drought. These costs are also not included in the retail price of gasoline or autos – but must be borne by society. It is also proper to factor in the huge amounts of money spent on energy security, including a military presence in the Middle East, and subsidies to corrupt local regimes.

The need to bring into perspective and account for hidden costs hasn't quite hit the minds of heads of state, nor has the idea of internalizing costs directly connected to risks been applied by the banking industry with regard to the exposures it is assuming. Yet the issue of hidden cost hangs over the Western economy, and those costs can be enormous. For example, a credit institution carries exposure to single names and therefore principal risks, and risk factors (see Chapter 8) which have to be measured across all relevant instruments traded with that counterparty. Exposure comes from lending, options, futures, forwards, credit default swaps and other instruments. As market prices change there is an aggregate effect on portfolio values associated with a single name (or group).

The chairperson, board members and CEO should not only require that the bank tracks the maximum amount it could lose if all underlying assets of each middle to major counterparty became nearly worthless, but also to be informed ahead of time as exposure and/or the visibility of the counterparty's default point increases. Positions and limits should also be controlled in connection with the liquidity of the parties. All material positions should be kept under constant scrutiny in the light of changing market conditions, and each commitment must be subjected to targeted processes, which include stress testing from both a business viewpoint and in connection with risk control.

An example where risk is a cost that might turn projected rewards on their head is the maturity of OTC-traded derivative financial instruments. Prudent management enters into derivative contracts maturing within a period of up to five years. One of the better known companies has established maturity limits for the following classes of derivatives:

- interest rate swaps for assets: five years to maturity,
- interest rate swaps for liabilities: five years to maturity,
- currency exchange forwards for assets: one year to maturity,
- currency exchange forwards for liabilities: two years to maturity, and
- purchased options for assets: one year to maturity.

Specifically for currency exchange, well-governed companies ensure that the maturity limit does not exceed one year, but even that has often proved to be too long. To protect themselves from a rising exchange rate of currencies from countries to which they export large quantities of goods, companies buy forward forex contracts. This is no fail-safe approach, however; and many firms found out with some pain that exchange rates had moved in the opposite way to what they had thought. The difference was the real cost of hedging risk.

The importance of rigorous accounting standards

One of the big global banks looked at dividends paid by its risk management operation for every dollar invested in the control of risk, and came to the conclusion that, in reduction in losses, the benefit had been six dollars. The same institution also examined which acts significantly reduced expected benefits, and came to the conclusion that these included cases that had escaped the scrutiny of risk control. For example, the originator of a deal sold to its investment managers mispriced securities for which it had used a volatility smile.[17] Or, its relationship managers had made promises to the bank's clients that were difficult to keep.[18] Or its agents had outright failed to deliver on their assigned mission, with the result that important clients moved their accounts to another bank.

A finding that unsettled senior management was that the banks' early warning system, which was implemented across all of its global operations, was not working as expected. Three reasons were identified as being responsible for this failure: the first was lack of universal accounting standards, as each subsidiary employed the local financial reporting standards in the way that was is required by the law of the land, but failed to convert such reporting to the internal standard used by the bank's management information system.

The second reason for the early warning's failure was that country and local management did not pay enough attention to implementing the system, therefore there were gaps in the application. The third reason was related to the mathematical model adopted for alerts. Early warning models combine bank-level financial indicators, the most important among them being the balance sheet (B/S), and the P&L (profit and loss) statement (income statement). They also map into them other factors, such as macroeconomic conditions and selected market indicators. In this case, too, B/S and P&L figures largely depend on prevailing accounting standards, and these are not standardized globally. In addition, the model had failed to pay attention to choices made by investors that have a bearing on the bank's business.

Both P&L statements and balance sheets have their followers. Investors in debt instruments and preferred stock, as well as stockholders (common stock), pay more attention to the income statement. In contrast, short-term creditors and credit institutions that extend three to six months' unsecured loans, generally look at the condition of the balance sheet. The B/S and P&L do not move in the same way, however; the balance sheet may grow significantly with leveraging, but the cost of assumed risk depresses income and net profits decline, though creative accounting may carry out a 'facelift'.

Both balance sheets and P&L statements can be manipulated. In their excellent book *Security Analysis*, Benjamin Graham and David Dodd devote eight chapters to 'Analysis of the Income Account'. Their analysis is only nominally concerned with variations in the expense items and their relations to net sales. What they are aiming at is to acquaint the reader with *artifacts* and *window dressing* designed to misrepresent earnings and conceal losses from the public eye.

Creative accounting is the practice of mishandling corporate accounting. 'There are unbounded opportunities for shrewd detective work, for critical comparisons, for discovering and pointing out a state of affairs quite different from that indicated' according to Graham and Dodd, who further suggest that *profits* have been and still are subject 'in extraordinary degree to arbitrary determination and manipulation'.[19]

Another way that global companies have found to beef up their income statement is to navigate among and exploit the differences prevailing in accounting standards in countries where they operate. No matter how one looks at the issue of quarterly and annual regulatory reporting by international firms, one of the important requirements for comprehensive and comprehensible presentation is standards. Two references are outstanding:

- Universal accounting standards and procedures that are free of different parochial incompatible versions[20] or, even worse, contradictory accounting principles, and
- A high-powered risk measurement and management system that is globally applied, transparent and well understood by every user, including lawmakers, regulators, stakeholders and the accounting departments of the companies themselves.[21]

Indispensable in a regional or global economy, universal accounting standards have, however, been *fata morgana* – no more than an illusion. Apart from the differences between US GAAP and IFRS,[22] all countries using IFRS (and some big ones don't) have the freedom of producing their own versions – apparently to make the standards simpler, but really to protect the competitive interests of 'their companies'. This disregards the fact that without a universal accounting standard it is not possible to manage systemic risk, investors and other stakeholders can be cheated, and if measurement are imprecise, politicians will have a free hand to take steps which twist the economy.

Because of these and other reasons related to balance sheets, P&L as well as effective risk control, I do not have the slightest doubt that convergence of accounting should top the agenda of regulators, nudging away from home-grown standards towards global ones. For example, one of the most controversial issues is how to report financial assets: whether at fair value[23] or amortized cost.

Up to April 1, 2009, America's FASB firmly backed fair value by marking to market, arguing that doing otherwise made creative accounting much easier. Opponents of fair value accounting think that revaluing at times of meltdowns makes banking crises more severe. In spite of political pressure from the Obama Administration (and a temporary suspension of marking to market) FASB dug in its heels, calling for most financial instruments to be given at fair value in regulatory reporting.

IASB has made a split: loans and loan-like equivalents held to maturity may be marked at amortized cost, while frequently traded instruments should be marked to market. That, however, leaves a huge loophole where financial trickery can have a ball. Trillions of OTC derivatives will be reported at historical cost, which becomes a myth as market conditions change, and big global companies such as AIG and Lehman Brothers, which were bankrupt, (not to mention plenty of other salvaged by taxpayers' money) would look like the kings of the market.

Fair value accounting provides the most transparent view of a company's accounts and best serves investors. What its opponents argue – that it exacerbated the 2007–12 financial crisis by reflecting irrational market behavior rather than the underlying value of assets – is misplaced, because what really brought doomsday were the gambles of the big global banks, not fair value accounting *per se*.

At the heart of all these arguments lies the fact that being able to compare accounts across borders has become indispensable. A standards *uniformity* not only ensures a better understanding of what is written in financial accounts but also provides the information necessary for more efficient capital allocation. In addition, with globally uniform accounting standards, companies can less easily pick their regulators to suit themselves. All that fair value does is to say how inordinate and irrational are some of the risks being taken.

Part V

Basel III Should Also Address Big Spending by Central Banks

11 By Salvaging Overleveraged Banks, Sovereigns Propagate Global Systemic Risk

Collusion between sovereigns and the banks

The legacy of the ongoing financial crisis, which started in 2007, has been a series of imbalances which continue to damage the global economy; most particularly, the economies of Western countries. Quite often, the way these imbalances are handled has been a desperate effort to avoid default, and this is providing the opportunity to some of the market agents to play the system.

In addition, because of the prevailing small margin for error and a relatively low Western economic growth, even those 'solutions' that were adopted did not turn the situation around. Trying to fight a debt crisis through more debt and timid or dysfunctional debt control policies has led to a loss of central bank credibility and brought other problems into being. Critics pointed out that, if big spending by sovereigns and central banks spurred growth, we should be in the middle of an economic boom. But we are not.

Nor have we reached the end of the tunnel of pumping public money into self-wounded big private global banks. In early April 2011, following a second series of stress tests, the European Central Bank lined up 90 banks in its jurisdiction for capital examination,[1] and this prompted credit institutions to attempt to strengthen their capital adequacy through the markets:

- Germany's Commerzbank sought €8.5 billion (US$12 billion),[2]
- Italy's Monte dei Paschi di Siena wanted €2.5 billion (US$3.6 billion), and
- Italy's Intesa Sanpaolo sought €5 billion (US$7.2 billion).

In retrospect, the governments' actions of merging into one big bank another that was badly damaged, to avoid pouring taxpayers' money into the latter, proved to be a deceitful course. On April 11, 2011, in its interim report, the British Independent Banking Commission stated that the government was wrong to merge HBOS into Lloyds TSB.

This merger has been an example of the over-concentration of credit services. It gave the combined institution a 25 percent share of the British retail banking market, a near monopoly, at least in some areas of the UK. The Commission also suggested that retail banking and investment banking should be separated from one another and handled by different institutions – which is precisely what the now repealed Glass–Steagall Act had done in the USA. Another most interesting initiative by the Commission has been that of underlining the need to overhaul the way banks work.

Unavoidably, the integral part of the necessary overhaul is the strengthening of capital reserves. If the status quo of thin core capital margins continues to prevail, then the likelihood of banks coming back to the government for more handouts rises significantly – and one crisis is followed by another. Paraphrasing Thomas Malthus: capital-hungry banks feed themselves on public money, thus bringing their sovereign to its knees. At this point, overleveraged sovereigns who cannot make ends meet take loans from the banks and edge them closer to the financial abyss.

In a couple of installments Ireland put €32 billion into its ailing banking industry, and thought that was sufficient. But in early April 2011, as the situation continued to worsen for the terminally damaged Irish banks, the government had to pour into the derelict institutions further billions of euros, eventually making a total of €70 billion. A huge amount of money for a small economy.

The after-effects are well known. The already high and rising sovereign debt, which is acute on both sides of North Atlantic, is having a very negative effect on prospects for the stabilization of the financial system. There is also negative feedback from the period following the crisis as countries are either reluctant or unable to take the necessary steps to radically restructure the banking sector, which could lead to a robust growth path.

One of the reasons for the negative feedback is the conflict of interest among sovereigns, banks and some other parties. Governments rescued banks from the threat of outright bankruptcy in 2008, but banks have also been big buyers of government bonds. This is particularly true in Europe, and is the reason why sovereign default might cause a new banking crisis.

Credit institutions are ever ready to lend to sovereigns, not only within their home jurisdiction but also cross-border. The big Spanish banks have been overexposed to Portugal, and without an immediate loan of over €100 billion[3] (US$145 billion) by euroland and the IMF, Portugal might well go bankrupt. When it comes to exposure, a similar question can be asked of pensions funds. Several countries who struggled to fund themselves put their hands into their pension-fund pockets, posing the question, 'Who is supporting whom?'

Alliances are formed out of both greed and misery. 'Help me to help you,' said US President Barack Obama to the 13 top bankers he invited to the White House on March 27, 2009 (more about this in

Chapter 12). The miscreants met their benevolent sovereign, and they knew they were off the hook. The way Simon Johnson and James Kwak put it:

> The Wall Street banks are the new American oligarchy ...
>
> Over the past thirty years, they had become one of the wealthiest industries in the history of the American economy, and one of the most powerful forces in Washington ...
>
> The *ideology* of Wall Street ... became the consensus position[4]

This collusion between sovereigns and banks is unhealthy. The former depend on the latter for cash, while the latter are counting on the government to save them from bankruptcy by using taxpayers' money. The global banking system is still faced with the unsustainable burden caused by the very risky exposures entered into not only prior to but also during the financial crisis. In early February 2011, as social unrest led to a regime change, it was revealed that of a US$43.3 billion aggregate bank exposure to Egypt (as of end of September 2010) comprised:

- French banks shared among themselves US$17.6 billion,
- British banks, US$10.7 billion,
- Italian banks, US$6.3 billion, and
- American banks, US$5.4 billion.

While banks from 18 countries were exposed to Egypt, those from the four countries listed carried among themselves the 80 percent of debt capital and French banks were exposed to the Egyptian government for nearly half that amount. In addition, when taken together, Egypt's foreign debt and the upheaval that led to the ousting of President Hosni Mubarak's (at the cost to the economy of an estimated US$400 million per day) justifies the dictum that countries can become bankrupt in a matter of weeks if the markets close to them.

There is plenty of evidence that countries, including Western countries, are not free from that kind of risk. Greece and Ireland are just the first examples. The real problem is much more fundamental and widespread, but is underestimated by chiefs of state, finance ministers and central bankers. The most basic problem confronting the West these days lies in comparative disadvantages that derive from:

- an anemic economy overburdened with unaffordable entitlements,
- nineteenth-century social policy, which is unsustainable in the modern economy,

- other comparative disadvantages such as high labor costs and structural inefficiencies,
- the irresponsible spending of scarce money, from recapitalizing banks to bombing Libya,[5]
- long-standing threats to competitiveness by developing nations, and
- an overburdening bureaucracy at all levels of the economy mixed with intensive lobbying at every hub.

Sprawling government deficits make sad reading, whether we are talking about the USA or the EU. In both cases, sovereign credit concerns continue to linger because of extremely high budget deficits. In 2010, the negative budget balance was 10 percent in Spain and 9 percent in France (though 'only' 5 percent in Italy and 4 percent in Germany). Ireland topped them all with an unprecedented 32 percent as a result of the torrent of money it threw at its problem banks.

In the USA the Federal Reserve adopted a policy of rapidly monetizing the Treasury's stock of debt – misnamed as quantitative easing (QE) (see Chapter 12) – by printing money to buy it. As in the case of Japan, the US government's costs of funds remained artificially depressed by means of rock-bottom interest rates, but many economists think that the strain will be taken by both the forex market and inflation.

With the 2007–12 crisis, Western sovereigns rushed to pull out of the financial abyss the big global banks that had slipped there because of their faults. These were (and still are), however, institutions that had reached the point of *non-viability* and their financial health cannot be restored by throwing public money at the problem.

The bail-ins of taxpayers and investors

Government overspending and life support for self-wounded banks were exceptional cases 20 years ago, but at the time of writing, they can be found all over Europe and America. Growing government deficits spread like an epidemic. There are more pensioners, health care is more expensive, more bank governance is needed, and more money is spent without a thought about return on investment (ROI). Since the bursting of Japan's bubble in 1991/2 its banks have consolidated but also remained on the sick list, its equities market suffered more than a two-thirds decline, the value of its real estate caved in by 70 percent, and its industrial companies fought a rearguard action to retain their markets.

How fast and how far one can go under is further documented by the fact that Japan used to be synonymous with the export of consumer electronics. But after the economy's decline in the 1990s and the first decade of the twenty-first century Japan became a net importer of televisions, stereos and other mainstay audio-visual products, as industry data suggest.

This trade gap reflects the weakening grip of Japanese manufacturers on the global consumer electronics market, and shifting business strategies that have seen companies move production overseas to cope with an overvalued yen.

At the same time, a near-zero interest rate policy practiced for far too long by the Bank of Japan has given rise to a carry trade that is very profitable to international speculators, but not to the Japanese. A yield of 1.2 percent is not attractive to investors, while foreigners run a significant currency risk in taking on yen denominated assets. The Japanese sovereign is at pains to roll over its gigantic pile of debt, which at the time of writing amounts to an estimated 20 times the state's revenues. Every 1 percent change in the weighted average cost of capital for the Japanese government is nearly equal to 25 percent of its tax revenue,[6] and by the end of 2012 even a small rise in interest rate costs could be fatal to the government's ability to pay its bills, and yet this rise is inevitable.

At the same time, however, the banking crisis is far from being over. In mid-April 2011, the IMF warned about the precarious state of European banks, the British banks' significant exposure to property loans, and the fact that billions of the credit institutions' debts will be maturing over the next two years. Banks imprudent enough to neglect the urgent need for recapitalization are finding out belatedly that, while market liquidity is high, at close to zero interest rates, capital is as scarce as hens' teeth, and making bondholders pay for the economy's and the banks' own mismanagement is not necessarily a brilliant idea.

The relatively recent concept of *bail-ins* was explained in Chapter 4 in connection to contingent convertible instruments. In this section we shall look at contrary opinions. Bailed-in with contingent convertibles (CoCos) will be investors who made a deliberate decision to buy these instruments. In contrast, taxpayers were bailed-in against their will (and against any good sense) when sovereigns created the (wrong) policy of salvaging big global banks that were too big to be saved.

An argument frequently heard recently is that bail-ins were invented following public anger because investors who lent the money that enabled banks to gamble in trading and make bad loans have so far suffered very little. Lawyers, however, warn of a highly confused situation before a court of law, because bail-ins are not traditional bankruptcies, which have strict rules and a court-supervised process that sees creditors ranked in order of repayment precedence.[7]

A bail-in would happen before bankruptcy, with regulators having the power to impose losses on bondholders while leaving untouched other creditors of a similar stature. 'The idea that within the class you could discriminate at someone's discretion is very scary,' said Richard Holden, an insolvency partner at Linklaters.[8] Other legal experts warn against thinking a bail-in will be a sort of treatment for banks falling on hard times.

As the careful reader will recall, a bail-in emulates the financing of a restructuring plan agreed by its creditors *ex ante*, with results being imposed by a pre-established protocol. Over a very short period, creditor claims against the bank would be reduced and CoCo bond holders will be in the front line of losses in a similar way to equity owners.

This is a very significant change for bond investors who traditionally enjoyed more freedom of action. Even if today there is a demand for the early issues of CoCos, investors burned in a bail-in cannot be expected to rush to buy contingent instruments again, just as a bank suffering a run and being taken into regulatory care would not be able to obtain loans from other banks. Nor will confidence be reinstated quickly, even if the wounded bank's core Tier 1 capital were to rise to 25 percent.

In addition, banks whose unwise rescue consumed an inordinate amount of public money might not find willing investors for a bail-in no matter what amount of interest they pay. An example is the Irish Nationwide Building Society (not a major player) whose bail-out consumed €2.3 billion paid by the Irish government. (The bank is now under state control, but in the future will probably be re-privatized and re-mismanaged.) Another, even greater, disaster with an insatiable appetite for public money has been the Allied Irish Bank.[9]

Complaining in particular about the eventual bondholders' pain will be those investors who buy CoCos of banks that typically finance most of their lending through bonds. If the risks of bond investors rise they will charge higher interest rates, with the result that the banks' borrowing costs rise and this rise will be priced into the costs of mortgages and other loans. This is one of the basic arguments lobbyists are using against bail-ins.

Those who support the thesis that pain should be shared (the *pros*), answer that there is nothing wrong with all shareholders participating in the losses created by a downturn. And they add that the broader concept of bail-in is deeper – partly borrowed from sovereign debt restructuring, which might include a sovereign's selective default on various classes of its obligations. Critics respond that sovereign debt investors may find that they are simultaneously being bailed-out and bailed-in.

In the opinion of those promoting them, bail-ins are a concept contributing to the control of system risk, intended to allow banks to fail while still maintaining financial stability – at no cost to the taxpayer. By reducing the par value of the senior debt of a troubled bank, regulators hope they will have an easier time steering it toward solvency.

Critics say that bail-ins have the potential to catalyze a bank run. Therefore, loss-absorbing contingent capital (see also Chapter 4) is going to become *concern capital* and, depending on incentives, it may even trigger at an early stage while the bank is still a going concern.

These two opposite viewpoints might come close if one were to project credit substitution together with visible sovereign action. According to some experts, the latter will continue being essential to crisis containment and in particular the restoration of confidence. Nevertheless this is not the prevailing opinion.

Another school of thought would like to see a two-step approach implemented, with clauses included in bail-in indentures reflected in pricing to different levels of risk capital. Higher-interest bail-in options could be invoked as a first resort in terms of bank resolution – while 'senior' bail-in bonds paying less interest would be triggered as a last resort.

A two-step approach can provide regulators (and bankers) with greater flexibility, but the bigger question is whether bail-ins at large could help the authorities to contain a banking crisis. They have not yet done so to date with the 2007–12 crisis, despite the fact that it has now been raging for some four years, and trillions have been spent through a fire brigade approach with taxpayers' money. Bail-ins, guarantees, work-outs, credit substitution and other procedures may make nice reading but they are not the universal remedy for financial ills. They are only one of the treatments, and on their own they make a rather small contribution.

It is therefore not unreasonable to think that the bail-in debate and sovereign-related action will continue to hang over the market. It is not possible to see with any real clarity how this issue will translate into solid regulatory rules without the experience gained from years of implementation and, most important, court decisions in different jurisdictions.

The biggest problem is the mass effect

When, in the late nineteenth century, the Bank of England saved Barings Bank from bankruptcy (damaged by the default of municipalities in the USA and other loans) this was a once-in-a-century case. Indeed, it is still featured in the annals of finance and the economy as an extraordinary event.[10]

These days, such formerly extraordinary events have become daily business, with all this means in moral hazard. As common citizens wait for the government's State Supermarket[11] to take care of all their wants through *entitlements* and free services for everybody, private banks expect the sovereign to feed them with public money no matter what mistakes they make.

After its 2008 bail-out through a massive injection of public money, Citigroup split itself into a *good bank* and a *bad bank* under the same holding. The bad bank still represents 20 percent of its assets and accounts for a third of its capital requirements. Add to this Royal Bank of Scotland and Commerzbank (which followed a similar policy) as well as HSBC (which was not bailed out but is running down a ring-fenced portfolio of sour housing loans in America), and bad-bank assets in these four institutions alone amount to nearly US$1 trillion (more on bad banks in Chapter 12).

All this alchemy has become necessary because at the time of writing banks are so often getting into big trouble. The reasons for doing so in such a massive way are lust, greed and carelessness, and such cases are multiplying. Since nobody has ever been punished for wrongdoing in this modern age, there could be no other outcome even if the sources of banks' financial troubles have somewhat changed. In the early part of the twenty-first century they were subprime mortgages, household loans and derivatives, but now, more than ten years into the century, the bulk of losses come from commercial property as well as from consumer loans and derivatives.

US commercial mortgage maturities are expected to peak in 2013, and as borrowers are not in the best of financial health, there is a widespread fear in the market that banks will foreclose on insolvent borrowers and start a fire sale. The banks themselves are projected to have in 2013 their own peak of loans to pay or to rollover (if they qualify for new loans), followed by life insurance companies and plenty of other institutions. That is why, in my book on *Sovereign Debt Crisis*,[12] I projected that the real depth of the crisis will most probably come in 2014.[13]

In addition, most credit institutions expect continued heavy write-downs in 2011, though they also hope to see an improvement after that. This improvement may well be smoke and mirrors, however. Citi's bad bank shrinks by only 10 percent a year as 'assets' mature. Only by the end of the second decade of the twenty-first century it might be out of the tunnel *if* new loads of pseudo-assets are not added to current ones.

Over and above serving wounded 'assets' come the requirements posed by new capital rules. European banks may need €355 billion (US$515 billion) according to a new stress scenario from the European Central Bank. Worse yet, this may well be an underestimate because, like the first stress test, the second has been very mild.

Precisely because British regulators want the banking industry to survive they are demanding a significant increase in capital mandated by Basel III (which by any count is inadequate). At stake with higher capital requirements is *return on equity* (ROE), the traditional measure of bank profitability. In the grand casino years of 2004–7, ROE hit 20 percent.

According to analysts at Morgan Stanley, Basel III rules and other regulatory changes are projected to lop off some 7 percentage points from the 13 percent average ROE achieved in 2010.[14] Banks could do better than that if they recast their business models, essentially by taking even more risks; or, alternatively, the math could be made to lie, and this is precisely what British regulators don't want to see. They want the big global banks to put on the table higher equity ratios than baseline Basel III capital, and because of this they are coming under attack by the banks, investors and international peers chiding the Bank of England and the FSA over their (correct) stance on bank capital.

Particularly objectionable to those who would like to see the financial earthquake repeated, is a proposal by a Bank of England advisor, calling for the doubling of new internationally agreed capital ratios. This idea of higher capital ratios appears to have gained ground. Lord Turner, chairman of the

FSA, has stated that large, systemically important financial institutions must hold additional core capital beyond that internationally implied by Basel III.

To appreciate the reasons for this stance, the reader must think of the €355 billion capital gap projected by the ECB, which is very conservative. Other estimates of the capital gap of European banks put it at more than €1 trillion and apply the golden rule that, when there are many unknowns in a budget, what the financial plan foresees will often be doubled.[15] Nobody has yet found out where the money will come from, and it is unlikely that the answer will be from investors happy to be bailed-in.

Not only there are so many cash-hungry mouths of banks and sovereigns to be fed with good money, but in the global courtyard there also are more and more, larger and larger financial entities. In terms of their size, it is enough to point out that each of the better-known global banks is bigger than the majority of UN member states. Governments and banks compete for cash wherever they can find it, and sovereigns are peddling their bonds in the capital market, as well as borrowing from credit institutions.

Take Italy and Lehman Brothers as examples. At the time it descended into the abyss, Lehman's exposure amounted to about US$600 billion. On January 1, 2011, Italy's debt was roughly €2 trillion, or US$2.7 trillion at the then prevailing exchange rate. Other things being equal, as measured on an economic Richter scale, if it becomes bankrupt Italy's impact on the global financial market could be 4.5 times as great as Lehman's.

Outstanding credit default swaps (CDSs) positions and spreads provide a fairly dependable pattern of sovereigns' strengths and weaknesses. It is interesting to note that investors have taken out more insurance against default by Italy than for any other country. In notional principal amounts:

- Italy leads the pack with US$28.5 trillion and a spread of 180 basis points (bp),
- Germany, Brazil and Spain follow with about US$15 trillion in CDSs each, but their spread varies widely. It is only 43 bp for Germany, 117 bp for Brazil and 206 bp for Spain (worse than for Italy),
- France (with a smaller economy than Germany) has about US$13 trillion and a spread of 71 bp, and
- the UK features slightly over US$10 trillion in CDSs and a spread of 73 basis points.[16]

Like Greece, Portugal and Spain, Italy has missed deadlines for cost-cutting and revenue-raising because of bureaucratic foot-dragging. Pension reform, health care restructuring and the uplift of education to make it more competitive are still awaiting decisive action. The same is true of a program for raising revenues and cutting the budget deficit as a share of GDP (Italy's public debt now amounts to more than 120 percent of GDP, third after Japan and Greece).

Investors doubt if such a huge debt can ever be repaid in full because it is intolerably high. This crisis, however, lies in the future, while currently *Italy's risk* is not worse than that of some big global banks and is much better than that of other euroland members. By mid-April 2011, ten-year government bond yields had hit 13 percent for Greece, over 9 percent for Portugal (and for Ireland), but only about 4 percent for Italy – almost at par with the UK.

This is not comforting news. Banks and sovereigns in the market for money should pray that investors expect no default. If they do, the interest rate they will ask to put money on the table will reach for the stars. And with so many private, public and sovereign entities looking for cash in the market, investors will have plenty of choice in their bets.

Whether the borrower is a big bank or a sovereign, investors will be pricing-in the next risk on the horizon and the next crisis. Of course, if they do so for profligate Italy, Spain, Portugal, Ireland and Greece, it will be silly not to do the same for greedy, over-leveraged big banks.

In conclusion, the purpose of this comparison between cash-hungry mouths is to focus on the fact that artificial dichotomies between new financing schemes for banks and those for sovereigns will not hold for long. At the end of the day, it is the same money markets and capital markets for which debt will be issued, and the same investors who will be asked to come forward with their assets and put them at risk.

There is no alternative to fiscal discipline

Both in America and in Europe falling tax receipts, unsustainable entitlements that keep on increasing, ill-conceived rescue packages for financial institutions and extensive debt-financed economic stimulus programs have led to fiscal deficits that are historically high for peacetime. There is no end in sight to soaring government debt and liabilities amassed by big global financial institutions.

Fiscal discipline is not just the best way, it is the *only* way that could lead us out of the deep trouble in which we find ourselves. 'How deep' was explained by ex-Federal Reserve governor Frederic Mishkin who, on March 28, 2011, said that the 2007–12 economic and banking crisis was worse than the Great Depression in the 1930s.

But, so far at least, in spite of this grim reference to economic real-time, there has been neither fiscal discipline by government nor a return to high standards of credit and prudent trading by banks. Irresponsible statements are still having a field day – such as President Obama's declaration that he will reduce the US deficit by 2031.[17] He did not, of course, bother to explain *how* the deficit will be reduced while it is still going up and new commitments are being made.

All over the world, practically all projections point to the fact that debt ratios will be rising in relation to gross domestic product (GDP). Since the unwise refinancing of private banks with public money, sovereign debt, as a whole, continues to increase and in several countries more than 50 percent of it is held abroad. That has been one of globalization's negatives. At the end of 2010, foreign-held government debt stood at:

- 51.4 percent for France,
- 54.9 percent for Ireland,
- 55.5 percent for Italy,
- 59.9 percent for Portugal and
- 94.2 percent for Greece[18] – a very large amount.

In contrast, the share of government debt held abroad was a manageable 18.5 percent for the UK, rising to 26.7 percent for the USA. It stood at 31.1 percent for Spain, but has increased since the end of 2010 as the Spanish government has been going to the capital markets to finance its new deficits. In addition, Spanish banks have €323 billion (the equivalent of 31 percent of GDP) in loans to property developers. If construction is added to that figure, the Spanish exposure rises to 42 percent of GDP, thus beating Ireland's.

With practically no hope of reversing the situations described in the preceding chapters, all that governments are doing at taxpayers' expense is essentially buying time. One is allowed to ask: time for what? There is only a slim hope that greedy banks or highly indebted economies will become strong and prosperous in a few years – boosting their exports and closing their fiscal and current-account deficits. The new culture is that of spending money, not of creating wealth.

In euroland, for example, the only way to reduce the costs structure of countries inside the common currency is the so-called *internal devaluation*, which requires very slow or nil price and wage growth but fast productivity growth, which in turn means outright declines in prices and wages as well as permanent street demonstrations. But neither politicians nor the public are in the mood to do something for their country. They would rather bet on the (irrational) hope that current debt levels will not increase significantly, and a miracle will make them more acceptable and affordable.

A different way of looking at this issue, however, is that taxpayers have not ended up paying for the mistakes of bankers and politicians – and this evidently includes the debt culture. Debt is treated as if it were a national treasure, even if it hides a swarm of nasty surprises. According to economists, on average, as at December 31, 2010, the Western countries' public debt was 50 percent greater than it was in 2007, and more than 200 percent higher than the average debt burden in emerging countries.

Such a profligate spirit has set in at a time when the Western world's growth prospects are deteriorating. With fiscal deficits still widespread and much short-term debt coming due, the sovereigns' needs for financing are rising. A projection by the Institute of International Finance (IFF), the

Washington DC-based financial analysis lab of big global banks, is that, by the end of 2011, America needed to raise over US$4 trillion, European governments collectively required some US$3 trillion, and Japan had to raise funds worth more than 50 percent of its GDP.

That is the same as stating that 2011 was going to experience some severe sovereign debt shock, unless governments take very drastic measures to re-establish fiscal discipline – including significantly reducing entitlements and (at long last) letting self-wounded big banks fail. Neither seems likely. In practice, the only positive sign came in mid-2010 when, to enable them to form a government, the Dutch parties agreed about three things:

- health care costs must be brought down,
- the retirement age had to be raised, from 65 to 67, and
- savings in government spending needed to be in the €15–20 billion (US$16–19 billion) range for 2011.

In contrast, in spite of a recent very modest rise in the retirement age, France still features retirement at 55 for bus drivers and at 60 for everyone else – levels established in 1982 by the populist right-wing politician François Mitterrand, who needed a boost to his credentials as leader of the Socialist Party. (The restructuring of the retirement age by a mere two years by Nicolas Sarkozy was long overdue, but it was still too little and will not come into effect until later in the present decade. But still labor unions revolted and demonstrators blocked streets and clogged traffic, costing other people hardship, time and money.)

All over the Western world short-sighted politicians fail to appreciate that run-away government borrowing crowds out more productive investments. Unprecedented US budgetary deficits ridicule Obama's claim that America needs to 'out-innovate, out-educate and outbuild the rest of the world'. Such generalities, and the men behind them, don't even try to explain how that could be done – or how what is so lightly promised might be funded.

Spend, spend, spend policies aside, governments don't have a stellar record on the effective use of public money. A report by the 2011 World Economic Forum in Davos put America in the 68th position in the world for the effectiveness of its public-sector spending, and other Western governments did not fare so much better either.

Many profligate policies find their origin in failure to count the total cost of an operation and judge the cost/effectiveness of its deliverables before a final decision is made. The Irish government's decision to provide blanket coverage of the debt of Irish banks was by no means an outlier. Nor are similar moves by the American and British governments an exception. What follows is another example of the (many) origins of political risk.

Some economists and financial analysts say that what happened in early 2007 was programmed 14 years earlier under Bill Clinton's presidency.

According to this school of thought, the agent of the coming catastrophe was Roberta Achtenberg, appointed in 1993 as assistant secretary of the Department of Housing and Urban Development.

Here is how Lawrence G. McDonald, a former trader at Lehman Brothers, describes the way that tsunami started: 'citing innate racism as one of the main reasons why banks were reluctant to lend to those without funds ... she set up a national grid of offices staffed with attorneys and investigators ... sometimes threatening, sometimes berating, sometimes bullying'[19] to oblige the banks to provide credit for mortgages to people who were unable to make a down payment and unsure about whether they might be able to service their mortgage in the future.

For the bankers, there was a silver lining as they eventually found that, for business and bonuses, the subprimes were a goldmine. Worthless mortgages were securitized, rated AAA for creditworthiness (rather than the CCC they deserved) and sold to correspondent banks and other financial institutions eager to divide them into new instruments to sell to their clients.[20] The practice was unethical but it produced a swarm of upfront 'profits' which justified extraordinary bonuses for the bankers themselves.

The power and novelty of securitized financial instruments, which made them sell like hot cakes, as well as their high leverage and price volatility, unleashed the destructive power of this high-flying 'business'. To make matters worse, sovereigns, central bankers and regulators adopted a 'wait and see' attitude. An example is Alan Greenspan's arguably naïve view that bubbles in financial markets could not be identified in advance, and even if they could, would prove more costly to pre-empt than to clear up after they had burst.[21]

Contrary to what Alan Greenspan has said, post-mortem bubbles *can* be detected as they build up, proof being that speculators join them. What is needed is vigilance by central bankers, regulators and sovereigns, as well as some powerful risk pricing models. In my book, *Risk Pricing*,[22] I have suggested the use of quantum electrodynamics. This is one of the most advanced theories in the physical sciences, allowing the building of solid models whose employment will be commensurate in sophistication to that of novel financial instruments with their rocketing risks.

Big bank bail-outs have been the ruin of sovereigns

According to estimates which pre-dated the recent severe economic and banking crisis, in the early years of the twenty first century the Venezuelan banking crisis cost 20 percent of that country's gross national product (GNP), and 30 percent of Chilean GNP.[23] In Peru, too, on the heels of the banking crisis triggered by the failure of two credit institutions, the bail-outs and a fiscal crisis represented a great drain on state funds.

The Peruvian government attempted to deal with the growing fiscal deficit by issuing bonds on the global capital market to the tune of US$3.2 billion, thus increasing the country's foreign debt by that amount. To the dismay of the indebted sovereign, the Peruvian debt service has been consuming 25 percent of the national budget.

The message conveyed by these statistics is that heads of state should have known about the dismal after-effects from observing other nations' experience with run-away liabilities, and yet they plunged blindly into similar crises by trying to salvage shot-by-shot their country's entitlements and its self-wounded big global banks. Moreover, neither the central bankers of these sovereigns nor supranational organizations, such as the IMF, rang the alarm bell in time – and this is true all the way to the big bubble that brought down the banking system.

This is what transpires from a critical report from the IMF's own independent evaluation office, published on February 9, 2011. According to this report, the IMF was late in spotting the severe interconnected problems in the Western economies. Almost up to the financial earthquake of Fannie Mae, Freddie Mac, AIG (salvaged at the eleventh hour through US taxpayers' money) and the Lehman bankruptcy, IMF's management was confident that the US had avoided a hard landing.

Many economists and central bankers also adopted the wrong hypothesis, that the worst was behind them. 'Group thinking' limited their ability to identify correctly the mounting risks. IMF's analysis and economic modeling, for example, focused largely on traditional macroeconomic approaches and failed to spot the huge risks building up in financial systems in countries such as America and Britain, according to that report. There was also a naïve admiration of light-touch financial regulation on both sides of the Atlantic, which ended in disaster.

More ominous is the finding by the IMF's independent evaluation office, that the Fund often seemed to champion the American financial sector and the authorities' policies, because its views typically paralleled those of the US Federal Reserve. By contrast, critical voices within the IMF's staff and from outside were ignored because they were not from the mainstream.

What makes the impact of these findings so much more significant is that the same attitude prevailed among central bankers, regulators and government officials in many jurisdictions. Whether this came from the wrong belief that the market can take care of itself – an outdated intellectual approach – or from a shortage of suitable expertise is less important than the fact that those responsible for monitoring systemic risk failed in their mission.

The excuse that they did so in the name and for the sake of free enterprise is not acceptable, because when the crisis hit all their actions were against a free market's basic principles. They did not allow insolvent companies to drop out of the market, thus creating room for new and more capable market players. Instead, they filled the coffers of failing institutions with other people's money.

The principle followed by Western governments in the first decade of the twenty-first century was reminiscent of the Soviet command economy, where a dying institution is helped in every way possible to survive. The moral risk involved jeopardized the stability of the financial system, harmed the national economy and led to contagion.

There is no free market principle which states that individual financial institutions should not collapse, though every care is taken to contain the spread of a fallout. A lesson taught by the result of over-leveraged sovereigns rushing to save over-leveraged banks is that governments threw money at the problem in a state of panic because they had not studied a priori an exit plan.

Only after the crisis hit, did the complexity of unwinding bank failures became one of the key topics discussed at central bank meetings, because it was recognized that rather than being 'too big to fail', mammoth global banks are, on the contrary, 'too big to be saved'. In the meantime, however, bankers were given the message that if they are too big to be allowed to go bankrupt, then, either explicitly or implicitly, taxpayers' money will bail them out and they will be able to continue their business as usual.

One of the problems during the 1990s and 2000s is that, as the banking industry continues to consolidate assets held by banks that are 'too big to fail' this is raising by so much the propensity of sovereigns to come to the global banks' rescue. Opponents to this policy, which makes a mockery of free markets, advocate letting some big banks fail if they deserve to do so – even at the risk of some short-term financial problems.

According to the views of true free-market advocates, this is the only means of eliminating the general perception that large banks will receive special treatment if they become troubled. And let us not forget that bank bail-outs are by no means risk free. They have many hazards, and there is an ongoing discussion as to which way the risk are greater: on the failure side or in the salvage.

A not insignificant number of central bankers fear that widespread bank failures will trigger a financial crisis that will destroy the global financial fabric. But opponents of salvage operations using public money point out that this has created a most curious *big business entitlement*, with private firms as beneficiaries, and over and above that it presents a moral hazard.

In turn, this moral hazard ensures that financial irresponsibility has developed into a fundamental problem associated with the fact that the resolution or restructuring of complex global financial groups is confronted by diverse laws and regulations in the different jurisdictions in which they operate. Globalization has created significant home–host supervisory challenges (Chapter 7).

A critical issue closely linked to a suitable crossborder resolution mechanism is who will pay for this: only the shareholders (and perhaps the sovereigns) in the country of origin or those in the jurisdictions in which it operates, as well as possibly where the bank has local investors. Also, how much should the financial industry as a whole contribute to these costs? Should transborder banks contribute to deposit insurance schemes in different jurisdictions? Should they include different jurisdictions as beneficiaries in their living wills?[24]

As the case of British and Dutch operations by Icelandic banks that collapsed demonstrates, deposit insurance costs matter, and who pays for other peoples' misbehavior or incompetence is a critical issue that has to be confronted head-on. Despite all sorts of assurances that bankers 'have learned a lesson from the current deep crisis' and that regulators will be 'smarter and more alert', big global institutions (and many other banks) are certain to get into trouble again, as they always have done. The way to protect taxpayers is to compel banks to have capital reserves and liquidity deep enough to withstand higher losses and longer freezes in financial markets (see above).

It would be unwise to forget that the record of bank capital rules is very poor, because no sooner have those rules have been confirmed than banks begin to play the system – as they did with Basel I and Basel II. Unreliable financial reporting is another headache. Five days before its bankruptcy, Lehman Brothers allegedly boasted a Tier 1 capital ratio of 11 percent. That was a big lie, but regulators chose not to apply the Sarbanes–Oxley Act, which would have brought its CEO and CFO to court and from there (most likely) to prison.

Taken together, the failure to observe and honor established capital rules by the banks' big brass, and the political will's failure to apply the law of the land, have created a nightmare for bank supervisors: if they have already tried and failed to make capital rules foolproof, why should they do better this time? If governments are ready to spend public money to rescue self-wounded institutions and let wrongdoers go free, why should they worry about being too slack in their supervisory duties?

In the drifting economy of the State Supermarket in which Western economies have landed,[25] it is pathetic to see sovereigns trying to be everything to every person and to every company. Instead, what is needed is disciplining business behavior, while minimizing the burden on taxpayers. Instead of throwing money to the four winds, sovereigns should pay attention to growing social ills such as severe income disparities.[26]

Forward, backward and forward again in financial regulation

The banks have been helped, with taxpayers' money, to recover from their own errors and misjudgments. Up to a point, but only up to a point, this might have been necessary because banks play a vital role in the economy, even if they had engaged in irresponsible activities. In the USA, banks benefited from different government programs – TARP being one of them (see Chapter 12). It is therefore proper that Congress and the government take back some of the enormous economic cost the banks have caused to society. But this is not to the liking of the big global banks, which raise massive objections through their stable of lobbyists and political friends.

Globally, banks battle against Basel III. Even if they have failed to provide convincing opposition to reforms by the Basel Committee for Banking Supervision, they have succeeded in trimming several of the Basel III provisions (as we have seen from Chapter 4 onward) – and in several cases they did so in partnership with governments, particularly in downsizing regulatory capital.

There was a time when such an adverse reaction to rules and regulations by those who should be subject to supervision activities was unthinkable. Like so many other processes, however, bank regulation is no longer what it used to be, and lobbying is the reason for this change, as documented in Chapter 2.

A hundred years of regulatory history in the USA provides evidence on how a determined government can get results. The first stepping stone was the 1913 Federal Reserve Act, which created the US central bank.[27] It was followed in 1933 by the Banking Act known as Glass–Steagall, after its authors, which introduced federal deposit insurance (see Chapter 12) and segregated commercial from investment banking. Also in 1933 came the Securities Act, which improved financial disclosure as well as requiring that securities sold across state borders be registered with the federal government.

A year later, in 1934, Congress voted in the Securities Exchange Act, which created the Securities and Exchange Commission (SEC). In 1940, the Investment Company Act came into force, in response to a wave of Ponzi schemes. This gave the SEC authority over mutual funds. Three decades later, in 1970, the Securities Investor Protection Act was passed. This created a body of safeguards protecting private accounts, and established financial responsibility rules at securities firms.

In 1974, the Commodity Futures Trading Commission Act was enacted, creating the CFTC to regulate futures markets. But after that, the pendulum swung the other way: in 1980 came the Depository Institutions Deregulation and Monetary Control Act, which deregulated savings account interest rates and enforced minimum capital requirements for banks. The cost of Depository Institutions deregulation hit the American taxpayers to the tune of US$800 billion as savings and loans (thrifts, savings banks) turned themselves into junk bond fans. This and other scams led many of them into bankruptcy and some of their bosses to prison.

What happened with the thrifts provided evidence that new legislation may demolish what previous laws had provided. In terms of moving backward, though, nothing really competes with the damage created by the 1999

Financial Services Modernization Act (Gramm–Leach–Bliley) which – with Bill Clinton's signature – repealed Glass–Steagall, allowing commercial banks, investment banks and insurers to merge or acquire one another.

This unwarranted lowering of regulatory fencing initiated the big stakes in banking games and speculations. Another disastrous piece of legislation was the 2000 Commodity Futures Modernization Act, which exempted OTC derivatives from government oversight, doing so while the stockmarket's earthquake was shaking the US economy and public confidence all the way to its roots.

Engineered by pretty much the same demolition squad of politicians, the 1990s and 2000 deregulations were an unmitigated disaster for the American economy. But the pendulum swung again in the opposite direction after the Enron, WorldCom and other scams, which had profited greatly from these deregulations. In 2002 the Public Company Accounting Reform and Investor Protection Act, Sarbanes–Oxley (SOX) was passed in response to Enron's bankruptcy.[28] SOX

- overhauled corporate governance,
- made the CEO and CFO responsible for their company's financial statements, and
- strengthened the role of auditors in overseeing accounting procedures.

With regard to banking legislation, the notable event of 2010 was the Wall Street Reform and Consumer Protection Act (FINREG; Dodd–Frank Act; see Chapter 1). In the original bills by Senator Dodd and Representative Frank, the proposed financial reforms aimed at avoiding future government bail-outs of 'too big to fail' financial institutions that had run into trouble and were (unwisely) rescued through massive amounts of taxpayers' money. The underlying concept has been to avoid 'repetition of the same' by creating a resolution regime which would assure that those who take hits are shareholders and bondholders – not taxpayers.

As with Basel III, however, the big banks lobbied aggressively for changes, to water down plans to ban deposit-taking institutions from conducting any proprietary trading, as well as a list of other risky trades. The Act gave SEC a boost and authorized the CFTC to take action on derivatives.

Another provision of the Dodd–Frank Act was that banks with more than US$100 billion of assets will be overseen by the Federal Reserve. This was judged as a regulatory reform representing partial victory for the central bank after months of criticism in Congress about the way it handled the economic crisis. Critics of this particular measure, however, have said that it compromises the central bank's independence (see also Chapter 12).

FINREG also pressed on with a new resolution regime aimed at dealing systematically with important institutions that are failing. In doing so, it aimed to allow the government to wind up a credit institution quickly to avoid contagion spreading through the financial system. It was designed to prevent the repeat of highly costly bail-out, in the style of Fanny Mae, Freddie Mac and AIG. Only time will tell whether this goal has been attained.

The bad news is that because of intensive lobbying by the banking industry, not every outstanding problem in the financial industry was addressed by FINREG. Hedge funds are still able to follow the course they choose with minimal or no supervision, offshores have virtual immunity from regulation, and the wisdom of following universal accounting standards (see Chapter 10) has not been promoted, even if a globalized economy makes this a 'must'.

As for capital adequacy and liquidity, this has been Basel III's remit. Chapter 4 highlighted part of the big global banks' negative reaction to Basel III. One of the lobbyists-and-governments campaigns against Basel III, which was left to this chapter to cover, is that, against Basel's proposal that banks stop counting minority-owned stakes as part of their equity capital, but they continue to recognize the entire potential losses of any subsidiary.

What regulators have essentially been saying is that banks need to depend on their country-of-origin capital and they should expand as far as this allows them to go. Among central banks, the Bank of Italy has made clear it is not happy with the rule, writing that it expected the Basel Committee to consider partially recognizing minority interests. The French and German governments joined in the chorus and eventually minority owned stakes were partially recognized.

This is counterproductive in financial stability terms, because there were good reasons behind the concept of tightening the capital rules for subsidiaries that are partly owned by outside investors. It would have stopped banks from including the equity they hold in subsidiaries as minority owners in the core Tier 1 capital ratio.[29] The negative aspect has been that this came at a time when banks needed to raise more funds to meet regulators' demands. Regulators answered the banks' complaints by saying that discounting minority interest stakes makes sense because a bank could be fully liable for its subsidiaries' losses. In contrast, minority-owned equity might not support losses elsewhere in the financial conglomerate.

A totally unjustified reaction by big global banks to Basel III rules has been that they and their customers 'would be harmed' by higher capital ratios. That complaint is widely shared in the banking industry and is a red herring. Low capital reserves are harmful because banks take so many risks. Leverage ratios of over 30 are common, and this means that even small variations in asset values can turn into disasters. If big global banks cannot rely on governments to save them, they should carry large capital buffers to protect themselves against losses and drops in confidence.

Equally important is where and how banks hold their assets. Those who say that a quarter of their assets is in 'low-risk, liquid form', such as government bonds simply forget that sovereigns can become bankrupt. Since

Basel III aims to remedy past failures, the definition of capital has to be much stricter. Indeed, there should only be pure equity in Tier 1. At the same time, risk accounting should not be dependent on the bank's own internal models because this makes it so easy to play the system.

Risks taken on by gamblers acting legally inside the system

In a far-sighted article published in April 2010, well before the Basel III rules took shape, Martin Wolf, the *Financial Times'* senior economist, warned that:

> the real catastrophe ... is the risk taken on by the gamblers working legally inside the machine ... big institutions are, at one and the same time, the house, the biggest players at the gambling tables, agents for the other players and, if all goes wrong, beneficiaries of limited liability and implicit and explicit government bail-outs.[30]

In one paragraph, Wolf encapsulated

- the situation we are in,
- the big casino of the modern economy,
- the fact that embezzlement has been legalized, and
- the reason for that is that sovereigns and bankers support one another during the good times, and in bad times the taxpayer foots the bill – not just once but many times over.

With legal hazard being so widespread, the reasons for fair play have weakened. Let's start with the so often toted consumer protection that so many governments talk about. The best protection is provided not by voting in new laws that remain dead letters, but by informing the citizen about the *downside of debt*. Governments don't do this because they are themselves so much in debt, yet citizen have a right to know about the unexpected consequences of new financial instruments, the fact that leverage kills assets, and that employment in the global economy can in no way be guaranteed.[31]

Debt's downside is spelled out by these three points, and its after-effects are no different, whether we speak of families, banks or sovereigns. Because for a large number of cases the decision to become leveraged is deliberate, it is appropriate to appreciate *ex ante* that everyone is responsible for his/her own acts and on no condition should the many pay for the greed and errors of the few.

As far as big global banks are concerned, this explaining by central banks and governments should be done *now*, because when banks start to make money again they will pay it out in bonuses. They will not hold on to it. This is written in full appreciation of the fact that top managements in credit institutions are not inclined to listen. They should, however, pay attention to the Bank of England's recent financial stability report, which argues (correctly) that the least painful way for banks to build up the capital they need under Basel III is by retaining more of their earnings.

As the careful reader will recall from this book's previous chapters, it has been a major mistake (and a great weakness of Basel III) to give banks until 2019 to build up their capital to the newly required levels. Such a 'long grace period' will not really be to allow banks to rebuild that capital gradually, though, but rather to continue business as usual, which means gambling and paying oversized bonuses.

It is ridiculous but true that outsize bonuses and the depth of the economic crisis are correlated. In 2001, Wall Street firms paid US$13.0 billion in bonuses, which is a lot of money. This was reduced by about 30 percent to US$9.8 billion in 2002, but rose to US$15.8 billion in 2003, US$18.6 billion in 2004, US$25.6 billion in 2005, and reached an astonishing high-water mark of US$34.3 billion in 2006. Even in 2007, the year of the disaster, US$33 billion was spent on bonuses; reducing to US$17.6 billion in 2008 (in the depth of the crisis) but rose again to US$22.5 billion in 2009 and stood at US$20.4 billion in 2010[32] in spite of governments prompting the big banks to reason, and the wide public outcry against spending through sovereign debt to feed lust and greed.

This is no time for complacency. At a time when the US Treasuries have been downgraded to a negative outlook,[33] both bankers and government officials should worry that while the financial industry improved its ability to absorb losses compared to the 2008–9 first dip of the crisis, the interconnectedness of the global banking system will amplify losses when a new financial earthquake hits the markets.

Moreover, by all indications this new financial earthquake is not going to wait until after 2019, when Basel III comes in full swing. My guess is that it will take place in 2014, give or take a year. When it happens, it will hit with force those banks that don't have enough equity commensurate to their liabilities – and, as the Lehman Brothers failure has shown, normal bankruptcy procedures do not work for complex institutions. Instead, they take along with them plenty of investors and other institutions as the contagion spreads.

Therefore, in the article mentioned above, Martin Wolf advised that it is wise to ensure that banks hold a large stock of assets that are not too complex to value by lenders of last resort. He also (aptly) made the point that attached to trading strategies are easy gains and easy losses. This in itself is a basic reason why regulators should impose much higher capital and collateral requirements against trading in derivatives.[34]

Bankers typically answer that there is nothing to worry about, because they know what they are doing. But do they? There are reasons to doubt that they do, even with regard to long-established product lines. Some years ago, Deutsche Bank founded its own insurer but discovered that it was not easy to develop. Therefore it bought Deutscher Herold, a well-known insurance firm, only to discover that it was not easy to run. To solve its problem, Deutsche Bank exchanged Deutscher Herold for the asset management of Zurich Insurance.

A very similar story happened with Allianz Insurance, which bought Dresdner Bank only to discover that it was not easy to run a commercial and investment bank. So it exchanged Dresdner Bank for the asset management operations of Commerzbank.[35] The moral of these stories is that nobody knows exactly how a financial company will perform in the future even in a domain very similar to the one in which it traditionally operates. Think what can happen when many unknowns increase the complexity of management decisions, and the financial institution is highly leveraged, thin in equity capital, loaded with liabilities and lacking cash.

There is an almost unlimited supply of examples of errors of judgment by the banking industry. High loss severity estimates are not only connected to subprimes and Alt-As[36] but also to consumer loans and credit cards. In 2009, for US banks, consumer loans represented an estimated cumulative 11 percent of the loan book, which means billions of dollars in red ink.[37]

The question raised by these statistics is the quality of judgment of those who establish loan objectives and approve these loans. The reader should also notice that most of the above loans have been securitized, sold to investors who lost plenty of money with them, and contributed the lion's share of the reason behind the deep economic crisis we are in at the time of writing.

The events that preceded and followed the descent to the abyss in 2007 and subsequent years, leave no doubt that regulators are right when they impose higher capital requirements on big global banks. 'We want to preserve the freedom to go beyond the absolute minimums – in particular in relation to our approach to systematically important banks,' said Lord Turner, chairman of the FSA in an interview prior to his annual policy speech to City of London bankers.[38]

Lord Turner was right when he said in this interview that the economy would not be immune to delays in making banks safer. Preventing the next crisis would probably require making unpopular decisions today. Raising capital requirements has never been a cozy affair, while not doing so immediately is tantamount to inviting systemic risk.

If the needed changes are being trimmed and supervisory authorities as well as accounting standards bodies and other government agencies agree to long implementation delays, then we are talking of *regulatory risk*, which should not be confused with *market disruption risk*. The latter refers to the potential for major disruptions in activities such as market making and price quoting. The effects of *regulatory risk* can be wide, deep and long-lasting.

12
What Is the Point of Central Banks' Interventions?

The independence of central banks is a myth

There is a saying in the financial industry that, while central bankers have not been perfect, politicians have been worse. When governments took responsibility for decisions that should have been made by the central banks, or dominated central banking policies, they created a devastating inflation that:

- Destroyed savings,
- Distorted incentives, and
- Imposed the worst sort of taxation on the whole population.

Governments have also proved themselves incapable of maintaining a balanced budget. Investors in government debt who have a short memory of the sovereign's profligate policies, frequently assumed that any deficit in the government's accounts would be temporary and ultimately be made good. But with only rare exceptions, the striking feature since the 1980s in Western countries has been the persistence of (and steady increase in) government deficits.

It looks as if Western governments want to prove that Lenin was right when he stated his famous dictum that the most effective way to destroy a society is to destabilize its currency. Critics say that, because of their policies, sovereigns are displaying cognitive dissonance in economic and financial matters, the worst case being that they have taken the central bankers along with them. That is the only way to explain

- steady fiscal deficits,
- very low interest rates over long periods of time, and
- quantitative easing, whereby the central bank prints money to buy government debt because nobody else wants it.[1]

On March 2, 2011, in an interview with *Bloomberg News*, Bill Gross of Pimco stated that foreign investors (unnamed but probably China, Japan and Germany) had bought roughly a third of US government bonds. And since nobody else wanted them the Fed was printing massive money to buy the other two-thirds.

In the short term, rising public deficit crowds out corporate bonds. In the medium- to longer term, as sovereign bond yields fall massively, investors keep away from them. This has a direct effect on the financial industry as banks mark down their holdings of government debt that has lost value. It also creates a vicious cycle, as the downgrading of sovereigns raises their funding costs. Such events reinforce negative feedback loops between the financial and real economy sectors, and have an adverse impact on economic factors as well as on the stability of the financial system.

Even as a warning about potential channels of contagion, this vicious cycle has two other after-effects with a longer-term impact. It drives home the message that, in the absence of significant fiscal tightening, the economy will continue to deteriorate. And it raises the question as to how independent central banks really are.

These days, the main reason for this question about Western central bank independence is their controversial decision to buy government bonds to calm unsettled debt markets. While the Fed, and to lesser extent the ECB, say that what they are doing is injecting liquidity into the financial system[2] and capping the potential rise in interbank funding costs, the reality is quite different. Central banks help the sovereigns to continue to be profligate.

Jean-Claude Trichet, the president of the ECB, half admitted this when, in early 2011, he said that the monetary institution cannot solve the problems of euroland governments for them. (This was most likely said with reference to Portugal, whose government's bonds the ECB continued to buy.) In contrast, Ben Bernanke has not even bothered to explain why he sticks to a policy which destabilizes the dollar and keeps it on a course of steady decline.

If central banks were truly independent, they would not have rigged the yield curve, keeping short-term rates artificially low and inducing banks to make money by buying longer-dated government bonds, as well as engaging in direct purchases of sovereign debt. This is a dangerous policy which produces a severe risk with regard to the monetary institution's independence. It also raises two most basic queries: Has central bank independence been genuine? Or has it been nothing more than a myth?

'The actions of the Reserve System depend on whether there are a few persons in the system who exert intellectual leadership and who these people are,' says Milton Friedman. 'Its actions depend not only on the people who are nominally the heads of the system but also on such matters as the fate of particular economic advisors.'[3]

In 1920, Benjamin Strong was the Master of the US Central Bank, albeit from his position as president of the New York Fed. In the recent history of the Federal Reserve, Arthur Burns and Paul Volcker were strong leaders of the Fed. Alan Greenspan and Ben Bernanke, particularly Bernanke, have been weak chairmen – and therefore the Fed's policies have drifted.

To prove his thesis that *personalities* rather than *statutes* make a difference, Friedman has taken as an example Emile Moreau, the governor of Banque de France from 1926 to 1928. Over that period, France established a new (and lower) parity for the franc as well as returning to the gold standard. Moreau was asked by Raymond Poincaré, the prime minister and former president of the Republic, for a large amount of money that the government needed. Moreau refused.

By statute, the Banque de France was not an independent central bank at the time that this happened, and its governor did not refuse the government's request to leverage it by being based on statute. Indeed, he did not need a statute, because he had the strength of *personality*. Poincaré, the prime minister, also had a strong personality but he accepted Moreau's verdict, probably because he believed the latter was right in refusing the loan. Compare to this Bernanke, George W. Bush, Jr. and Obama.

In direct contradiction to the policy of central bank independence defended by Emile Moreau in the course of the 2007–12 economic crisis, central banks in the Western world have joined governments in misusing public money through stimulating the economy, supporting failing banks and so on – with results that have been widely disappointing. A great deal of newly printed money has been thrown to the four winds. With this sort of unwise subservience to the commands of over-leveraged sovereigns, Western central banks have painted themselves into a corner. They have lost their independence, and when they started to realize that they could not continue to contribute to the currency's instability, they found it difficult to reverse course.

Neither the Federal Reserve nor the Bank of England turned around and adopted prudent monetary policies. For their part, the sovereigns find it difficult to decide what to do next. They are looking for something that is neither risky economically nor hard politically – and they find nothing.

There are no easy choices. Adopting a balance sheet restructuring policy might increase joblessness, leading to higher benefit payments and an adverse public reaction. On the other hand, it is becoming increasingly clear that adding to the debt assures sluggish growth as well as creating a vicious cycle, preventing sovereigns from cutting their deficits significantly.

Belatedly, both politicians and central bankers have come to appreciate that unless there is a rapid recovery, the debt will keep piling on and making the current problems harder to solve. But they find it difficult to decide on the fiscal monetary policy that will right the balances. To help them clear their minds, instead of looking to J. M. Keynes they should have followed Marriner S. Eccles' policies.

Personalities, not scripts, assure central banks' independence

In his book entitled *Inflated*, R. Christopher Whalen gives a first-class American example of what is meant by central bank independence. In 1948, US President Harry S. Truman declined to reappoint Marriner Eccles, a long-standing Fed chairman, appointing instead Thomas McCabe. But when Truman asked the Fed to maintain a cap on interest rates, chairman McCabe refused to do so.

Joined by other members of the Federal Open Market Committee (FOMC), McCabe and Eccles (who was still a Fed governor and member of FOMC) faced off populist political pressures from Treasury secretary John W. Snyder and the president. Their decision was not to support artificially low interest rates.[4] Compare this to what is happening today with the Bernanke Fed.

Eventually (in 1951) McCabe was forced out of the Fed, and Eccles quit. But the new Fed chairman, William McChesney Martin, upheld the central bank's independence. The way McChesney Martin looked at inflation in his acceptance speech, should be required reading by all central bankers and all economists:

> Unless inflation is controlled, it could prove to be an even more serious threat to the vitality of our country than the more spectacular aggressions of enemies outside our borders.[5]

Ben Bernanke had a different schooling. On July 13, 2011, he was quoted as saying that printing money guarantees a good income for the Treasury.[6] This is an evident absurdity because it disregards the mountain of negatives associated with turning the Federal Reserve's presses at high speed – all the way from inflation to destabilizing the dollar.

Nor did the rest of Bernanke's comments that day give a sense of confidence to those who heard them. Everything he said was wrapped in a sheet of 'ifs', and every statement included something and its antithesis, practically weighted on equal likelihood. That is the best way to destroy confidence in financial stability and to pull the rug from under the currency – hitting two birds with one well-placed stone.

It is not the job of the central bank to play 'me too' by subduing monetary policy in an (ill-fated) attempt to help the government maintain a semblance of fiscal balance. The evidence can be found all over as, since 2008, the relaunching of the economy has been a chimera. The refusal to maintain fiscal balance has been a deeply engrained characteristic of less developed countries. Now, it has also become a Western landmark. This is particularly true of democracies, because the people who vote governments 'in' and 'out' are convinced that they are entitled to an ever-increasing standard of living, But, at the same time, they are unwilling to pay for it – while they revolt against huge government deficits.

The result of living way beyond one's means is deficits accumulating at all levels of society: the governments, the corporates and the households. It needs no explanation that the after-effect is a looming hyperinflation whose cost is paid by everybody, particularly by those who are economically weak. The steady erosion of the value of money eats away at the purchasing power of the very consumers who press for more entitlements. This wrong policy is also reducing employment opportunities and longer-term economic growth.

The central flaw in Keynes' thinking, the American economist, Henry Hazlitt, once said, was his unwillingness to acknowledge that the high unemployment in the UK in the 1920s and in the USA in the 1930s, was caused by government intervention, including the empowering of labor unions, which made many prices and wages inflexible. Hazlitt also forecast that the American policy of flooding the world with dollars – through loans, grants and other measures – would not generate wealth in the USA nor in the recipient countries. The events of the first decade of the twenty-first century have proved that Hazlitt was right.

To a very substantial extent, the cases discussed here are political decisions and belong to the realm of the legislative and executive arms of the government. The central bank should play no role in them. But the way that R. Christopher Whales looks at the Fed's actions gives plenty of food for thought:

> In the decades since its creation, the US central bank has evolved into a lobbying and advocacy organ for the banking industry, with Federal Reserve governors and senior officials toying the large bank party line as they testify before Congress... The Fed has come to shield the banking industry from scrutiny by the public and Congress.[7]

Summing up the message conveyed by the above comments, one can see that there were good reasons why Milton Friedman did not believe in the 'independence' of the central bank. He stated, in no uncertain terms, that 'One defect of an independent central bank ... is that it almost inevitably involves dispersal of responsibility ... the central bank is hardly ever the only authority in the government that has essential monetary powers.'[8] In Friedman's opinion, to have not only the form but also the substance of an independent monetary authority, the Fed would have to concentrate all the debt-management powers of the sovereign – including the creation and destruction of government-issued money.

Another technical defect pointed out by Friedman in connection with an independent central bank is that invariably it will strongly emphasize the opinions of a whole coterie of bankers. This happened under the chairmanships of both Greenspan and Bernanke. From the property and junk bond fiasco of the late 1980s, and simultaneous savings and loans debacle, to the stock market crash of 2000 and the deep economic crisis of 2007–12 engineered by SPVs and subprimes, the Fed's independence was compromised by inaction, and taxpayers have ended up footing trillion-dollar bills through a loose monetary policy and the collapse of their investments in real estate.

Economists who are convinced that 'independence' is a myth and not a reality, point out that the reserve banks' powers, as centralized monetary institutions, themselves derive from the government; and therefore from politicians. As such, they are wide open to manipulation by politicians for electoral ends. This introduces a bias toward big spending and inflation – precisely what we are getting these days from 'independent' central banks.

In addition to the reasons presented so far, the independence of the central bankers' monetary policy is also constrained by governments' desire to hold down exchange rates. This forces the monetary institutions to engage in heavy foreign exchange intervention that inflates money supplies. To sum up, the independence of monetary policy is no self-evident truth, its key variables being:

- personalities,
- liquidity constraints,
- credit policies,
- forex policies,
- bubble puncturing policies (when practiced),
- political commitments and pressures, and
- plain old politics beyond immediate political pressures.

A 2007 IMF study ranked 163 central banks according to their political autonomy based on such factors as how officials are appointed, whether interest rates have to be approved by the government and so on. The result demonstrated that emerging countries' central banks have become more independent since the 1980s, though they remain less so than the Fed, the Bank of England or the ECB. Since 2007, however, there have been plenty of reasons to believe that this argument should be revised. Western central banks have not really demonstrated their independence.

Measures by central banks have been ineffectual

A central bank's assessment of its monetary policy stance focuses on the latter's effect on economic, financial and monetary developments. Such an assessment involves an examination of whether the most likely after-effects are in line with the central bank's objective(s), and whether or not they constitute the most effective way of reaching them.

Typically, the best assessment in shaping monetary decisions is broad-based and forward-looking, reflecting long-standing policy principles and experience. It also incorporates all information relevant to the formation of views on opportunities and risks associated with each projected course of action. The alternative is inaction, caused either by a 'wait and see' attitude, indecision, or different conflicting objectives.

Conflicting objectives can create a dangerous situation. The statutes of the Federal Reserve, for example, prescribe two goals: *monetary stability* (by far the most frequent aim of a central bank); and *full employment*. These contradict one another. A loose monetary policy could, up to a point, promote employment, but in contrast, a tight monetary policy constrains the money supply and has a negative effect on employment.

Most important, however, creating employment is a political rather than a monetary decision. Indeed, it is a political decision affected by both social issues and the state of the economy. In the USA, less than 2 percent of the workforce is engaged in agriculture and about 6 percent in manufacturing. Where can new jobs be created when jobs in the service sectors are being eliminated, either by technology or by cost-cutting?

Nor is the strategy 'jobs now, deficits later' making sense – because both missing jobs and growing deficits are permanent rather than temporary challenges. Instead, what is happening as a result of attempting to reconcile conflicting aims are monetary policies that inflict pain on savers, and in particular on seniors.

Central banks have no business replicating the political decisions of governments, and even less in showing the way. Under this perspective should be seen the May 2010 reaction of Axel Weber, then president of Deutsche Bundesbank, who publicly opposed the ECB's decision to start buying the bonds of euroland's profligate countries' governments. Such a policy, he believed, was intruding dangerously into fiscal matters of sovereigns sharing a common currency, and it was doing so without any hope of influencing them.

Though the name of the game is different, there have been important similarities between what the Fed and the ECB have done by buying government debt. The Fed's quantitative easing (QE) bought government bonds with newly printed money, while the ECB's purchasing of Portugal's and other peripheral countries' bonds was fomenting political spending policies, and at the same time steering the central bank into treacherous political waters.

The way a feature article in *The Economist* put it: 'A common theme among the most vocal critics is that QE is some sort of voodoo monetary policy.'[9] The article went on to say that this was nonsense, but it admitted that there are worries about its effects, ranging from the fact it does not work, in fact, sending inflation spiraling. The article also spoke of growing unease within the Fed itself. Tim Hoenig, president of the Federal Reserve

Bank of Kansas City, has recently stepped up his criticism, calling QE a 'bargain with the devil'.

Critics also point out that a government facing the imminent exhaustion of its financial resources should not use the central bank as a milk cow. Rather, it should put its house in order. If it doesn't, the moment will come when it is no longer able to inject cash into the economy without the monetary institution's presses working overtime. Dollars, euros and pounds cannot buy yesterday, nor can they 'buy' a better life tomorrow.

As far as reigniting the economy and making governments more thrifty is concerned, the Fed, the ECB and the Bank of England have been 'pushing on a string' (an expression that is gaining wider usage: if you push on one end of a piece of string, nothing happens at the other end). True enough, the monetary policy of Western central banks face very difficult choices. With the unemployment rate still stuck near recessionary highs and with structural headwinds, some central bankers believe it is much too early to withdraw monetary and fiscal stimuli. But as Milton Friedman aptly put it in his time: a full employment policy leads to inflation, and inflation hurts everybody, particularly those who are economically weak.

The Fed launched a war on deflation by forcing investors to reduce their cash holdings. Subsequently, it engineered asset price reflation, first in bonds, then in equities and commodities. That was the thesis supported by a Bank of America Merrill Lynch commentary[10] as well as by a number of other analysts. From March 2009 to March 2011, which means two reflationary years later:

- global equities doubled,
- inflation expectations rose above 2.5 percent,
- gold reached for the stars, and
- oil prices jumped well above US$110/bbl (for WTI, while for Brent it went beyond US$123/bbl).

The Fed seems to be very relaxed about inflation and is not concerned about the rise in commodity prices, but this is not the way the market looks at these two issues. Not only are investors becoming nervous about the prospect of inflation, which pushes up the price of gold and other dollar-denominated commodities, but they are also jittery about the fact that nearly 70 percent of new Treasury issues are being bought by the Fed through QE, thus ballooning the monetary institution's balance sheet.

In both sides of the Atlantic, central bankers, the public and politicians are suffering from monetary, bail-out and fiscal fatigue. Past stimuli have not worked as intended by igniting strong growth. The argument 'it would have been much worse without the stimulus' is impossible to prove and tends to obscure the fact that a long, painful exit strategy is needed, with an end to bail-outs, a withdrawal of liquidity by the central bank and raised interest rates, and balancing the sovereign budget cannot be achieved without serious deficit reduction requiring shared sacrifices, with cuts in entitlements as well as defense, complemented by tax increases.

It is indeed curious that neither at the sovereign nor at central bank level do the top players appreciate that it is not possible to fight a debt problem with more debt. Japan has tried that unwise strategy intensively and after two decades it has yet to show any signs of success. In addition, it is not possible to fight moral hazard with more massive moral hazard created by the rescue of banks that are too big to be saved.

All this probably forms part of the background that led Henry Sender to publish an article entitled 'Faith in the Bernanke Put Could Be Bad for Your Health'. The Federal Reserve, says Sender, seems bent on driving share prices higher through rates so low that Pimco's Mohamed El-Erian describes them as *confiscatory*; the market is rigged against small investors, and episodes like the May 2010 flash crash provide evidence that 'the deck is stacked against them'.[11] It would have been much better if, rather than trying to save profligate governments, their entitlements and 'dear banks', by superleveraging the money supply, central banks based their advice on IKEA's philosophy of lean operations, shrewd tax planning, and tight management control.

Prime ministers, ministers of finance and central bankers do many things they later regret. A good example is that of Salmon P. Chase who, as Secretary of the Treasury in the Lincoln Administration, issued the greenbacks. Subsequently, as Chief Justice of the US Supreme Court, Chase ruled that constitutional provisions were violated by their issuance.[12]

A similar case exists today with debt, debt and more debt. The market has got the feeling that some dysfunctional, runaway machine has been placed in gear and nobody knows how to stop it.

The 'negative synergy' of monetary policies

Central banks are supposed to be paradigms of virtue, teaching all other banks the importance of knowing what their capital is really worth, of safeguarding their assets, of appreciating their limits and, most important, of being fully in charge of their exposure. Central banks are also expected to be in full control of their balance sheets.

If this had been the case since 2007, it would have been a demonstration of the 'positive synergy' that exists between monetary policy, sound management of financial affairs and the well-being of the economy. Instead, what the economy has got is a 'negative synergy', characterized by the loose monetary policy of the main Western central banks, and the inflation of their balance sheets, albeit at different levels of 'out of control' conditions.

Let's face it, since 2007, the Bank of England, the Federal Reserve and the European Central Bank (in that order) are no longer in charge of their monetary policies and balance sheets. This contrasts markedly with the course followed by the Bank of Japan, even if the world's No. 2 industrial power is in no better state than America or Europe. Taking the total assets of the these four monetary institutions as the 100 percent level of reference, from 2007 to March 1, 2011:

- The assets of the Bank of Japan fluctuated between 85 percent and 115 percent of that 100 percent frame of reference.
- From mid-2007 to mid-2008 those of the Bank of England oscillated between 120 percent and 130 percent, then in September/October 2008 they spiked at 340 percent, were reduced to 220 percent and subsequently drifted upward to a band of 310–325 percent.
- Up to September 2008, the Federal Reserve kept its assets below the 110 percent level, but then they suddenly zoomed up to nearly 260 percent, came down to 220 percent and then (with QE) drifted upward to 300 percent, with a tendency to increase still further. This is, indeed, a highly inflated balance sheet.
- From mid-2007 to mid-2008, the pattern of the ECB's assets paralleled that of the Bank of England, but then the two patterns became unstuck. The ECB's assets increased by 'only' 180 percent in September 2008 (an example of virtue compared to the other two central banks) and subsequently fluctuated in a band between 160 percent and 190 percent of the previously mentioned 100 percent reference marker.[13]

These are dramatic examples of the 'negative synergy' in monetary policy among central institutions considered to be the guardians of financial stability. The often heard excuse that the reason has been a bad economic situation 'which is now improving' does not hold water. If the economy and the conditions in the financial markets were indeed improving, then the three main Western central banks should by now have radically reduced their balance sheets – which they have not done. Instead, the trend toward greater leverage continues, particularly by the Fed.

This is highly regrettable for the Western economy as a whole, and for the three central banks themselves. By their actions they are documenting Milton Friedman's aphorism that, contrary to what is often claimed, Western central banks have no political independence.

The tipping point in the central bank's leverage was probably reached on October 13, 2008, when the CEOs of the nine foremost US commercial and investment banks) met at the Treasury at the invitation of Henry Paulson, then US Treasury secretary. Also present at that meeting were Ben Bernanke of the Fed, Timothy Geithner of the New York Federal Reserve, and the bosses of the Office of the Comptroller of the Currency (OCC) and the FDIC. In short, the top brass of the government, the monetary institutions and bank supervision.

The offer the government made on that infamous day of October 13, 2008 to which all those present consented, was one that the CEOs of private, badly wounded commercial and investment banks could not refuse: 'Very cheap capital',[14] and a great deal of it. It was offered to the banks as manna from heaven with no strings attached. No conditions or constraints accompanied this huge handout of public money, and with this an unprecedented opportunity to reform the banking industry and put it to work for the economy – rather than the reverse – was lost.

One can understand that, during a severe economic, financial and banking crisis, governments and central banks adopt unconventional monetary policy measures; and that they do so on an unprecedented scale. But doing this on such generous terms constitutes a scandal. For all the public money loaned by the Treasury to the self-wounded banks, they were asked to pay a paltry five percent interest rate. In contrast, Warren Buffett, the only private investor who ventured to put money into one of these banks that had destroyed its balance sheet, demanded and received a 10 percent interest rate.

These scandalously generous lending terms began a phase where the 'negative synergy' of monetary policies spread to other government deals; for example, handouts to the auto industry. It also found imitators in Europe; the UK being an example. No wonder that, with cheap public money coming from heaven, the mammoth global banks emerged even bigger, much more powerful, and highly profitable to their executives, rather than to their shareholders and the public.

Nor were the gifts being made by politicians running the Treasury department, Exchequer and Ministries of Finance short-lived. Once it got going, this policy of patronage continued even though practically everybody privately admitted that it could go on for ever. Critics are now saying that the medicine administered was worse than the disease.

There is no doubt that, during a severe crisis, central banks have to take measures aimed at stabilizing the financial markets and preventing the real economy from drifting into a depression. But when these measures are prolonged, their after-effects can be deeply unsettling to the economy. They disadvantage large sections of the population to serve the interests of an oligarchy.

As the March 2011 *Monthly Bulletin* of the Deutsche Bundesbank aptly remarked:

> As a 'long-term medication', they would have harmful side-effects. Generous liquidity operations allow even those banks that are no longer able to raise any funds in the private funding markets to continue operating. This runs the risk of necessary restructuring in parts of the banking system being delayed or not taking place at all.[15]

Moreover, so as not to be left behind by the new culture which looks at financial stability as a nonentity, the mints of developing countries are also working overtime. From 2006, the annual growth in China's M3 measure of broad money supply has speeded up significantly. The same is true of Russia's and India's money supply.

In the global economy, the broad measure of money supply in emerging economies increased about three times as fast as it did in the Western world. Adjusted for inflation, this money growth is alarming. Because of interdependencies, the fact that the world's money supply is growing at its fastest (in real terms) has been and remains a danger signal.

Developing countries complain that the West's monetary policies export inflation to them. This is partly true, but it is also partly because their own surplus money growth, over and above the increase in their nominal GDP, creates inflation which (as is to be expected) they find difficult to control.

Ironically, the surge of developing economies makes their monetary problems worse than they otherwise might have been. In the latter part of the twentieth century, rapid monetary growth in emerging countries was of little concern to the central banks of the West. A monetary deluge in Indonesia, for example, simply caused hyperinflation there. But now these countries play a much larger role in the global economy, and crossborder financial flows are also much bigger.

This is another way of saying that the freedom of US monetary policy is, up to a point, constrained by the monetary and exchange-rate policies of the BRICs: Brazil, Russia, India, China and other countries whose weight on the global economy has significantly increased since the end of the 1980s. This in no way means that the monetary policy of some countries is 'wrong' while in others it is 'right'. What it means is that there is a 'negative synergy' when we think of the global economy as being *one world.*

The power over the economy: funds rate, discount rate and inflation

The first three sections of this chapter carried the message that, while they share the same label of *central banks,* no two monetary institutions share the same goals, the same functions and the way in which they operate. Nor are they alike in terms of their charter and the authority they exercise.

On the other hand, as monetary institutions, central banks do have some common characteristics. If a general statement is to be made establishing what a central or reserve bank does, or at least is supposed to do as its primary function, then such a statement will include five main areas:

1. Deciding on monetary policy.
2. Issuing money.
3. Acting as a lender of last resort.

4. Exercising bank regulation and supervision.
5. Functioning as the bank of the government.

The fifth area of duties is important to some central banks. Examples of acting as the government's bank include handling the payroll of public servants, retirees, war veterans and so on. Also, performing some commercial transactions on behalf of the sovereign. Some central banks also assume other roles.[16]

Regarding function No. 4 in the short list above, there is no universal rule that commercial banks and universal banks fall under direct central bank supervision. When, toward the end of the twentieth century, the Labour government in Britain made the Bank of England an independent central bank, it took away from it bank supervisory duties and integrated them into the Financial Services Authority (FSA). But in 2010 the Conservative–Liberal government reversed this separation of duties and brought the FSA under the wing of the Bank of England.

In the USA there have been four major commercial and retail bank supervisors: the Federal Reserve; the Office of the Comptroller of the Currency (OCC, under the Treasury),[17] the Federal Deposit Insurance Corporation (FDIC) and the Office of Thrift Supervision (for savings and loans). In 2010, FINREG strengthened the Fed's authority over bank supervision but also instituted a Coordination Council of Supervisors under the Treasury.

Also in the USA, the Securities and Exchange Commission (SEC) has supervisory duties over investment banks and other financial institutions such as publicly quoted companies. The states of the Union also have bank supervisory duties, and this mosaic not only is ultimately ineffectual but it also creates plenty of opportunities for banks to cherry-pick their leaders.

In other countries, different financial institutions are regulated either by the central bank or some other government appointed authority. Not only does the regulatory and supervisory structure of the banking industry vary from one country to another, but also in need of supervision and regulation is a large and growing group of non-banks. These include, for example,

- insurance companies,
- credit card companies,
- postal banks,
- cooperative unions,
- department stores with credit lines,
- mutual funds,
- pension funds, and
- hedge funds.

To put it another way, the notion that central bank authority covers the whole financial industry, let alone that it holds veto powers in relation to other regulators, is false. Nor is a central bank (nor should it be) directly involved in the ongoing competition between different financial institutions as they divide among themselves the different segments of the market. Typically, such a division changes over time and has many overlaps.

While a central bank might make a contribution to the existing pattern of duties and segments among different parties, it does not lay claim to the role of arbitrator. Quite the contrary, in fact – it lays claim to monetary policy functions, but the way of executing them varies between jurisdictions.

I have chosen the Federal Reserve as an example. Monetary decisions are taken by the Federal Open Market Committee (FOMC), which consists of twelve voting members: all seven Fed governors plus five of the 12 presidents from the Federal Reserve district banks. The FOMC holds regular meetings every six weeks, at which it sets the short-term Federal Funds Rate (FFR). This is the most important interest rate controlled by the Federal Reserve. It is the widely watched interest rate that applies to banks with reserve deficiencies which need to acquire capital temporarily.

FFR applies to overnight loans by the Fed to commercial banks. In a functioning financial market, banks charge each other that rate. But it may be that the interbank market freezes, as it did in late 2008. Or for creditworthiness reasons, banks apply a premium when lending to individual wounded institutions – or, alternatively, to the banks from a country with known credit problems. The *Japan premium* of the 1990s is an example.

Controlling the FFR is the key to the Federal Reserve's power over the American economy, because it provides control over credit conditions. Conducted through the New York Federal Reserve, the open market operations of the Fed, which consist of buying and selling US Treasury bonds, cause an increase or decrease in the FFR. The Fed's *Primary Discount Rate* is the one it charges on emergency loans when banks borrow directly from one of the 12 regional Fed banks.

In the 1990s, the computer systems of the Bank of New York failed. Neither credits nor debits could be processed, but the institution had claims to meet. To honor its obligations it borrowed an undisclosed amount from the Federal Reserve of New York, which it repaid two days later when its IT system was again up and running. For this two-day loan, the Bank of New York paid the New York Fed interest of around US$55 million.

Among themselves, Funds Rate and Discount Rate define the cost of money in the USA, but they don't need to move in unison. For example, in late February 2010, the Funds Rate was kept at 0 percent by the Fed while the primary discount rate was raised by a quarter, from 0.50 percent to 0.75 percent (still at a trivial level).

In the general case, the central bank provides discount credits by buying securities before they mature and deducting an interim interest charge for the remainder of the maturity period. The interest rate applied is, as a rule, the discount the reserve bank itself fixes. Discounted securities are held in its portfolio until maturity and are then presented for payment. When the central bank buys the securities, the monetary base[18] increases, but in contrast, when it collects payment on them, the monetary base narrows.

Advances against securities imply that the debtor deposits certain securities as collateral. In principle, secured advances are to be used only for short periods in order to tide over liquidity shortages. Down to basics, the reserve bank is under no obligation to discount, but it has the possibility of influencing the recourse to discount credit, not only by fixing the discount rate but also by varying the discounting limits, or changing the eligibility requirements for the securities discounted.

In the case of the Federal Reserve, buying or selling government bonds in open market operations has been the typical process by which it manages the monetary base of the American economy. However, debates in academic and economic policy circles have been raging for years about whether it is possible any longer to measure the monetary base accurately, given the complexity of the modern economy.

This has led to the policy of targeting specific interest rates, rather than tinkering with monetary base numbers. The Fed can influence rates not only through open market operations but also by means of the discount rate controlled by the Board of Governors. The announcement of changes in discount rate has long been the principal means used by the Fed to communicate its interest rate policy, though this is no longer true today. The problem with targeting interest rates alone, and failing to keep a close watch over the monetary base is that it leads to bubbles and inflationary pressures when interest rates are kept too low for too long – while the monetary base expands through quantitative easing financed by keeping the central bank's printing presses busy. This is one of the most fundamental criticisms made of the monetary policy followed by the Bernanke Fed.

In addition, very low short-term interest rates held over a long timeframe are encouraging banks to take on liquidity risk, thereby increasing dependence on volatile market developments. And since the central bank does not control long-term interest rates, which are set by the market, a large gap between short-term and long-term interest rates is creating an incentive for banks and other financial market players to delay the adjustment of the short-term profile of their funding, and continue with maturity transformations on a large scale, which exposes them and the economy to significant risks.

The reader should notice that interest rate risk also constitute the greatest individual source of risk for other financial industry sectors; for example, for life insurance companies. In the event of unfavorable market developments, income from investments may no longer be sufficient to make agreed guaranteed payments to policyholders and other commitments. The life insurers' treasury comes under stress if funds are continuously invested at a very low interest rate.

Nor should the risk of inflation be taken lightly. Inflation destroys the value of fixed investments, reduces take-home pay and in particular penalizes the weaker members of society – acting as the taxation of the poor. 'What creates inflation?' Arthur Burns, the former chairman of the Fed, asked his students at Columbia University, answering his own question with the statement: 'Government deficits create inflation.' To the negative effect of government deficits should be added very low interest rates and a rapid increase in the monetary base.

Britain, among other Western nations, has faced this triple whammy. In late January 2011, Mervyn King, the governor of the Bank of England, warned that inflation in Britain could reach 5 percent in the coming months, and that real wages in 2011 would be no higher than those six years earlier. This is something that has not happened since the 1920s,[19] and is the direct result of erroneous monetary policies.

Deposit insurance and bad banks

Economic history suggests that, in periods of rising markets and significant financial activity, credit criteria are bent or are completely forgotten. With market players in high spirits, market instability becomes endemic. Then come recessions, panics and depressions. The social costs of banking panics are high, and in the front line are depositors. In the good years, depositors don't have the power to impose constraints on the bankers' activities, but in bad years they lose their savings, other assets (which may be in marginal accounts), and even their homes.

Deposit insurance was invented in the early 1930s, in the wake of the First Great Depression, to provide depositors with some statutory rights over the money they entrust to the banks.[20] Through it they are protected up to a given level which varies across jurisdictions and over time. There is a rationale behind this kind of protection, depositors are typically short of detailed information about the financial staying power of institutions where they hold their current accounts and a direct effect of this is that it takes only a niggling doubt (on their part) about adverse changes in the value of a bank's assets, to spark off a run.

Widespread bank failures can lead to a vicious spiral of default and falling prices, as in America in the 1930s, when a third of all banks collapsed and the monetary authorities were not in a position to prevent a savage deflation. In the aftermath of the First Great Depression, the Roosevelt Administration instituted a scheme of government guarantee in case of a bank's insolvency. The capital came from *ex-ante* contributions by banks to the Federal Deposit Insurance Corporation (FDIC), at that time a new agency.

What the FDIC and other *deposit insurance* schemes guaranteed from the start is that small depositors would get their money back if the bank where it was deposited failed. This premise, however, has been exploited all the way. In the early 1930s, relatively small amounts of money were involved and the scheme focused on the *depositor* as a physical person. More than five decades later, in the late 1980s, the savings and loans (S&L) crisis revealed that deposit insurance served the speculator.

This is not a criticism of deposit insurance, but rather of the way that governments allowed it to develop. The need for it came from the risks that banks take with loans and other instruments, as well as their proprietary positions and OTC trades. But because of the way it evolved over the years, it became the subject of gaming by banks and depositors, as well as contributing to moral hazard.

During the late 1980s in the USA, when the guaranteed sum of deposit insurance stood at US$100,000 per account, plenty of speculators (and some high net worth individuals) opened accounts in a number of S&Ls up to the guaranteed amount. Their aim was to benefit from higher interest rates than those paid by banks while also being protected by deposit insurance. When several of these S&Ls became bankrupt, they recovered their money through the FDIC.

More recently (as noted in Chapter 7) in the UK, the Netherlands and other EU countries, retail customers opened accounts with IceSave, which offered a 5 percent interest rate. When it crashed, central banks and other government agencies in EU jurisdictions compensated depositors, but then their governments asked that Iceland's taxpayers return the money – to the tune of £3.5 billion (US$5.6 billion) for the UK and the Netherlands alone.

Another, more far-reaching, way that deposit insurance has contributed to moral hazard is that, because of it banks became separated from their obligation to be extremely careful with the way that they used depositors' money. This made them careless, not only with regard to borrowers' creditworthiness but also about running out of capital or liquidity. A bank's capital and reserves are a buffer. What it lends out or commits in derivatives trades is in truth the depositors' money.

Deposit insurance also makes it politically safer to let banks fail, because it compensates depositors even if it caps the guaranteed amount of deposits. Also, with proper and timely adjustment of the *ex-ante* deposit insurance premium, it does not place the cost of compensation on the taxpayer, as is the case with the unconditional salvage of failing self-wounded banks. As these references suggest, by now, deposit insurance is no longer just the common citizen's protection. Not only does the limit continue to be raised, but also some governments – for example, the Irish – have been guaranteeing all deposits, no matter the amount.

In fact, even if there is a limit to deposit insurance, the average American or European citizen does not have even 10 percent of that amount deposited in cash. No wonder, therefore, that regulators are contemplating removing the implicit guarantee that bank creditors will get all their money back in case of bankruptcy.[21]

While this will settle some of the issues connected to moral hazard, it is not clear if in economic terms it will be good or bad. Deposit insurance contributes toward financial stability because it reduces the likelihood of a sudden, massive withdrawal of deposits by clients. But at the same time it reduces the incentive for banks to improve their governance and for investors to take a prudent approach when choosing a credit institution.

Typically, today's statutory deposit guarantee schemes are regulated and supervised by governments. In the European Union they are regulated by the EU Directive on Deposit Guarantee Schemes, but there is no wider harmonization. For example, there are currently some 40 such guarantee schemes in the EU supporting a diverse range of investors and deposits to varying amounts – though the European Commission aims to harmonize deposit protection.

Opinions differ as to whether or not the concept of a *bad bank*, which is becoming rather popular recently, should be seen as a king-sized extension of deposit insurance for credit institutions. To begin with, the term bad bank is a misnomer. What it means is an independent financial company that is either spinoff from a bank in deep trouble; or against a nominal payment (provided typically by the government with taxpayers' money), it takes over bad loans and other underwater investments from an institution's portfolio, thus allowing it to clean up its balance sheet, and start anew as a *good bank* (also a misnomer).

The deep economic and financial crisis of 2007–12 has prompted some countries to establish *bad bank* schemes to enable credit institutions to remove from their balance sheets assets that are at risk of severe impairment. Typically, though not exclusively, this transfer involves portfolios of loans, securities and other holdings such as investments in commercial and industrial firms.

Since transfers of loan portfolios to *bad banks* are a sort of loan sale, their impact is removed from the originating bank's dubious assets, which have to be written off. At the same time, it buys breathing space, since the new entity (presumably) is under no pressure to go ahead with fire sales. It can wait until market conditions improve to get its money back.

In the 1990s, Sweden's Securum, the *bad bank* carved out of Nordbanken, was able to dispose of the non-performing assets it was entrusted with at about 75 to 80 cents to the kroner; they would have fetched much less than 50 percent in a fire sale. Securum, however, was very well managed, which is not the general case with *bad banks*.

Not all the assets in a portfolio of dubious securities are able to fetch 80 cents to the dollar. Many economists and financial analysts worry that that what can be found in the vaults of the Fed, the Bank of England and the European Central Bank is useless paper. An Italian banker characterized these positions as garbage worse than that littering the streets of Naples.

Unfortunately, this is not a joke because since 2008 all three central banks have been dousing the financial system with liquidity and buying up the government bonds of troubled countries and the most dubious assets of commercial and investment banks. This risks turning each of these monetary institutions into a *bad bank* in which rotten assets are piled high. We shall see.

The troubled assets relief program

The US Troubled Assets Relief Program (TARP) was initiated under the Bush Administration and it continued a lavish spending of taxpayers' money under the Obama Administration. This has been the Treasury's pet project.[22] The idea behind it was to recapitalize banks and enable the banking system to continue functioning.

Instead of putting the assets of self-wounded credit institutions and investment banks into a *bad bank*, it poured cash into banks with troubled assets. How successful has it been? To its critics, the answer is obvious. The government's decision to force America's nine largest banks to accept US$125 billion in taxpayers' funds during the crisis of 2008 did not restore confidence in the banking system; it undermined it.

Richard Kovacevich, former chief executive of Wells Fargo, disputes the government's argument that the bail-out was a success. 'People are ... bragging about restoring health to the banks,' he told the *Financial Times*. 'Baloney'.[23] Kovacevich agreed in principle with the notion of the sovereign extending temporary help to some banks, but said that the TARP program that was forced on his and other institutions exacerbated the industry's problems because it did not distinguish between healthy and troubled entities.

Citigroup, J.P. Morgan Chase and Wells Fargo each received US$25 billion. The Bank of America was given US$15billion, and US$10 billion was reserved for Merrill Lynch (which had agreed to be acquired by BofA[24]). Another US$10 billion were pumped into Goldman Sachs and the same amount into Morgan Stanley. The Bank of New York Mellon and State Street Bank received US$5 billion between them.

What the former CEO of Wells Fargo objected to in particular was that, given the magnitude of these indiscriminate infusions, investors concluded that every bank receiving the government's bail-out funds must be in trouble. As a result, the share price of Wells Fargo and other banks fell almost 80 percent from the time the program was announced until early March 2009, when the drop in the market started to find its lowest point, and some time later equities began to recover.

At least in private, Ken Lewis, Bank of America's CEO, criticized the government's (alleged) arm-twisting which pushed it to complete its acquisition of Merrill Lynch, despite misgivings over the latter's mounting losses.

Lawsuits, probes and recriminations followed. Lewis was stripped of his chairmanship and later announced his retirement. Merrill's write-offs forced the Bank of America into taking a second tranche of TARP capital, and the repayment was to be funded, at least in part, by a huge US$18.8 billion capital-raising.

While the big banks CEOs were not happy with TARP, though not everyone voiced their objections, most Americans saw it as an unwarranted bail-out of Wall Street fat cats at a time when unemployment had hit 10 percent. (The same is true of the rescue of the auto industry and of any other industry sector where the sovereign is interfering seriously with the way a free market works.)

The US$700 billion for the Troubled Assets Relief Program was aimed at those folk. A pragmatic way of looking at the TARP is as evidence that America (as well as Britain and euroland) has a thinly capitalized banking system that is being allowed to earn its way back to health on the back of taxpayers, with ominous effects on the increase of national debt in Western nations, and interest payments for rocketing sovereign debt that will weight heavily on future state budgets.

For their part, many financial analysts have pointed out that, since Congress passed the huge US$700 billion financial bail-out, the institutions considered 'too big to fail' have grown even larger and have in no way restrained the lavish pay of their executives. It was also said that the office of Neil M. Barofsky, the special counsel of the TARP, was investigating 77 cases of possible criminal and civil fraud, including tax evasion, insider trading, improper mortgage lending and payment collection, false statements and public corruption.

Scandals associated with the TARP are highly counterproductive because, among common citizens, this program is far from being popular while in some quarters it is seen as the mother of all US government plans aimed at saving the big global financial institutions from self-destruction. In an interview given on June 25, 2009 on Bloomberg, Warren Buffett counseled patience, pointing out that deleveraging is a slow process; it cannot be done in short time. He then quoted a friend of his who said that leverage is something that smart people don't need, and dumb people have no business using.

But they did. So much so that as the TARP deadline approached, at which time the spigot of cash was going to be turned off, several people asked for it to be extended, saying that some banks would be vulnerable to a relapse. The Treasury responded to these worries. The program was due to expire at the end of 2009 but was extended until October 2010 to continue bailing out the banks. It was also widened, with Obama wanting it to provide loans to small businesses.

How successful has all that effort been? A report from a congressional panel that monitored TARP said an effective assessment of the program was hampered by the Treasury's 'failure to articulate clear goals or to provide specific measures of success'.[25] Tim Geithner, the Treasury secretary, told Congress that banks were returning the money they had obtained under the scheme. But was that enough evidence that the TARP had had a real beneficial effect on the banking industry?

Optimists said that one piece of evidence that the TARP had been successful has been that it made a profit of US$10 billion for the taxpayer. In a letter to the *Financial Times*, however, Christopher Whalen suggested that, at a time of zero interest rates and quantitative easing, such a reckoning seems suspect. He asked the provocative question: 'Shall we not first subtract the value destruction of lengthening the duration of the credit adjustment process to suit the convenience of the bankers and their political masters?'

If he were the Treasury secretary, says Whalen, he would subtract the losses to the Federal Deposit Insurance Corporation and private investors in banks to date before declaring victory, especially with credit loss rates still rising.[26] Other critics of the treasury's enthusiasm of the TARP's profitable outcome made similar comments.

One of the none too favorable commentaries has been that, if results for US salvaging operations are judged in unison, as should be the case, then there is no reason to crow about them. Even if TARP investments did eventually make a profit, losses from the bail-out of the automotive sector, from AIG, Fannie Mae and Freddie Mac should also be taken into consideration.

Still another critical commentary has been that if the TARP was so profitable, there would have been less of a reason for the Obama Administration's attempt to raise up to US$100 billion from a fee on banks to cover losses in the TARP bail-out fund. And, by January 2010, red ink was still flowing, lending support to this so-called *Obama Tax* (which has more or less faded into oblivion).

A good reason why it is not easy to sort in a clean way the financial 'pluses' and 'minuses' of the TARP is that the Obama Administration has used money returned by banks for other bail-outs, such as that of GM and Chrysler, which were not part of the original US$700 billion authorized by Congress. When everything is counted, there is a loss of US$120 billion or so.[27] This may also be the deeper reason why the Obama Tax had short legs. Banks would not pay for bail-outs – whether they were their own or those of other industrial sectors.

To save or not to save failed banks?

Though the TARP was a life-saver thrown to the self-wounded big global US banks by the Bush Junior Administration, the Obama Administration, too, went for it in full force. Its formal commitment took place on March 27, 2009 at a White House meeting. Simon Johnson and James Kwak make three points about that event which have entered the chronicles of how governments bend over to please special interests:

1. 'My administration is the only thing between you and the pitchforks,'[28] said Obama to the top bankers who gathered around him on March 27, 2009.

That is true of every government that tries to have it both ways: skewing its decisions toward the big and powerful while trying to maintain its appeal to the common citizen – and instead of exercising leadership, ending up as 'soft wax'.

2. 'Banks used huge balance sheets to place bets ... that ultimately poisoned the global economy.'

In the 1950s, US President Dwight Eisenhower spoke of the *Industrial–Military* complex. Four decades later, in 1998, Jagdish Bhagwati identified the new oligarchy as the *Wall Street–Treasury* complex.[29] The March 27, 2009 meeting crowned this oligarchy as the government's partner.

3. 'In the process they grew so large that their potential failure threatened the stability of the entire system, giving them a unique ... leverage over the government.'[30]

With the rapid growth of economic power and its effective translation into political power, we no longer have a banking industry at the service of the people and their government. Rather, it is the common citizens, their money, the central bank and the government at the service of mammoth financial organizations – whose power grab has been helped by a huge and reckless speculation, too politically powerful to be reigned in, and ironically, the descent into the abyss of the economy that permitted already big institutions to become much more powerful by absorbing at bargain basement prices failed big banks, while the liquidity was provided by taxpayers' money.

As David Cho noted in an article in the *Washington Post*: 'Those mergers were largely the government's making ... The bailouts skewed the financial industry ... J.P. Morgan Chase, Bank of America and Wells Fargo were each allowed to hold more than 10 percent of the nation's deposits despite a rule barring such a practice.'[31]

Plenty of financial analysts and economists reckon that the lessons from the waves of bank failures that preceded the TARP were not properly learned. Prior to the 1988 debacle of the US S&L, FDIC had resisted heavy pressure to bail out a smaller bank called Penn Square. Shortly afterwards, however, letting a bank the size of Continental fail led to the reverse policy. Continental was saved because of its links with other banks, and the panic that would ensue if it collapsed.

To pull the bank up from under, the FDIC bought a bundle of Continental's bad loans and injected money directly into the bank. Shareholders and managers suffered, but Continental's creditors did not. In the end it was possible to maintain public confidence but this does not mean that salvaging self-wounded banks is a good policy:

- It creates moral hazard,
- significantly lowers the level of self-discipline,
- costs taxpayers and governments a mountain of money, and
- forges special links between sovereigns and big banks.

Crises that have hit the financial industry, the frequency of which continues to increase, have provided a wealth of documentation that the secret of sound bank regulation is to force financial institutions to build up capital and reserves in good times to enable them to get through unscathed in bad times. But the lesson that politicians drew from the most recent crisis had precisely the opposite effect. They pressed for delays in significantly strengthening capital requirements but, moreover, did notice that banks got into trouble because the penalties for bad lending decisions and highly risky trades had not been severe enough, and watered-down Basel III provisions put in place in account for the fact that banks are masters of gaming capital regimes which requires them to raise equity and pay premiums when losses are high.

For example, the only lesson that the Treasury (and its OCC), the Federal Reserve and other bank regulatory agencies seem to have retained from the S&L banking crisis of 1988, is that fire brigade approaches have the advantage of not requiring a priori decisions. They work by default. All that is needed is to reinvent the Resolution Trust Corporation (RTC), a government body set up in a hurry to deal with the fallout of the S&L bankruptcies.[32] This led straight into the next big banking crisis.

The RTC absorbed hundreds of distressed S&L. It did not have to pick and choose the assets it would acquire; everything was thrown in, including the kitchen sink. It should be said, however, that those assets were infinitely simpler than the tangled instruments banks and non-banks (for example AIG) had to shed in the course of the 2007–12 economic crisis. Even so, the history of the RTC says something interesting about how fast salvage cost escalates, and the fact that taxpayer-financed salvage ventures are 99 percent politics and 1 percent everything else.

This does not mean that, when hell breaks loose, after years of excesses, leveraging and speculation, government intervention is not warranted. But because practically all intervention by sovereigns in the markets has moral hazard associated with it, it should be immediate, well-focused and flanked by its indispensable alter ego of bringing those responsible to justice.

In plain talk, a sovereign's intervention favors some agents of the economy at the expense of others. Whether the private firms being salvaged by public money are insurance firms, railroads, motor vehicle firms, small S&Ls or big global banks, getting them out of trouble is nothing but a taxpayer-funded mopping up of toxic debt. This might be a result of high leveraging, derivatives that turned on their head, loans that went sour or mortgage-related plays such as the subprimes.[33] No matter what is its origin, huge amounts of unpayable debt are choking the financial system.

In more ways than one, regulators, central banks and the government are part of the mismanagement. After having given free reign to the banks for years and looked the other way while systemic risks mounted, the sovereign and its agents want to provide a floor to asset values to keep them from falling farther. This rewards poorly managed institutions, enabling them to work through the debris and try to avoid collapse by means of other people's money.

Critics say that at the horrendous expense of public funds and in violation of free market principles, two different Bush Administrations – almost two decades apart, the Clinton Administration and the Obama Administration have focused on maintaining an unbalanced status within the financial sector. They simply reinvented the wheel of a very Japanese approach to solving a credit crisis, by throwing money at the problem. By so doing they prolonged the credit crisis and waited for their credit cycle to reignite.

In the meantime, small to medium-sized banks were allowed to fail. Experts did not doubt that banks would go to the wall. As a Merrill Lynch research paper put it, 'Applying 1989's failure rate to today's banking universe suggests that approximately 280 banks and thrifts could possibly fail'[34] (in the course of the 2007–12 crisis). Merrill's forecast was pragmatic.

Both in the late 1980s and at the end of the twenty-first century's first decade, the proverbial fire brigade approach was used, with much public money being spent to put out the banking fire. The fact that regulators looked the other way was believed to be because they knew that banks could further wound their precarious balance sheets if the law of the land was applied. This increased the taxpayers' costs, as the most dubious 'banking assets' could be found in the financial institutions' vaults.

Excesses have also arisen because of a growing tide of speculation, while at the same time deficit financing became second nature for Western sovereigns. Congress authorized and the government spent hundreds of billions of dollars to salvage banks and other entities. Then the Federal Reserve bought Treasury bonds by printing money.

A recent economic analysis by a major bank has put this in perspective:

> risk premium [is] reflecting the rising credit risk of holding US Treasury debt under current trends of budget deficits. Willingness and ability to pay timely interest and principal defines sovereign credit risk. As the US debt is denominated in its own currency, impairment of ability to pay implies the Fed forgets how to run its printing presses.[35]

This study goes on to state that only by setting the fiscal policy on a unsustainable path can this unwanted outcome be avoided. It also points out that, in the long term, credit risk in holding US debt is really reflecting inflation risk. Most particularly the likelihood the government will eventually need to resort to higher levels of inflation in order to ease its debt burden.

In conclusion, financial market uncertainty will not disappear until there is evidence that the US, European and other sovereigns are living within the limits of a balanced budget, and that the financial industry is not taking more risks than those it can afford in relation to its capital. This means that not only entitlements have to be re-dimensioned, but also extravaganzas such as re-inflating the treasuries of self-wounded big banks are strictly avoided. The likelihood that all this will happen is not high.

Conclusion: the perfect storm

It was an aphorism of Oscar Wilde's that the truth is rarely plain and never simple. Many financial analysts and well-known economists are of the opinion that the problems the East and West, in particular the latter, are faced with at the time of writing have their origins in the late 1970s/early 1980s deregulation. Some time during that period, big global banks became a state-within-the-state. By the second presidency of Bill Clinton, through the two terms of Bush Junior and under the watch of Barack Obama, the 'big guys' became much bigger and took it upon themselves to run the government.

Some analysts follow Sherlock Holmes' maxim in their reasoning: when you have eliminated the impossible, whatever remains, however improbable, must be the truth. The way that Simon Johnson and James Kwak put that evidence, 'By the late nineteenth century, the Senate had become known as the "Millionaires' Club"; buying political support with cash was considered an extension of normal business practices.'[36]

In Washington and in Brussels, lobbyists are working overtime on behalf of those who benefit handsomely from the large handouts of the different governments, while the common people want the State Supermarket to enlarge its entitlements. It is therefore not surprising that the leverage ratio of Western economies continues to increase beyond the level that proved to be plainly unaffordable. The pressure is kept alive by the overwhelming presence of embedded interests.

As the reader will remember from the early chapters of this book, on December 17, 2009, the Basel Committee on Banking Supervision published a consultation document that was more stringent than many bankers had expected. Among other things, Basel called for a shake-up in the way that banks' capital is measured. But the lobbyists reacted immediately, supported by sovereigns afraid that the derelict banks in their jurisdictions could not meet the new capital requirements. In the aftermath, the implementation schedule of Basel III has unwisely been lengthened to 2019, and the banks themselves are busy developing derivative instruments able to challenge the new capital rules even before they have been fully implemented.

All this created many mixed messages about governments' and central banks' willingness, let alone ability, to improve upon the current chaos characterized by a mismanaged economy and free-wheeling banking. Trimming an already mild Basel III is tantamount to continuing to live on imaginary money. That's politics, and *politics is a profession in which it is vital to say imaginary things with total certainty.*

* * *

Dr Ben Bernanke once stated that the Federal Reserve has an unlimited ability to print money. That is a fundamentally false statement. 'I print money as much as I please' has been the not-so-famous *Bernanke put* – the notion that, if trouble occurred in the banking industry, its CEOs 'will do what they have to do' while the Federal Reserve will always be ready to come to their rescue.[37]

Dr Paul Volcker, who, as chairman of the Federal Reserve, launched the successful fight against the ruinous inflation of the 1970s, has been of precisely the opposite opinion. In his words: 'The truly unique power of a central bank is the power to create money, and ultimately the power to create is the power to destroy.'[38]

Nearly two years prior to the start of the 2007–12 deep economic and banking crisis, David Rosenberg, North American economist of Merrill Lynch, wrote a prophetic essay entitled 'Bracing for the "Perfect Storm"[39] which predicted a triple whammy facing the US economy – namely, weakening home prices, Fed-induced yield curve inversion and a period of continuing high energy prices. To these three horsemen of the Apocalypse has been added a fourth: a high gear of speculation.

Left unchecked and fed by huge amounts of borrowed money at higher and higher leverage ratios, speculation produces destructive financial crises. As the odds mount, the storm will roar back in full fury, engulfing not only the banking industry but also the whole economy. At the time of writing, the leadership of the Western world, and its policies, has failed. The time has come for radical change.

Epilog

Basel III, the Dodd–Frank Act (in the US, 2010) and the Vickers Commission reforms (in Britain 2011) seem to provide a quantum leap step towards an increased credibility of banking regulation. On the contrary, however, they postpone some key regulatory issues, and leave open the door to the devil of financial regulation: the politicians.

Most politicians still live in the past, when free market ideologies created *banker hubris*. Politicians gave the bankers free reign and awarded them moral legitimacy, since they seemed the only people 'wise enough to understand money.' By so doing they destroyed the credibility of the financial system.

With the banking industry's self-inflicted wounds leading to the huge economic and banking crisis which started in 2007 came the time to tame the banks. That's what the Dodd–Frank act aimed for: 'In America banks typically held about $30 in assets for each $1 of their equity, while some European banks stuffed their balance-sheets with up to 80 times more assets than equity,' said *The Economist* (September 10, 2011).

The only country in Europe which, so far, has put up the needed effort to right the balances has been the UK. This was the remit of the Independent Commission on Banking (better known as the Vickers Commission). One of its major goals was to prevent future bank bailouts at taxpayers' expense.

The time to act was none too soon: 'The assets – and liabilities – of British banks exceed £6,000 billion ($9.7 trillion), four times the country's income,' wrote John Kay in *The Financial Times*. Kay added: 'Only if traditional retail banking is ring-fenced can taxpayer guarantees be limited to personal and business depositors, and government funding of the banking system be directed to the needs of the businesses that create jobs and growth '(*The Financial Times*, September 14, 2011).'

That's what the Vickers Commission recommended, but Basel III did not even suggest anything like that because, as a successor to Basel II and Basel I, its roots lie in the late twentieth century – not the twenty-first century. Therefore, as this book has explained, its regulatory armory is incomplete. In its mid-September 2011 report the Vickers Commission provided an answer to the query 'How can a bank be world class and protect the taxpayer?' and the answer is to:

- ring fence the bank's retail activities,
- have the retail and small business banking under a separate board of directors from the investment arm, and
- endow retail operations with equity capital equal to at least 10 percent of risk weighted assets.*

The weakness of IBC's proposals is that the transition period is too generous. Banks will have until 2019 to put the new structure in place, while a couple of years should have been plenty.† This is also one of Basel III's weaknesses. Till then we may have

* Still, this may not be enough in case mortgage banking gets in very deep trouble, as has happened with the Bank of America and with Hungarian real estate.

† As taught by the experience of World War II. When US carriers returned to Hawaii in bad shape after the naval battle of the Coral seas the American engineers decreed

one or two new severe and unmanageable banking crises. These delays are imposed by the politicians who talk too much and do too little.

Since 2007 we have seen one crisis summit after another bringing together chiefs of state, central bankers and finance ministers in their worst possible role – that of firefighters. These costly and largely useless meetings were accompanied by public statements which:

- sounded hollow, and
- did not strengthen the global economy and its finances.

Basel III – which is due to be introduced on a step-by-step basis beginning in 2013 but not completely implemented till 2019 – does nothing to change central bankers' role. As this book has brought to the reader's attention, Western central banks have more or less lost their independence. Political action is also discredited because the rule of law, for instance the Sarbanes–Oxley Act in the US, has been observed neither by banks nor by sovereigns.

No wonder, therefore, that on both sides of the North Atlantic, in Europe and in the US, the financial industry remains under pressure from several sides. Trimmed regulatory measures, losses from government bond holdings, the threat of a double-dip recession and tension on the interbank market come at a most critical stage of a delayed and timid restructuring process of the banking sector.

On September 21, 2011, the International Monetary Fund said that, according to its estimates, European banks were undercapitalized by euro 300 billion, in large part due to the credit crisis. The European banks' exposure to peripheral euroland countries alone stands at euro 650 billion and is partly responsible for this shortfall. To Greece alone French banks have a euro 42 billion exposure, German banks euro 18 billion and British banks the equivalent of euro 10 billion: *Euronews*, September 28, 2011. By being themselves so much indebted, governments, which as late as 2008 have rushed to fill the gaps in the banks' coffers, have to think thrice before repeating their generosity, with taxpayers' money, of course.

Money is not the only missing link to the route of sound governance, as the problems faced by banks today have no resemblance to those of the 1980s. Critics say that lessons learned from some of the most damaging cases of the deep 2007–12 economic and banking crisis have not been translated into Basel III rules. An example is provided by the Bank of America, which in mid-September 2011 stated that:

- five out of six of its divisions earned almost $6 billion,
- but the losses from its mortgage operation were horrendous and the bank may be indebted to the tune of hundreds of billions of dollars (*The Economist*, September 17, 2011).

Lawsuits against the Bank of America range from litigation in state courts over mortgages sold to investors with allegedly faulty representations in regard to their quality, to alleged violation of federal underwriting laws and irregularities in foreclosure procedures. The large number of these financially dilapidating failures comes from

---

that they needed two months to work on them. Admiral Nimitz gave them three days. The engineers met the challenge and the carriers participated in and won the Battle of Midway.

Countrywide, a hard sales mortgage institution Bank of America acquired after its bankruptcy – but is now responsible in front of the courts for its liabilities.

Mortgages of course have been bread and butter business in banking, what is new is that losses can reach astronomical levels. A new regulation which does not put position limits and associated legal penalties to oblige accurate and timely recognition of such losses, as well as of potential losses and litigations, leaves the gates open to new forms of speculation.

Neither is Basel III making provisions for loans-*and*-foreign exchange shocks such as Hungary's real estate mortgages and consumer loans. Between 2004 and 2008 Hungarian home owners financed their loans in Swiss francs to the tune of florint 4 trillion, because Swiss franc interest rates were so much lower than those of florint loans. At the time, this represented 25 billion Swiss francs with an exchange rate of 160 florint to the franc. Today there are 240 florint to the franc, with a corresponding 50 percent increase in the debt of Hungarian citizens.

In the frontline are Western banks, as 80 percent of Hungary's banking is foreign owned. (Austrian banks account for 27 percent and German for 21 percent.) To this frontline has been added political risk, after the Hungarian government's intervention:

- leading to a combination of loans-*and*-foreign exchange-*and*-political risk, and
- providing one more evidence that much more than what Basel III mandates is necessary to tame the jungle of global banking.

The list of reasons why 'more', much more, is necessary in prudential rules is inexhaustible. Incomplete financial information is another example. Central bankers and regulators from several countries have warned that rules to safeguard against systemic risk posed by the vast $6 trillion over-the-counter (OTC) derivatives market are undermined by potential *data gaps* in the information held on trades.*

In late August 2011 the Bank for International Settlements (BIS) made the point that a global well-defined set of data must be reported by banks on their OTC derivatives trades. It needs no explaining that much greater detail than is currently available on highly risky bank-to-bank trades, as well as full transparency for regulators of all banking transactions, should be an integral and important part of any package of financial reforms. That is not yet the case.

Expect the unexpected should be the guiding light of all regulation after Heraclitos, the ancient Greek philosopher, who said that everything changes and we can never step into the same river twice. A tough, just and universal regulation is to the banking industry's own interest. By wheeling and dealing over the last three decades banking has become a damaged brand, weakened by its own errors of judgment and style as well as by the politicians' deadly embrace.

Wise people learn from their errors and do not repeat them. *If* banks and regulators postulate a system that depends on every party always following the right policies, *then* sooner or later they will find that no such workable system exists. And so will the sovereigns.

---

* For instance, details on exposure amounts, posted collateral, market values of open transactions and reference data on affected parties in the event of default by a counterparty (*The Financial Times*, August 28, 2011).

Notes

Introduction

1. Bank for International Settlements, *81st Annual Report*, Basel, June 26, 2011.

1. Basel III: An Overview and a Warning

1. *The Economist*, May 14, 2011.
2. Originally, this concept was known as *precommitment*, but the term was dropped because some central bankers objected to it.
3. When properly used, mathematical artifacts are powerful tools. But they are also a double-edged sword.
4. As an excuse, many banks said that it was not their executives and risk managers who abused the system but the 'models'. In reality, financial models of the riskiness of loans failed because their developers based them on data gathered in an unusually benign economic climate. The excuse that is now being used speaks volumes about the *model illiteracy* of those who have commissioned them.
5. *The Economist*, May 14, 2011.
6. D. N. Chorafas, *IT Auditing and Sarbanes–Oxley Compliance*, Auerbach/CRC, New York, 2009.
7. *Financial Times*, July 22, 2011. Barney Frank is a member of the US House of Representatives and former chairman of the House Financial Services Committee, 2007–11.
8. *The Economist*, July 16, 2011.
9. D. N. Chorafas, '*Risk Pricing*, Harriman House, London, 2010.
10. The term generally appears in connection with 'sovereign debt', but its bearing is much larger, ranging from sovereign policy such as quantitative easing (QE) to the existence and authority of an independent – therefore *sovereign* – state.
11. David Packard, *The HP Way: How Bill Hewlett and I Built Our Company*, Harper Business, New York, 1995.
12. Jean-Pierre Soisson, *Charles Quint*, Grasset, Paris, 2000.
13. *Financial Times*, July 22, 2011.
14. Above the minimum requirement of 7 percent.
15. Basel Committee on Banking Supervision, *Resolution Policies and Frameworks – Progress So Far*, BIS, Basel, July 2011. The same Basel document also states that if the biggest banks continue to take on risk they could be hit with an even higher charge of 3.5 percent.
16. The terms *metrics* is broader than 'measurements' deliberately used because it denotes not only measured quantities but also the process of measuring and decision lying behind it.
17. *Financial Times*, July 2, 2011.
18. Chaired by John Vickers.
19. CRD4 will become European Union law after approval by the European Council and European Parliament.

20. The majority of people who know and use statistics have learned to think in terms of a normal distribution where 99.7% of measurements, or events, lie between 'plus' or 'minus' three standard deviations from the mean. Whatever falls outside is an *outlier*, a term which has a much wider connotation.

2. Finance and Banking Are Time and Motion Machines

1. D. N. Chorafas, *Economic Capital Allocation with Basel II: Cost and Benefit Analysis*, Butterworth-Heinemann, London/Boston MA, 2004; and D. N. Chorafas, *Operational Risk Control with Basle II: Basic Principles and Capital Requirements*, Butterworth-Heinemann, London/Boston, MA, 2004.
2. *Bloomberg News*, March 10, 2011.
3. Ibid.
4. William Greider, *Secrets of the Temple*, Touchstone/Simon & Schuster, New York, 1987.
5. In some countries, the USA and the Federal Reserve being a prime example, the central bank's charter requires it to pursue both financial stability and full employment – which are contradictory goals.
6. One of the worst government scandals of 2010 took place inside the city of Bell, one of the tiniest local governments. Bell is a blue-collar neighborhood within the vast conglomeration of Los Angeles, whose city elders (eight of whom are now awaiting trial) paid themselves outrageous pensions and salaries of up to US$800,000 a year, thus robbing residents in countless innovative but unethical ways (*The Economist*, November 20, 2010).
7. *Financial Times*, February 21, 2011.
8. Ronald Reagan had famously said that the worst sentence in the English language is, 'I come from the government and I am here to help.'
9. D. N. Chorafas, *Managing Risk in the New Economy*, New York Institute of Finance, New York, 2001.
10. Real estate values have been both at the origin and in the sequel of the crisis.
11. D. N. Chorafas, *Risk Pricing*, Harriman House, London, 2010.
12. As of mid-December 2010, Picard had reportedly recovered US$2.5 billion, which suggests that some parties would rather pay and keep their secrets.
13. Ironically, this coincided with the second anniversary of Madoff's 2008 arrest.
14. For example, HSBC hired KPMG to do full-scale diligence examination of Madoff's operation after it bought the Bank of Bermuda, which served as the custodian for a series of billion-dollar 'feeder' funds.
15. *The Economist*, December 18, 2010.
16. Ibid.
17. Jean-Pierre Soisson, *Charles Quint*, Grasset, Paris, 2000.
18. John Lanchester, *IOU: Why Everyone Owes and No One Can Pay*, Simon & Schuster, New York, 2010.
19. In a derivative financial instrument the *underlying* may be a specified commodity price, share price, interest rate, currency exchange rate, index of prices, or something else properly identified by the transaction. Typically, though not always, the relationship prevailing between the underlying and the derivative is not linear (see D. N. Chorafas, *Derivative Financial Instruments*, McGraw-Hill, New York, 2008).
20. Statistics by *Financial Times*, December 17, 2010.
21. D. N. Chorafas, *Financial Boom and Gloom: The Credit and Banking Crisis of 2007–2009 and Beyond*, Palgrave Macmillan, Basingstoke, 2009.

22. Barings' operation in Singapore had followed a similar policy. Barings crashed.
23. Largely thanks to Bill Clinton and George W. Bush, the latter conceivably being the worst president in American history (so far) – unless Barack Obama overtakes him.
24. *The Economist*, June 13, 2009.
25. *Financial Times*, September 30, 2010.
26. Procter & Gamble, one of the most solid companies in the Dow Jones, lost 37 percent of its value before recovering.
27. CNBC, October 1, 2010. Allegedly the basic reason which turned the model on its head was a sloppily executed sell order of one mutual fund group (reportedly Waddell & Reed), when the market was already jittery because of economic turmoil in Europe.
28. Nathan Miller, *F.D.R.*, New American Library, New York, 1983.
29. Gates and his company were fully entitled to pay what allegedly was greenmail, even if this refusal was against the embedded interests of the political machine.
30. The most recent financial regulation in the USA, also known as the Dodd–Frank Act.
31. D. N. Chorafas, *Sovereign Debt Crisis and the New Normal*, Palgrave Macmillan, Basingstoke, 2011.
32. *Financial Times*, May 17, 2010.
33 In America, the Dodd–Frank bill did succeed in reminding the banks of their responsibilities to retail clients through provisions for consumer protection, but though a popular theme this was watered down by lobbyists.
34. *The Economist*, March 12, 2011.
35. Ibid.
36. *The Economist*, February 26, 2011.

3 Global Banking and Systemic Risk

1. And, according to some accounts, it flourished particularly in the second millennium BC.
2. *The Economist*, August 7, 2010.
3. D. N. Chorafas, *Globalization's Limits: Conflicting National Interests in Trade and Finance*, Gower, London, 2009.
4. The letter of credit, for example, was invented in medieval times in conjunction with trade fairs in Lyon.
5. For example, through the Black–Scholes option pricing algorithm for derivatives.
6. Douglas Porch, *The French Secret Service*, Macmillan, London, 1996.
7. European Central Bank, *Financial Stability Review*, June 2011.
8. *The Economist*, January 15, 2011.
9. See Chapter 1, in the section on dark pools, special purpose vehicles and flash crash.
10. D. N. Chorafas, *Energy, Natural Resources and Business Competitiveness in the EU*, Gower, London, 2011.
11. Based on a scenario in which the non-OECD countries' share of world trade and global GDP is kept constant.
12. *EIR* (*Executive Intelligence Review*), January 1, 1997.
13. The *risk of contagion* starts as an idiosyncratic problem that becomes more widespread as the reasons for financial imbalances and other negative factors persist and accumulate.

14. D. N. Chorafas, *Globalization's Limits: Conflicting National Interests in Trade and Finance*, Gower, London, 2009.
15. As contrasted with the more classical multinationals, which concentrated on manufacturing and trade.
16. A bank typically holds only limited cash reserves, since normally only a small proportion of its accounts are closed on any given day. As a result of a sudden demand for account closures, the bank finds itself in payment difficulties and is forced to raise money instantly from other banks and from its creditors in order to serve its customers.
17. BIS, *79th Annual Report*, Basel, June 29, 2009.
18. Also called regulatory capital arbitrage.
19. D. N. Chorafas, *Rocket Scientists in Banking*, Lafferty Publications, London/Dublin, 1995; and D. N. Chorafas, *Stress Testing: Risk Management Strategies for Extreme Events*, Euromoney, London, 2003.
20. DTAs were a Ponzi game, but nobody was punished for it.
21 *Bloomberg News*, March 18, 2011.
22. Basel has not yet clearly decided how to handle these perpetuals in the confines of Basel III. One of the opinions is that in the first year they should be reduced in terms of value in Tier 1 by 10 percent.
23. But included an option to stop coupon payments to investors.
24. D. N. Chorafas, *Financial Boom and Gloom: The Credit and Banking Crisis of 2007–2009 and Beyond*, Palgrave Macmillan, Basingstoke, 2009.
25. Which evidently contrasted with the hype that these were Tier 1 capital, but nobody seems to have noticed.
26. Which a disgusted Irish citizen wrote on his big cement truck which, in mid-2010, he drove up the steps of the Irish parliament.
27. *The Economist*, November 27, 2010.
28. D. N. Chorafas, *Modelling the Survival of Financial and Industrial Enterprises: Advantages, Challenges, and Problems with the Internal Rating-Based (IRB) Method*, Palgrave Macmillan, Basingstoke, 2002.
29. Rather than using them to control their exposure.
30. D. N. Chorafas, *The 1996 Market Risk Amendment: Understanding the Marking-to-Model and Value-at-Risk*, McGraw-Hill, Burr Ridge, IL, 1998.
31. *The Economist*, February 21, 2004.
32. D. N. Chorafas, *Sovereign Debt Crisis: The New Normal and the New Poor*, Palgrave Macmillan, Basingstoke, 2009.
33. *The Economist*, October 24, 2009.

4 Basel III Is a Grand Compromise, Not a Bold Initiative

1. The RFC was established in 1932 by the Fed to channel US$1.5 billion of taxpayers money into the banking system. US$1.5bn was big money at the time. Ten years later, the cost of the Manhattan Project was US$2 billion, and was considered to be a large amount.
2. The Basel Committee represents 27 countries and regions, including the UK, China, France, Germany, the Netherlands, Japan, Sweden, Switzerland and the USA.
3. Which was supposed to be a significant improvement over Basel I, but became subject to extensive regulatory arbitrage.
4. CoCo structures so far available are Lloyds' enhanced convertible notes (ECNs) and Rabobank's senior contingent note (SCN).

5. Crédit Suisse may issue as much as US$30 billion in CoCos over several years to replace a portfolio of hybrid securities that will no longer qualify as capital under Basel III rules.
6. *Bloomberg News*, February 12, 2011.
7. Also, if a conversion takes place, this is likely to be interpreted by the market as a crisis signal, thus increasing market pressure on a given institution.
8. Basel II specified 8 percent capital adequacy for international banks and 4 percent for local or national, but the dichotomy was different than the one this paragraph suggests.
9. *Financial Stability Review*, Deutsche Bundesbank, November 2010.
10. D. N. Chorafas, *Sovereign Debt Crisis and the New Normal*, Palgrave Macmillan, Basingstoke, 2011.
11. GAAP and IFRS have significant differences, but there are other standards as well as IFRS versions. The French, for example, have one that is not totally compatible with what the IASB has designed. D. N. Chorafas, *IFRS, Fair Value and Corporate Governance: Its Impact on Budgets, Balance Sheets and Management Accounts*, Butterworth-Heinemann, London/Boston, 2005.
12. D. N. Chorafas, *IFRS, Fair Value and Corporate Governance: Its Impact on Budgets, Balance Sheets and Management Accounts*, Butterworth-Heinemann, London/Boston, 2005.
13. Europeans are divided on the question of whether to tax banks to pay for future financial rescues.
14. This chapter was released on January 11, 2011.
15. *Financial Times*, January 11, 2011.
16. *International Herald Tribune*, December 18, 2009.
17. Asian credit institutions also have problems with Tier 1 and Tier 2 capital.
18. This could be decided on a discretionary basis by a public authority, or be subject to certain rules. For example, according to how much a set capital ratio is being undershot, or by the level of the bank's equity prices.
19. Rules credited to Puggy Pearson, who dropped out of school at 11 but won the World Series of Poker in 1973.
20. For instance, including losses occurred over the last five years by an acquired company, provided the acquiring company has recorded taxable benefits in its financial statements – or vice versa.
21. *International Herald Tribune*, October 26, 1995.
22. *Financial Times*, August 24, 2010.
23. Bank of America Merrill Lynch, *French Banks*, January 29, 2010.

5 Is It Possible to Regulate a Global Financial Market in Perpetual Change?

1. Isidor F. Stone, *The Trial of Socrates*, Little, Brown, Boston, 1988.
2. The term hedging is itself a misnomer, typically chosen to give confidence but without considering that hedges have a nasty habit of becoming asymmetric. See D. N. Chorafas, *IFRS, Fair Value and Corporate Governance: Its Impact on Budgets, Balance Sheets and Management Accounts*, Butterworth-Heinemann, London/Boston, 2005.
3. The crucial question is: can the institution afford the risks it is taking, without going cap-in-hand to the government for taxpayers' money?
4. *Bloomberg News*, February 11, 2011.

5. D. N. Chorafas, *Sovereign Debt Crisis and the New Normal*, Palgrave Macmillan, Basingstoke, 2011.
6. And not with precision, which hides the grand design by being too specific.
7. D. N. Chorafas, *Risk Pricing*, Harriman House, London, 2010.
8. Widely known as *Città Salaris*, the complete title of this small and powerful look is *La Città del Sole e Poesie*. First published in the mid-sixteenth century. Recent edition by Feltrinelli, Milano, 1962.
9. Like the big global banks did, both individually and by establishing the Institute of International Finance (IFF) in Washington, DC.
10. Back in the late 1980s, in his lectures at ETH Zürich, Professor Wirth used to say: 'Today, programming in COBOL is a criminal offense!' Cobol was then a 30-year-old obsolete 'language'. Think of programming in COBOL in the twenty-first century, when knowledge engineering can do the job at much lower cost, offer higher performance and in a fraction of the time.
11. Forget Madoff. As far as falling into the law's catchment area, he was an exception, and paid the price for himself and for all the others.
12. With elected separate domiciles in Paris, London and Frankfurt, respectively.
13. The centralized Five-Year Plan initiated by Stalin in 1928.
14. David E. Hoffman, *The Oligarchs*, Public Affairs, New York, 2002.
15. Ibid.
16. Basel Committee, *Implementation of Basel II: Practical Considerations*, BIS, July 2004.
17. D. N. Chorafas, *Economic Capital Allocation with Basel II: Cost and Benefit Analysis*, Butterworth-Heinemann, London/Boston, 2004.
18. Inaugural address, January 20, 1953.
19. *The Economist*, March 27, 2010.
20. *Financial Times*, September 28, 2009.
21. The European Union's directive, which includes market discipline.
22. A similar reason complicates the application of indicators based on observed market prices.
23. D. N. Chorafas, *Energy, Natural Resources and Business Competitiveness in the EU*, Gower, London, 2011.
24. The relationship between the compliance function and internal audit is addressed by several jurisdictions, but there are no general rules on how to go about it (Basel Committee on Banking Supervision, *Implementation of the Compliance Principles*, August 2008).

6 Capital Adequacy and Liquidity: the Devil Is in Their Detail

1. An example is provided by the contagion effects following the collapse of the investment bank Lehman Brothers and the impact this had on other banks as well as on the global economy.
2. Milton Friedman, *Dollars and Deficits*, Prentice-Hall, Englewood Cliffs, NJ, 1968.
3. *The Economist*, October 30, 2010.
4. That is the classical bank practice of taking in deposits and lending most of them out in the form of riskier and longer-term loans.
5. *Financial Times*, December 17, 2010.
6. *Bloomberg News*, October 4, 2010.
7. European Central Bank, *Annual Report 2002*.
8. Some regulators are much more prudent than others. The People's Bank of China (PBOC) raised reserve requirements on banks six times during 2010, obliging

them to set aside 18.5 percent of their deposits, which was a record ratio (*The Economist*, January 8, 2011).

9. 'I said Yalta, not Malta,' Stalin cabled to Churchill and Roosevelt when the two Western political leaders met in Malta to get ready for the coming meeting. And they went to Yalta.
10. The capital components under Basel II were: common equity, retained earnings, minority interests, some preference shares, and deductions.
11. Basel Committee on Banking Supervision, *An Assessment of the Long-Term Economic Impact of Stronger Capital and Liquidity Requirements*, BIS, Basel, August 2010.
12. Basel Committee on Banking Supervision, *International Framework for Liquidity Risk Management, Standards and Monitoring*, BIS, Basel, December 2009.
13. From January 1, 2018, banks must also meet the medium-term funding metrics: the Net Stable Funding Ratio (NSFR), the objective of which is to ensure that there are no inappropriate maturity mismatches between assets and liabilities over a one-year horizon.
14. Still, the Basel Committee eased its definition of how severe the outflows in such a crisis would be. It also allowed banks to count high-quality corporate bonds in addition to cash and government bonds.
15. European Central Bank, *Financial Stability Review*, December 2010.
16. Many banks do not seem to know the precise rules that govern payments connected to hybrid securities.
17. *Financial Times*, April 12, 2010.
18. As if this were not enough, the Bank of America projected that additional claims from other investors against loans sold by Countrywide could total between US$7 billion and US$10 billion.
19. *The Economist*, January 23, 2010.
20. Bank of America Merrill Lynch, *Weekly Strategy Insights*, October 12, 2009.
21. D. N. Chorafas, *Financial Boom and Gloom: The Credit and Banking Crisis of 2007–9 and Beyond'*, Palgrave Macmillan, Basingstoke, 2009.
22. The Geneva Association, *Progress*, No. 48, December 2008.
23. *The Economist*, January 24, 2009.
24. And sank both Fannie Mae and Freddie Mac.
25. E&Y says that it followed the rules laid down by FASB. FAS 140 allowed it to certify Repo 105 as it did. But in March 2010, a report into Lehman's bankruptcy by a court-appointed examiner stated that while E&Y had become 'comfortable' with Lehman's use of Repo 105 it did not examine the extent to which the investment bank used it to manicure its reported figures (*The Economist*, January 1, 2011).

7 Home–Host Issues Haunt Bankers and Regulators

1. Basel Committee, *Resolution Policies and Frameworks – Progress So Far*, BIS, Basel, July 2011.
2. D. N. Chorafas, *Globalization's Limits: Conflicting National Interests in Trade and Finance*, Gower, London, 2009.
3. The underlying assets were mainly collateralized debt obligations (CDOs) issued by other institutions. A settlement announced on March 28, 2011 provided most of the retail investors with a 70 percent to 93 percent recovery rate on their initial investment with an additional payment pushing the recovery up to 85 percent to 96.5 percent. *The Economist*, April 2, 2011.
4. Located on both sides of the state border, Calumet provided 'swing-door' protection to the underworld. When the Illinois police descended on the western part

of the city, gangs, prostitutes and traffickers just crossed the border into Indiana, and they did precisely the opposite when the Indiana police began to get active in the eastern half of the city – but only up to the border. It is curious that these two police departments never worked in unison.

5. *Bloomberg News*, January 29, 2011.
6. Who in the past had been no particular friend of marking to market.
7. *Financial Times*, March 21, 2011.
8. But did not seem to deny relationship lending.
9. *Financial Times*, February 6, 2008.
10. Statistics by *Financial Times*, February 14, 2009.
11. Nathan Miller, *F.D.R.: An Intimate History*, New American Library, New York, 1983.
12. Basel Committee, *Resolution Policies and Frameworks – Progress So Far*, BIS, Basel, July 2011.
13. D. N. Chorafas, *Sovereign Debt Crisis, the New Normal and the New Poor*, Palgrave Macmillan, Basingstoke, 2011.
14. ECB, *Monthly Bulletin*, October 2003.
15. *Financial Times*, March 21, 2011. More than one in four investors cited the risk of a sharp slowdown in Chinese economic growth as the biggest threat to markets, outstripping fears about political upheaval in the Middle East and North Africa.
16. The Zero fighters, the most feared of Japanese planes, were originally designed by Howard Hughes, rejected by the US military, but copied and manufactured by the Japanese.
17. Richard P. Feynman, *Adventures of a Curious Character*, W. W. Norton, New York, 1985.
18. *Bloomberg News*, January 30, 2010.
19. The rules were written by US regulators after financial reform legislation passed in the Dodd–Frank Act required an overhaul of the US$600,000 billion over-the-counter (OTC), derivatives markets.
20. *Financial Times*, December 17, 2010.
21. Done in the late 1970s by then US President Jimmy Carter.
22. *Financial Times*, January 22, 2011.
23. Tax-free reserves are legal in Switzerland but illegal in other countries; for example, in the USA, where the IRS interprets them as a way of hiding profits.
24. D. N. Chorafas, *Risk Pricing*, Harriman House, London, 2010.
25. D. N. Chorafas, *Stress Testing for Risk Control Under Basel II*, Elsevier, Oxford/Boston, MA, 2007.

8 The Concept of Risk Management Must Be Thoroughly Revamped

1. *The Complete Illustrated Lewis Carroll*, Wordsworth, Ware, Herts, 1996.
2. Dating back to the Middle Ages, when plays were performed by candlelight.
3. The currency of choice in preparing and presenting their balance sheet and income statement (P&L).
4. *The Economist*, March 5, 2011.
5. Equity prices of small-capitalization companies are more vulnerable than those of large-capitalization companies to adverse business and economic conditions.
6. There still are differences between finance, engineering, medicine and the physical sciences.
7. D. N. Chorafas, *Energy, Natural Resources and Business Competitiveness in the EU*, Gower, London, 2011.

8. Contracts for drilling units are generally fixed day rate contracts, and renegotiations or increases in operating expenditures affect their profitability adversely.
9. William Greider, *Secrets of the Temple: How the Federal Reserve Runs the Country*, Touchstone/Simon & Schuster, New York, 1987.
10. Antonio J. Ferreira, 'Family Myth and Homeostasis', *Archives of General Psychiatry*, 9: 457–63, 1963, p. 458.
11. *Financial Times*, November 17, 2008.
12. As the credit premium rises.
13. *BusinessWeek*, December 5, 1988.
14. For Greece and Ireland, the alarm bells rang at 7 percent. It was silly of Portugal to wait so much longer.
15. Therefore EVT studies should be seen as a source of information rather than a complete analysis, when assessing the overall levels of protection provided, for example, by different types of default estimates.
16. *The Economist*, January 24, 2009.
17. Something economists are now calling 'black swan fatigue'.
18. D. N. Chorafas, *Stress Testing for Risk Control Under Basel II*, Elsevier, Oxford/Boston, MA, 2007.
19. For example, in early April 2011 the European Central Bank lined up 90 banks in its jurisdiction for capital examination through stress testing.
20. *The Economist*, February 27, 2011.
21. *The Economist*, February 13, 2010.
22. This also happens with volatility estimates used in risk pricing, hence the term *volatility smile*.

9 Correlation Risk Overwhelms the Global Banking Industry

1. Each represented by a set of measurements.
2. $r_{AB} = \frac{S_{AB}}{S_A \cdot S_B}$

   where s_{AB} is the covariance of 'A' and 'B' and s_A and s_B, respectively, the standard deviations of set 'A' and set 'B'. The mathematical details are not part of the aim of this book. The covariance refers to the co-movement of the two variables 'A' and 'B'; for example, risks (or prices) pertaining to two different instruments which correlate.
3. Stochastic dependence may indicate that there *might be* a causal relationship, but much more research is necessary to find out whether this is true.
4. The Board of Dresdner Bank made that silly decision and it ended by wrecking the institution, whose remnants were merged into Commerzbank.
5. The master economic plan of the Soviet Union.
6. D. N. Chorafas, *Stress Testing for Risk Control Under Basel II*, Elsevier, Oxford/Boston, 2007.
7. The algorithm is:

$$CR(n) = \sum_{i=1}^{n} MA_i$$

   where n = number of biggest banks (3, 5, 7 or 10); MA = market share in percentage points.
   Source: Deutsche Bundesbank, *Monthly Report*, January 2002.

8. For example, the Herfindahl–Hirschmann Index (HHI), which is expressed through the equation:

$$HHI = \sum_{i=1}^{m} MA_i^2$$

where m = total number of banks in a given market. This algorithm represents the sum of squared market shares of all banks in a market. Squaring ensures that the larger shares are weighted more heavily. This approach is justified by the fact that their market weight leads to an unequal distribution of market shares.
9. See D. N. Chorafas, *Financial Models and Simulation*, Macmillan, London, 1995; and D. N. Chorafas, *Advanced Financial Analysis*, Euromoney Books, London, 1994.
10. A mean variance efficient portfolio is said to be one that cannot be outperformed by another portfolio in both risk and return. Admittedly, this is a vague notion.
11. As it did from July/August 2007 to the end of 2008/early 2009.
12. D. N. Chorafas, *Risk Pricing*, Harriman House, London, 2010.
13. The Delphi method has been used successfully with a variety of projects, originally developed (in the early 1960s) in connection with the Man-on-the-Moon project.
14. D. N. Chorafas, *Operational Risk Control with Basel II: Basic Principles and Capital Requirements*, Butterworth-Heinemann, London/Boston, 2004.
15. D. N. Chorafas, *Risk Pricing*, Harriman House, London, 2010.

10 Risk Control Requires Authority, Goals and Organization

1. *M. Pasteur: Histoire d'un Savant par un Ignorant*, J. Hetzel, Paris, 1883.
2. Ibid.
3. Ibid.
4. *'De devenir'*, in Louis Pasteur's words.
5. For example, solar movement is dissymmetric.
6. The emphasis in this equation is on a 'good hedge'. The problem is that – given asymmetries – it is not that easy to define it.
7. Bank of America Merrill Lynch, *Global Asset Allocation*, April 5, 2011.
8. D. N. Chorafas, *Rocket Scientists in Banking*, Lafferty Publications, London/Dublin, 1995.
9. For banks with assets over US$1 billion, this stands at about 20 percent.
10. D. N. Chorafas, *Risk Pricing*, Harriman House, London, 2010.
11. D. N. Chorafas, *Reliable Financial Reporting and Internal Control: A Global Implementation Guide*, John Wiley, New York, 2000.
12. Named after the physicist, Werner Heisenberg.
13. That is how risk adjusted return on capital (RAROC) works.
14. *Outstanding Investor Digest*, New York, September 24, 1998.
15. Ron Chernow, *The House of Morgan*, Touchstone, New York, 1990.
16. Paul Roberts, *The End of Oil*, Bloomsbury, London, 2004.
17. The term *volatility smile* first appeared in the mid-1990s in connection with the mispricing of options and other derivative instruments. Other things being equal, the lower a financial instrument's price, the more easily it will sell. For pricing purposes, banks ask brokers for their volatility projections, and the brokers often minimize volatility risk – that is the 'smile'. Needless to say, this can be very

costly for the banks. NatWest Markets became bankrupt because of volatility smiles.
18. Indeed, in some of these cases the bank had to pay penalties to the client because contractual investment targets were not kept.
19. Benjamin Graham and David L. Dodd, *Security Analysis*, McGraw-Hill, New York, 1951.
20. Which, for example, characterize IFRS.
21. D. N. Chorafas, *Risk Pricing*, Harriman House, London, 2010.
22. US GAAP and IFRS apply different valuation methods to different types of assets and liabilities. For example, one criterion that determines the valuation method is the intended holding period of the asset or liability. D. N. Chorafas, *IFRS, Fair Value and Corporate Governance: Its Impact on Budgets, Balance Sheets and Management Accounts*, Butterworth-Heinemann, London/Boston, MA, 2006.
23. Fair value is the price that would be received from selling an asset or paid to transfer a liability in an orderly transaction between a willing seller and a willing buyer.

11 By Salvaging Overleveraged Banks, Sovereigns Propagate Global Systemic Risk

1. *Bloomberg News*, April 8, 2011.
2. *The Economist*, April 9, 2011.
3. Officially €80–90 billion.
4. Simon Johnson and James Kwak, *13 Bankers*, Vintage Books, New York, 2011.
5. Quite apart from the social and policy issues raised by this irresponsible action.
6. *Financial Times*, February 21, 2011.
7. Moreover, those in each repayment group must be treated equally.
8. America has put in place bail-in-like powers as part of the financial reform Dodd–Frank Act in 2010. *Financial Times*, February 21, 2011.
9. D. N. Chorafas, *Sovereign Debt Crisis, the New Normal and the New Poor*, Palgrave Macmillan, Basingstoke, 2011.
10. Together with the decision by the Bank of England not to repeat for a second time its benevolence toward Barings when, in 1995, the British merchant bank lost all its capital in derivatives gambles on the Osaka and Tokyo stock exchanges.
11. D. N. Chorafas, *Education and Employment in the European Union: The Social Cost of Business*, Gower, London, 2011.
12. D. N. Chorafas, *Sovereign Debt Crisis, the New Normal and the New Poor*, Palgrave Macmillan, Basingstoke, 2011.
13. Give or take one year.
14. *Financial Times*, March 28, 2011.
15. Which Dr Neil Jacoby, Dean of the School of Business Administration UCLA and economic advisor to President Eisenhower, taught his students.
16. *The Economist*, October 16, 2010.
17. Comparable to Tony Blair's pronouncement, while he was Britain's prime minister, that he was going to cut CO_2 levels radically by 2050.
18. Deutsche Bundesbank, Financial Stability Review, November 2010.
19. L. G. McDonald and P. Robinson, *A Colossal Failure of Common Sense*, Crown Business, New York, 2009.
20. D. N. Chorafas, *Financial Boom and Gloom: The Credit and Banking Crisis of 2007–2009 and Beyond'*, Palgrave Macmillan, Basingstoke, 2009.

21. Greenspan, however, had second thoughts. As he confessed to Congress in the hearings of October 2008, bankers' behavior during the crisis had revealed a flaw in the model that defines how the world works. A flaw discovered too late.
22. D. N. Chorafas, *Risk Pricing*, Harriman House, London, 2010.
23. *EIR*, April 23, 2004.
24. D. N. Chorafas, *Sovereign Debt Crisis, the New Normal and the New Poor'*, Palgrave Macmillan, Basingstoke, 2011.
25. D. N. Chorafas, *Education and Employment in the European Union: The Social Cost of Business*, Gower, London, 2010.
26. A new survey by the World Economic Forum, discussed at its 2011 annual gathering in Davos, indicated that its members see widening economic disparities as one of the two main global risks over the next decade, the other being global governance.
27. Previous attempts, such as, for example, the nineteenth-century Bank of the United States, encountered fierce opposition and failed.
28. D. N. Chorafas, *IT Auditing and Sarbanes-Oxley Compliance*, Auerbach/CRC, New York, 2009.
29. Crédit Agricole and BNP Paribas, for example, had more than 13 percent and 12 percent of their equity, respectively, in minority hands.
30. *Financial Times*, April 28, 2010.
31. Therefore, when one is leveraged and unemployment hits, the whole family is under stress.
32. *The Economist*, February 26, 2011.
33. As of April 18, 2011. While US Treasuries still retained AAA status, their downgrade from a stable to a negative outlook was a worrying event in a nervous market. Indeed on August 12 2011, Standard & Poor's downgraded US Treasury Bills from AAA to AA+.
34. Aside from the fact that such activities should be moved on to exchanges.
35. The Geneva Association, *Progress*, no. 42, December 2010.
36. D. N. Chorafas, *'Financial Boom and Gloom: The Credit and Banking Crisis of 2007–2009 and Beyond*, Palgrave Macmillan, Basingstoke, 2009.
37. Bank of America Merrill Lynch, *Weekly Strategy Insights*, October 12, 2009. In comparison, losses for subprimes/second lien were 23 percent, and for credit cards 16 percent.
38. *Financial Times*, September 22, 2010.

12 What Is the Point of Central Banks' Interventions?

1. D. N. Chorafas, *Sovereign Debt Crisis, the New Normal and the New Poor*, Palgrave Macmillan, Basingstoke, 2011.
2. Banks, too, are dependent on ECB funding. Ireland's banks are an example.
3. Milton Friedman, *Dollars and Deficits*, Prentice-Hall, Englewood Cliffs, NJ, 1968.
4. R. Christopher Whalen, *Inflated*, Wiley, New York, 2011.
5. Ibid.
6. CNBC, July 13, 2011.
7. R. Christopher Whalen, *Inflated*, Wiley, New York, 2011.
8. Ibid.
9. *The Economist*, November 27, 2010.
10. Bank of America Merrill Lynch, *The RIC Report: Shocks 1 Stocks*, March 8, 2011.
11. *Financial Times*, November 27/28, 2010.
12. Milton Friedman, *Dollars and Deficits*, Prentice-Hall, Englewood Cliffs, NJ, 1968.

13. Statistics by Deutsche Bundesbank, *Monthly Report*, March 2011.
14. In the words of Vikram Pandit, Citigroup's CEO.
15. *Deutsche Bundesbank Monthly Bulletin*, March 2011.
16. For example, attempting to guarantee full employment, as the Fed does. This, as already noted, is a contradiction.
17. Which was the original supervisory authority.
18. The product of the monetary base and the velocity of circulation of money is a jurisdiction's money supply.
19. *The Economist*, January 29, 2011.
20. While many jurisdictions today have deposit insurance schemes, these are not clones of one another. The Swiss solution, for example, is different from the American one, or that of other countries. What exists is an insurance model guaranteed not by the government but by the Swiss Bankers Association (SBA) to a maximum amount of CHF 30,000 should a bank go into liquidation. Unlike the FDIC, the SBA will collect the funds after the fact, asking banks to contribute if necessary.
21. *The Economist*, May 29, 2010.
22. Not to be confused with TAF, which stands for the Term Actions Facility by the Fed, a program launched in December 2007.
23. *Financial Times*, May 17, 2010.
24. The merged Bank of America Merrill Lynch eventually received a combined US$45 billion.
25. *The Economist*, December 12, 2009.
26. *Financial Times*, April 12, 2010.
27. According to some opinions, the ultimate cost to the taxpayer of the banks' salvage alone may be some US$50 billion.
28. In Obama parlance, this meant popular anger sweeping the USA against the big global banks and their wheeling and dealing.
29. The term 'Wall Street' has been enlarged to include not only institutions with home offices in lower Manhattan but all US megabanks – and why not the big global banks in all other countries?
30. Simon Johnson and James Kwak, *13 Bankers*, Vintage Books, New York, 2011.
31. David Cho, 'Banks "Too Big to Fail" Have Grown Even Bigger', *Washington Post*, August 28, 2009.
32. The RTC, and in consequence TARP, were preceded by the Reconstruction Finance Corporation (RFC), a Herbert Hoover initiative aimed at stopping the snowballing of the economic crisis in the banking industry at the end of the 1920s. Hoover argued that restoring prosperity to banks and corporations would reinvigorate the economy. RFC channeled US$2 billion (big money at the time) to banks, railroads and insurance companies on the edge of collapse. A sister government agency, the Federal Farm Loan Bank was endowed with US$1 billion to help farmers avoid foreclosures. At the same time, the Fed expanded the supply of credit (Nathan Miller, *F.D.R.*, New American Library, New York, 1983).
33. D. N. Chorafas, *Financial Boom and Gloom: The Credit and Banking Crisis of 2007–2009 and Beyond*, Palgrave Macmillan, Basingstoke, 2009.
34. Merrill Lynch, *Investment Strategy Update – RTC II?*, September 18, 2008.
35. Bank of America Merrill Lynch, *Situation Room: Credit Risk of the US Is Inflation*, April 18, 2011.
36. Simon Johnson and James Kwak, *13 Bankers*, Vintage Books, New York, 2011.
37. Originally the same (wrong) idea was known as the *Greenspan put*, after its inventor.
38. *The Economist*, June 19, 2004.
39. Merrill Lynch, *Bracing for the Perfect Storm*, October 3, 2005.

Index

Made in the USA
Monee, IL
13 September 2026

62976822R00166